D0609184

OPENING GAMBITS

OPENING GAMBITS

ESSAYS ON ART AND PHILOSOPHY

MARK KINGWELL

KEY PORTER BOOKS

Library and Archives Canada Cataloguing in Publication

Kingwell, Mark, 1963-
Opening gambits : essays on art and philosophy / Mark Kingwell.

ISBN 978-1-55470-073-8

1. Art and philosophy.   2. Aesthetics.   I. Title.
N70.K46 2008   701'.17   C2008-902090-1

ONTARIO ARTS COUNCIL
CONSEIL DES ARTS DE L'ONTARIO

The publisher gratefully acknowledges the support of the Canada Council for the Arts and the Ontario Arts Council for its publishing program. We acknowledge the support of the Government of Ontario through the Ontario Media Development Corporation's Ontario Book Initiative.

We acknowledge the financial support of the Government of Canada through the Book Publishing Industry Development Program (BPIDP) for our publishing activities.

Key Porter Books Limited
Six Adelaide Street East, Tenth Floor
Toronto, Ontario
Canada M5C 1H6

www.keyporter.com

Text design: Martin Gould
Electronic formatting: Alison Carr

Printed and bound in Canada

08 09 10 11 12 5 4 3 2 1

For James Lahey

CONTENTS

PART TWO: **Philosophy After Art**

Introduction: Puzzles and Plays: Philosophy as/and/of Art

"The truth of art lies in its power to break the monopoly of established reality (i.e., of those who established it) to define what is real. In this rupture, which is the achievement of the aesthetic form, the fictitious world of art appears as true reality."
—Herbert Marcuse, *Aesthetic Dimension* (1978)

i. Irony

Søren Kierkegaard, celebrated as a master of irony, knew it was neither merely a literary flourish nor a cheap sense of knowingness or distance. Irony is, instead, a lever of insight, finding in the gap-spaces of thought something we had not thought to seek. And of course *eiron*, in Greek, means to dissemble, to open a space between said and meant, known and unknown, feigned and real. Philosophical irony, as distinct from spoken or dramatic kinds— and maybe especially as distinct from the what-the-hell knowingness too often called irony—is a matter of the seemingly innocent, even ignorant question that conceals in that seeming a prickly deeper intent. As an example, consider Kierkegaard's famous query: "Among the Christians, is there a Christian?" Such a question appears an obvious non sequitur—of course there are Christians! You just identified the category!—until we see that the validity of the category is precisely that which is being questioned. Among those who *call themselves* Christian, are there any—is there even one—who is truly such?

The essays that follow are concerned with two similar questions. One: among the artists, is there an artist? And two: among the philosophers, is there a philosopher? These questions are not pursued by the usual means of *sifting*. That is, I am not occupied with assessing specific examples of (people who call themselves) artists or (people who call themselves) philosophers, weighing up their individual contributions against some notional scale of validity of which I alone am possessed. You can find this sort of sifting; in fact, there is probably a surfeit of it, given that so much seems to hang on the two labels—artist, philosopher—even as so little consensus emerges with respect to what or who counts as such. Rival (people who call themselves) artists and (people who call themselves) philosophers are typically the people most interested in this project of screening, and that is no doubt part of what they, or perhaps anyone, would consider an aspect of properly being defined as one. An artist, among other things, judges art. A philosopher, even more clearly perhaps, judges philosophy. Both tasks involve judging the work of others, both substantively in their contributions and categorically in their license to contribute at all.

These kinds of judgment, substantive and categorical, are theoretically separable but in practice they run together: someone is judged not worthy to contribute because his contributions are too often bad; or a failure to establish the right to contribute sets off the contributions, however good themselves, as unconsidered. The worlds of art and philosophy are hypothetically open to any and all, but in truth the categories of artist and philosopher are limit loops that work to exclude some in the act of including others. That the debate continues, both within and without the loop, concerning the essence or nature of the souls who have gained entry, is a sign not of health but of an instability no amount of sifting will resolve. As a character in an Iris Murdoch novel notes of his (admittedly somewhat mystical) disillusionment with academic philosophy: "The modern world is full of theories which are proliferating at a wrong level of generality, we're so *good* at theorising, and one theory spawns another, there's a whole industry of abstract activity which people mistake for thinking."[1]

But we must be careful here not to overstate the negative case. Lots of interesting results may be generated by these twinned projects of sifting and generalizing, even if purists see the level of generality as wrong. It is well, for instance, to improve on the rigor of our discussions of what constitutes a belief even if most people do not follow the inquiry very far. But the basic situation is no bad thing either, especially if the structural instability of the system allows space for a different kind of intervention, which may be closer to what the character means (or anyway what I mean) by thinking. Not a sifting now, but a querying of the conceptual apparatus clinging to the categories themselves. In any event, the situation is now well entrenched and perhaps inevitable, a necessary starting point.

The art world, as I will suggest in what follows, is not one world but many, and the edges of these worlds are, despite all efforts to the contrary, porous. One might even say *because of* rather than *despite* such efforts: the energy of containment is precisely what sets free the chance of "illicit" entry. There can be no such thing as "outsider art," for example—no category of work classed under that name—unless there is a presumption of insideness, vehemently defended. This means that the art world(s) are subject to the vagaries of fashion—hardly a new claim, of course, but one that can usefully be explored by noticing the way position is established in any field rather than fingering certain artists, movements, or ideas as fashionable. Even less useful is the kind of wholesale condemnation of the idea of art to be found in some thinking, itself self-consciously fashionable, about the "conspiracy" or "piracy" of art. Such moves risk a fatal self-negation, despite all efforts to outdistance their overtaking. These critiques of art's attempts to appropriate the materials of the culture industry are correct in one respect: such appropriation never does, and never can, effect the *détournement* advocated by Guy Debord and the Situationist International. It is critique only in the sense, noted by Jean Baudrillard, that critique is "complicit with what it denounces." For Baudrillard, "critique always precedes what it criticizes." The paradox, or second-order effect, is that this is true also of this sort of critique of the art world!

The world of philosophy has been more successful in tightening its containment walls, mostly by means of the severe measures, and associated costs, of academic professionalization. Almost nobody lacking certain appropriate forms of accreditation—a doctoral degree, a university teaching post, a professorial title— is even considered a candidate for insideness. But here, too, the anti-contamination lines are quickly revealed as self-defeating, not because they're porous to outside challenge, but rather ensnared in their own contradictions. Philosophy-as-containment— serious, dry, objective—cannot control the collateral intellectual damage its questions cause. The more we try to batten philosophy down, the more it evades and proliferates. It is well to remember that the founding figure of one of philosophy's main traditions was himself a master of irony and instability. That Socratic impishness cannot be regulated. In a sense, it enacts, again and again, a different sort of situationist tactic, namely the *dérive*, or "drift," that stages the thinker's own disappearance in the act of thinking.

So, to ask whether there is an artist among the artists, or a philosopher among the philosophers, is always already to ask: *What is art? What is philosophy?* Before explaining why these two questions belong together, another caveat for what follows: Just as there is no screening of individual artists and philosophers against a scale of validity, there is likewise no general theory of art or philosophy, still less a philosophy of art, offered in what follows. Though there is what I hope counts as some sustained meditation on the nature of the work of art, you will find no single definition of art, nor even a set of necessary and sufficient conditions under which something is considered to be a work of art. Though there is a series of puzzles concerning the nature of theoretical engagement, or thinking, you will find no general account of what counts as a philosophical position or, still less, theory.

So no specific sifting, and no general theory. You might well be wondering what does lie ahead. What these essays amount to, or at least what I want for them, is a repeated attempt to find a third space for thought: not a middle ground, with its suggestion of bland compromise, or even the third language of Hans-Georg Gadamer's hermeneutical fusion of horizons, but something more like the middle voice of natural language, between active and passive, where a certain kind of truth may be allowed to emerge. (Martin Heidegger thought this truth was a fundamental ontological one, but we need not feel compelled to agree with him.) Such a space, if we can manage to clear it, is one of reflection that is neither preoccupied with judgment nor given to grand pronouncements about general natures and essences. Both of those projects, seemingly distant from each other, are in fact the same one, since the judgment side depends on norms taken from the general-theory side for its assessments of validity; while the general theory cannot generate those norms without reference to their actual or possible traction in given judgments on the specific.

This circle of specific and general is often thought virtuous, not vicious, and certainly it has generated lots of intellectual firewood. I will not try to settle the question of its virtue—a question beyond my means anyway—but, instead, simply try to hold away, or hover above, the vortex it usually exerts on thinking. If I have a general claim, it is implied rather than explicit. It is that art and philosophy at their best, and indeed in conjunction, offer the most revealing kinds of thought we can imagine.

ii. As/and/of

What, though, is the precise relationship between art and philosophy?

In a paper delivered as the 1984 presidential address to the

American Philosophical Association—the keynote to the keystone of the profession of academic philosophy—the philosopher Arthur Danto considered the topic "philosophy as/and/of literature": a conjunction of prepositions I have borrowed for my title here. Philosophy, Danto argued, though it comes in many literary forms, from dialogue to meditation to aphorism, is now mostly conducted in the form of the stylistically neutral academic journal article—or "paper," as we academics like to call them. Because these papers are, in their presumed aims and presumably at their best, transparent vehicles for argument, philosophy should not be seen as reducible to literature. The fact that Danto views this possibility as a reduction is the clue to the argument's interests. The reason philosophy is not literature is that philosophy, whatever else it does and in whatever style, makes truth claims; and that is precisely what literature does not, and cannot, do. The philosophical paper may be viewed as a kind of literary genre, with associated criteria of both class and success within the class; but if so, it is a genre that, as well as establishing an internal relation to the reader (what all literature does), seeks to establish an external relation to the world: "really to reveal us," in Danto's words, by "aiming at truth."[2] *Where are your papers?*

Danto does complicate matters by allowing that there is such a thing as "philosophy as an art"—truth claims done with aplomb or even genius, one imagines—and acknowledging that this paper-centered view of philosophy does tend to "flatten out" the deeper philosophical urges. And the differences between philosophy-as-literature and philosophy-as-art are considerable on any account. But his central position on the truth-claim issue is what concerns me here. It is a conservative position, if not a reactionary one. In the service of puffing up the scientific, or quasi-scientific or wishful-scientific, status of philosophical argument, Danto succeeds only in denigrating literature as devoid of cognitive substance. Or, if there is some sort of cognition available in art, it still can only be released with help, via the healing hands of interpretation: what Susan Sontag memorably defined as "the revenge of the intellect upon art."[3] Such an "explanatory" position—interested in deciding what art means—immediately invites the aggressive counterargument that, in seeking its demonstrable forms of truth, philosophy, like science, has missed the bigger human boat. "Truth is entirely and absolutely a matter of style," Oscar Wilde wrote in a satire on the triumphant naturalism of Herbert Spencer. That is why people prefer literary art to science: its charming lies are more comforting than science's aggressive claims of fact.

Well, perhaps. Both of these moves, or the one move with its two related consequences, betray a prejudice that gets philosophy and literature badly wrong. In fact, the basic impulse to rank order two realms of human reflection is itself badly conceived. While literature, like any art form, is never reducible to its mere propositional content—thinking so marks one of the ways we do violence to the aesthetic—it nevertheless carries substance of a kind that could not be carried any other way. (For more on this issue, see chapter 12.) And philosophy, in its making of claims, is always also a claim on the reader's attention, or should be, that cannot be conceived apart from its particular vehicle, with special benefits and drawbacks. This is all the more surprising in that Danto, in addition to being an acute philosopher of art, is a talented art critic. That is, he is practiced in the ways of seeing that art makes possible, as surely literature does too.

We do better, I think, to consider the as/and/of relation to be one that reveals kinship: it is a family resemblance function rather than a strict categorical differentiation, to use some philosophical language. Danto himself has argued that the general form of a philosophical problem is the situation where two things (experiences, claims, perceptions, intuitions, arguments) *appear* to be the same but are really different. He calls these "comedies of similarity." Teasing out the difference is philosophy's job. At its most ambitious and metaphysical, that teasing out leads to a phenomena/noumena boundary or a perceived-world/real-world ontology. This kind of systematic solution to the perceived problem is both controversial and unnecessary, since many such comedies are not based on levels of reality or their revelation. In art, for example, it is not a problem (except for aggressive Platonists) that the depicted chair is "not real." Nor is it even a problem, once we understand the nature of art, if a "real chair" is made into a work of art by being placed in a museum. This latter kind of case, where the object stays the same but depending on context is either a work of art or a "mere real thing," is a comedy that lasts. One cannot resolve the similarity issue categorically— either once and for all, or by categories. Its comedy depends on a kind of resolute irresolvability.

Philosophy and art pose a similar comedy of similarity, especially, but not exclusively, when conceptual techniques are in play. They are each a way of *going on*, of *creating*—I almost want to say, of *thinking*, but I realize that will make trouble when the notion of thinking in question is not yet clear. (Calling the thinking "Heideggerian" is a mixed blessing: accurate but obscure.) Furthermore, the banalities of much conceptual art muddy the waters around the question of how art might be a form of thought. I mean something closer to *playing*, though that, too, may be misleading if we associate play with pointless fun or mindless, unproductive activity. Play is of course much more than this. It is that form of goal-directed activity whose stated goal is not, or not always, the real point of the game. We can play silly games and dangerous ones, for stakes large and small. Many games, professionalized and commodified, lose their essence even as they achieve higher levels of apparent achievement. The very idea of a game losing its soul, that common complaint about professional sports, is evidence that we maintain a baseline belief in the value of play. A game gone bad, thrown, cheated or drugged offends a complex mixture of aesthetic, ethical and theoretical convictions, most of them unarticulated.

The idea that art is a high-level form of play, in the sense of its difficulty and capacity to challenge, is familiar enough. But what of philosophy? We do not typically talk about playing, or playing at, philosophy. Instead, we mostly speak of doing it—a suggestive difference of verb. *Doing* is equivalent in ordinary language to *working* (one does a job) or *performing* in the merely factual sense (one does a deed). It does not carry the other suggestion of per-form, which is to play (a tune) or play-act (a role). "Doing" also embraces less workmanlike uses: one does a drug, say; or, vulgarly, one does a person—which, it is worth noting, can mean either having sex with them or killing them! To speak of doing philoso-phy is to indicate a performance, as of a duty, but more deeply to suggest that philosophy is a form of work, a kind of intellectual bricklaying that justifies its apparent uselessness with the unques-tioned value of hard labor.

Again, I do not want to repudiate this conception of philoso-phy—there is nothing easy in grappling rigorously with concepts at the far end of a debate—only to loosen it, or expand it. What if we conceived of philosophy as a form of play, like art, that deals with central human concerns and forms of thought? What if rea-son itself were an art form? It would follow that the conclusions of thought would not always, or even frequently, have the assertoric shape familiar from logic or even the best-guess-so-far falsifia-bility of science; they would not be propositions. This can, and should, be somewhat unsettling. Lionel Trilling, recounting his first exposure to the work of Russian writer Isaac Babel, confessed that it upset him in part because his literary expectations "involved a desire for an art that would have as little ambiguity as a proposition in logic." Instead he found a form of art, and thought, that refused to do that, even unto the "revanchist" and "unpatriotic" silence that led to Babel's death in a Stalinist purge. "Intensity, irony, and ambiguousness," Trilling learned from Babel's example, "constitute a clear threat to the impassivity of the State. They constitute a *secret*." This secret is one that "implied there was more than one way of being. It hinted that one might live by means of a question."[4]

There is no quarrel, in these pages, with the State, just the state of affairs that works to render philosophy and art null—some-thing far short of a political purge, but dangerous enough after its own fashion. The essays in this collection are partly arguments about the kind of irony Trilling is describing, and partly attempts to produce examples of what I mean. "Attempted" because there is a basic difficulty in the notion of play, which any collision of art and philosophy is bound to bring to our attention.

I said that there is no philosophy of art in what follows, and no philosophy of philosophy. But the conjunction of essays on art and essays on, or around, philosophy does raise the question of *where to stand* in order to think. To put it another way, is it possible to intervene intellectually without committing oneself to a general program? The reason for wanting to do so is not to avoid intellectual responsibility but to take it on in a new way. Not standing still becomes a form of standing up, or maybe standing tall. As I discuss in one of the pieces included here, "The Theory Theory," once we begin the game of intellectual one-upmanship, there is no way to stop it. So we should not begin. But we must begin something, somehow. And so, what do we begin? *How* do we begin?

The fashionable irony of the savvy culture consumer is not the answer. Certainly none of the artists or thinkers discussed in these essays can be considered ironic in that banal sense. But it is the deeper irony of "living by means of the question" that they, and we, seek. Or so I shall argue. The difference I am after here may be communicated by means of a metaphor. In scholarly footnoting— an odd practice, really, when one considers it—there are two main strategies available. One, the more usual course of action, is a natural extension of the footnote as a basic citation device. This method uses the footnote to offer a sideline remark or meta-commentary on the main text. This is no more than obvious, and many texts usefully offer footnotes that run a commentary along the main argument. Lurking within the strategy, though, is a kind of self-defeat by means of infinite regress, rendering the whole idea of a unified text meaningless. If the main text can be annotated, why not annotate the notes? And if the notes can be annotated, why not also annotate the second set of notes? And so on, world without end—or at least until the vagaries of eyesight and typography make it impossible to go further. The novelist David Foster Wallace, himself a master of simulacral irony, has done this on the page, offering a visual deconstruction of textuality in the form of a foot-note *mise-en-abyme*. The text consumes itself, disappearing into a sense-swallowing swirl of letters and numbers.

Of course, once that has been done, there is not much point doing it again. One can return to simple footnotes, or to no footnotes, but the trick is spoiled because the hidden mechanisms have been revealed; it is, as one observer has said, like coming to the edge of an abyss, turning your back, and announcing you are on the other side. The second strategy, however, followed by Heidegger, for example, is to offer footnotes not as commentary and meta-commentary, but as against-the-grain alternative voices. The difference can be super-ficially hard to distinguish, but the effect accumulates: the footnote now destabilizes the text in a way that neither collapses back down to authority nor spirals away into nonsensicality. This text will not be mastered because it does not master itself. Instead, it surrenders the goal of mastery. In effect, the whole text now forces the reader to go back, again and again, seeking the meanings it offers. It makes the reader, over and over, an absolute beginner.

If we can think this way, we are doing something more inter-esting than "finding out what the text means." In a sense, interpre-tation is now impossible because, as Sontag noted decades ago, the notion of the master key, the revelatory gesture of reading it right, is no longer of interest. The logic of revealed depth, of latent con-tent lying beneath manifest content, is a presumption, or set of them worth querying or even abandoning. But in another sense, this querying is really just what interpretation ought to mean: a dwelling in the text or the thought, an engagement that is goal-directed but not final. The nature of play is that it stops only to renew at another moment. A given game, a particular engagement, comes to an end, perhaps even declares a winner; or the player makes the popular move of claiming his opponent is not playing by the rules and so stops the play; but the game itself is never over. One can always say, even in the most apparently final circum-stances, *Wait till next year!*

iii. Play

Hence the book's title, which is already a kind of play on words. In the game of chess, an opening gambit is a move, or series of them, whereby a piece, usually a pawn, is sacrificed to gain tactical advantage, known, of course, as *position*. But positions in chess are never stable, and the idea of position is one that needs playing with. A gambit is also a conversational intervention: an opening line or remark, to effect some reaction. In general, gambits are tricks or devices, or studied gambles. They are not deceptive for the sake of being so; they do not aim to fool, only to arouse a non-final outcome.

I also chose the title's form, a modified plural noun, to echo that of a previous collection of essays, *Practical Judgments*, to which this is a kind of companion volume. The reader might wonder why the "opening" comes second, after the so-called practical stuff, and gambits after judgments. The only answer is that, in philosophical thinking, it seems to me we are always, Merlin-fashion, working our way back to the beginning, the opening of the question. The previous collection was diverse and loosely collected around the theme of public engagement, while this volume has a stronger thematic core—art and philosophy at *play*—even while being more open-ended.

The book falls into two parts, related both by similarity and by contrast—seeking a sort of destabilizing either/or effect. The first part has nine examples of "philosophical" writing about modern visual art and architecture, including both general assessments (chapters 1 to 3) and engagements with specific makers (chapters 4 to 9). The second part of the book then takes up the issue of philosophy's relation to itself. That is, these latter essays address philosophy in terms of the possibilities and impossibilities of itself as an art form. Specific questions (love, happiness, law, fashion) bind together in a sense of what philosophical play is like. A general theme governing both parts of the book is that of *disappearance*: not only the mutation of the roles of "the artist" and "the philosopher," but also the basic ironic quest to find, among all the examples, an example of something. Motivating all these pages is a sense of discomfort with the idea of an art world or a conception of philosophy that does not, somehow, embrace the idea that a work of art may be an ethical occasion as well as a thing or mere experience. Friedrich Nietzsche's injunction to *make your life a work of art*, or Rainer Maria Rilke's more forceful command that *you must change your life* when confronted by certain forms of beauty, strike me as the gift of philosophy made concrete. (I cannot answer for the frequency of reference to *The Simpsons* in these essays, except to say that popular art, too, can make ideas concrete.)

As I discuss at greater length in "The Theory Theory," the final essay in the book, the phrase *ars longa, vita brevis* is frequently misunderstood. The common meaning given to it is that life is short while art endures. The original meaning, however, concerns study, in particular the study of medicine. Life is short, and the art of healing takes a long time to learn. Too long, in fact, for any one life to learn it all. I take the liberty of substituting philosophy for medicine, changing one kind of doctor for an even older use of the title, and suggest the same conclusion about thinking. Hence one opening gambit after another, and no end in sight except the provisional one of insight. So then to begin again, and again . . .

Notes

1. Iris Murdoch, *The Good Apprentice* (Penguin, 1987). The speaker, Stuart Cuno, is a mathematician as well as a philosopher.

2. Arthur Danto, "Philosophy as/and/of Literature," in Cornel West and John Rajchman, eds., *Post-Analytic Philosophy* (Columbia, 1985), pp. 63-83, at p. 83.

3. Susan Sontag, *Against Interpretation* (Farrar, Straus & Giroux, 1966). A nicely turned—if rather nasty—version of the Sontag position is offered by irony-enabled critic Dale Peck in his dismemberment of irony-deficient critic Sven Birkerts: "The Man Who Would Be Sven," in *Hatchet Jobs* (New Press, 2004), pp. 7-41, esp. p. 8 and p. 37.

4. Lionel Trilling, from his Introduction to the first English translation of Babel's stories (1955), reprinted as an Appendix to Isaac Babel, *Red Cavalry and Other Stories* (Penguin, 1994), pp. 340-65, at p. 345.

PART ONE:

Art and Its Objects

1. Art Will Eat Itself

On any given Saturday you may observe them, the pilgrims of art, haunting the long blocks of Chelsea in Manhattan. Rich and mostly good-looking, they are nevertheless a sad lot; in search of something they know not what. Less certain of salvation than the walkers reeling in the miles to Santiago de Compostela, driven by a sense of purposiveness without purpose, they go and go, following a trail mapped by *Artforum* and *The New York Times* Arts & Leisure section. Sometimes they are impressed, sometimes even moved. Sometimes they buy. But always there is a sense of thwarted longing, an itch of yearning not fully scratched. Is this all there is?

Every couple of years the pilgrims take a step back and wander the hangar-halls of the Whitney or the hills of Venice, the streets and alleys of Berlin, where things are not for sale, looking for the large vista, the big picture, the overview. What is art today? Perspective never comes, not least because they can't quite believe in big pictures like that anymore: they have been taught to distrust them, to question the metanarrative and universal claim. They are beyond that. And yet, even evaporated desire can leave a crusty residue of dissatisfaction, desire's precipitate. A sense of what it all means would be nice, wouldn't it, even if we are too sophisticated to say so? And there is an awful lot of rubbish to sort through, isn't there? Wouldn't it be good—wouldn't it lay a nagging problem to rest—if we could say, in some definitive fashion, what art is all about? But no. The thought self-destructs in the very act of being formed.

It is too simple to say the art world is in disarray, since by many measures it is in very good nick indeed. Despite constant and frankly structural complaints about gallery access, bad dealers, cabals and who slept with whom, the dissemination of art is relatively easy today. More art is produced and shown now than ever before in the history of human civilization. Art schools are thriving, at least in the sense of producing regular battalions of graduates to throng the warehouse spaces and downtown cafés of our cities. And the market for art, once considered so elite a preserve that democrats were driven to invent the public museum, is now within the reach of anyone with a few hundred (though better, thousand) spare dollars. It is, to be sure, a market that more resembles the distribution of stock, where mutual funds and day trading do nothing to alter the basic facts of wealth concentration except to provide a cozy illusion that those facts are alterable. But like finance, art has finally realized the dream of all aspects of achievement in the ambit of human life: it has become television.

Consider. A vast undifferentiated schedule is constantly available, always apparently growing, offering every species and manner of product. We believe there is wheat in there somewhere, occasionally even believe we have found it. This is good; and yet, the television-style art world often cannot avoid a descent into generalized banality and creeping depression. In most large North American cities, regular "international art fairs" are held, sprawling aesthetic trade shows where gallery owners crowd in next to one another on convention-center floors and flog their wares, spewing up everything from the shamelessly twee kitsch of Thomas Kincade, "painter of light," to neglected Marc Chagall lithographs and bits of compelling cleverness from (as it might be)

Kim Adams, William Wegman or Bruce McCall. These shows, with their unpredictable plunges from sublime to ridiculous, become exercises in vertiginous aesthetic profusion, channel-surfing for the cultured. You may turn any corner and come upon something good, but the sheer force of volume, for once honestly presented in a jumble rather than the self-conscious minimalism of the white-walled gallery, soon renders its banal essence. Armed with a glass of ubiquitous art-world white wine, Château d'Ennui, we wander the pallid partitioned corridors of post-historical art: art cut free from narratives of progress, beholden to no school or tradition, where anything and everything may be displayed. Any medium, any style, any subject. Ho hum.

The Whitneyites and other biennialeans may disdain these fairs, of course, but they are no freer of the facts than people who like to tell you they just watch public television. Mounting invidious distinctions do not confer genuine merit, only levels of membership. The Chelsea rangers are just the art world's equivalent of National Public Radio (NPR) tote-baggers, smug supporters in good standing, maybe with a credit card on file, who get the free gift—the mug, the T-shirt, the boxed videotapes—in recognition of their pledge.

Even blockbuster exhibitions of artistic virtuosity, such as the Gerhard Richter retrospective that graced the Museum of Modern Art (MOMA) in 2002, merely reinforce the current confusion. For all its hype and moments of genuine brilliance, the Richter show was a testament not so much to vision as to preoccupation. The shifts from figuration to abstraction, the self-conscious, often very beautiful renderings of blurred photographs, the effortless command of pigment: all of this tells us that Richter's true subject is not what he paints but that he paints. Richter may flirt with politics and memory in portraits of Baader-Meinhof terrorists or unsettlingly gorgeous images of American fighter-bombers, but these are merely exercises in technique; his real subject is always the medium itself. The swirling, chocolaty abstracts and gray-white, semi-figurative images that appear alongside the imagistic canvases make this clear. They are jarring and self-indulgent but illustrate a necessary point: paint, paint and more paint. In many ways the most striking, honest and moving work in Richter's oeuvre is *1024 Colors*, the massive installation of precisely pigmented panels that mimics the paint-chip catalogs artists and home decorators consult to choose shades.

Being interested in, even moved by, this kind of artwork is surely a sign of something that might be called sophistication or intellectual elevation; and indeed, shows like this slyly encourage a moment of "getting it" set on top of the sheer lusciousness of the works themselves. We engage in a form of second-order consumption all too typical of the postmodern condition, consuming our own cultivation as a by-product of some first-order experience—say, of beauty—understood to be insufficient by itself. This can be fun, if you know how to shop or surf, knowing for instance that Richter's color panels are an allusion to Ellsworth Kelly's 1951 work, *Colors for a Large Wall*; but recognizing allusions and supplying theoretical infill is just more NPR self-congratulation. If we were bolder and more honest, we would see the current aesthetic economy as the sign of a depressing endgame where art has lost its way and is too scared to say so, for fear of what the consequences may be. So-called fine art has struggled for centuries to free itself from the bonds of elitism and privilege, opening a larger and larger public sphere, only to find that the result was an empty and defeated art world. Three hundred channels and nothing to watch. It's a bit like the old rap against democracy: in the land where everybody's somebody, nobody's anybody. When anything is art, art risks being nothing.

It is no surprise that the very same period of art's meandering has shown a dearth of good thinking about art, for in a sense there is nothing to think about. Grand aesthetic theory is as certain a casualty of the war on metanarratives as any other kind of grand theory, ejected with other suspect detritus of the Enlightenment. G. W. F. Hegel could confidently place dramatic poetry and figurative art near the pinnacle of world-historical development, concrete, sensuous expressions of Spirit's inevitable progress towards full development. Along the way, of course, he put Egyptian, Greek and Roman art in their appropriate places well below German Romanticism, a move we would consider the sheerest hubris, the high-wire act of a bygone day. Even Immanuel Kant's more modest attempt to locate the faculty of judgment in a critical scheme of moral and epistemological presuppositions is now generally suspect, a piece of legerdemain too universalistic to swallow. Instead of comprehensive aesthetic theory, we have a theoretical free-for-all, a shopping mall of philosophical options. The assumptions of the art world are as jumbled as the techniques and works on offer, a mishmash of self-protection and uneasy accessibility. Aesthetic autonomy, yes, faculty of taste, no. Tortured romantic genius, yes, primacy of beauty, no. Politics, yes, responsibility, no. Versions of Clive Bell's Bloomsbury formalism somehow stagger on next to the crudest versions of Platonic art-as-imitation, both living hard by much half-baked constructivist radicalism and warmed-over anticonsumerist ranting.

That is surely one reason the most comprehensive aesthetic philosophy of recent memory is also the most deflationary: Danto's so-called institutional theory of art. Loosely combining ideas from logical positivists, Ludwig Wittgenstein, Heidegger and others, Danto analyzes the pop moment of Andy Warhol's *Brillo Box* as the end of art history. We must now accept that, logically speaking, art is anything that is accepted as "an object of rapt attention" in a conventionally structured institutional setting. The art world is a conceptual space, a linked series of locations and discussions, where things are given a certain status; but there is nothing inherent in the things that makes them art. You cannot look into the work of art and hope to find the quality or feature that sets it off from everything that isn't art. That quality or feature does not exist. We know this because anything can be art, including the most ordinary object. Therefore, art is simply whatever the art world talks about.

Danto is much reviled for the view—a Harvard colleague calls him a "master of the flat-footed assertion"—but the theory is hard to defeat. In terms of strict ontological ordering, there really is nothing intrinsic in a "work of art" that distinguishes it from the furniture of the world or "mere real things," to use Danto's phrase. Neither beauty nor genius are categories with the same logical extension as art; that is, art may include those things, but it need not. And they may occur in nonart contexts. They are neither necessary nor sufficient for something to be art. Other options likewise fail to define the conditions of art. Significant form, purposiveness without purpose, emotional communication, illumination of higher reality—all of these and more have been served up as the definition of art. But none succeeds, for there is always a new work (or even an old one) that surges past a given conceptual boundary. A Tracy Emin installation or Jeff Wall photograph of an unmade bed is still capable of arousing old-school outrage among editors at the *New Criterion* or *Daily Telegraph*, but their ire confesses its own past-it futility. Whatever you think of their works, these artists of the supremely ordinary reason far more clearly than their critics. They know the only quality exactly coextensive with the category "art" is "found in the art world."

The institutional theory is often seen as hostile to art or beauty, but that is a misconception. When philosophers write in this mood they are not trying to destroy practices, but rather simply to understand their underlying assumptions. They want to know what makes the concept of "art" tick. So the health or otherwise of the art world is unrelated to the truth of the institutional theory, since art still does whatever it does for us no matter what ontological status its objects enjoy. That's the theory, anyway. In practice, of course, matters are more complicated, since artists and viewers alike want art to *mean* something, usually something *deep*—the emphasis here expressing a sort of table-thumping frustration over articulating what deep meaning actually is. And yet the institutional theory tells them there is, there can be, no valid philosophical account of the deep quality that is supposed to satisfy this desire for meaning.

Hence the current art world stalemate, in which analytic

philosophers think they have said all that can be said about art, and yet everyone else keeps trying to say more. Logically speaking, criticism and evaluation of art remain distinct from philosophy of art proper, so most of the resulting voluminous chat about art is confused level-jumping, specific comments straining for an impossible generality—impossible because nothing general can be true enough to stand, and nothing true can be general enough to satisfy the craving. In the resulting vacuum of thought, art itself tries to take over the job of saying what it is about. Since good artists are often bad philosophers, the results are frequently excruciating. What is called conceptual art rises to the top, irritating and baffling by turns. From this vantage, the surest sign of the times is not someone like Richter—with his literally palpable technique—but instead the celebrated conceptual artist (Ian Carr-Harris, Jenny Holzer) whose work is either undergraduate-quality though beautifully presented, or else apparently random collections of objects and in-jokes incomprehensible without the exhibition essay. Or, all too often, both.

This conceptual option has only existed for a short time but its influence has been pervasive, to the point where conceptual art dominates the highest reaches of the art world's thinking. The rise of conceptual art in America during the 1970s is nicely analyzed by Alexander Alberro in his elegant but uncritical book on conceptual art in America, *Conceptual Art and the Politics of Publicity*.[1] Alberro does not eschew aesthetic judgment of works by such pioneering American conceptual artists as Dan Graham, Sol LeWitt and Joseph Kosuth, but rather concentrates mainly on the impresario role played by the New York dealer Seth Siegelaub. More than any other single person, Siegelaub may be credited—which is to say, blamed—for opening up a gallery market for heavily ideational works in the latter third of the twentieth century. Amid the swirling confusions of mid-1960s New York, where pop had softened up the boundaries of what could be regarded as art, he was perfecting the craft of branding *avant la lettre*, making his chosen clients into "the best dishwashing liquid around," to quote his client Lawrence Weiner. Siegelaub's artists were packaged and sold to a hungry public even as they created works of vanishing ephemerality that could not be: grids marked in fields, chunks removed from gallery walls, labels and contracts, a magazine ad proclaiming itself the artwork.

If one is inclined to be a little more cynical than Alberro, this marks the first coordinated instance of a now familiar experience: the art show as outright scam. In the three decades since Siegelaub's New York heyday, conceptual art has become a winking insult, a condescending piece of self-indulgence dressed up as a radical challenge to the staid old art world where things have to be painted and displayed and maybe even be the result of talent. There are exceptions, of course: Yoko Ono and her Fluxus Movement colleagues, for example, created remarkable works that combined witty intelligence and arresting beauty even as they played with the very idea of art. But now, for the first time in the history of art, art is available to anyone with sufficient self-regard or lack of shame. It's all about fronting, success gauged not by talent but by degrees of arrogance and self-promotion. "He was the advertising agency," Weiner said of Siegelaub in a 1971 interview, and it is a mark of how far marketing and the techniques of what was then known as Madison Avenue have come to dominate the art world that no one today can be surprised by the choice of metaphor.

This is, if you like, the fully rational outcome of a post-historical art world ruled not by aesthetic criteria but by the institutional imperatives of displaying, promoting, buying and selling. The artists tell us the work is secondary to its ideas, the experience secondary to the system of communication. These moves are swiftly self-defeating, of course, with nonshows of nonworks in nongalleries the new norm. They destroy all human connection to the art object and elevate the artist as that familiar type, the elitist democrat, decrying the "aesthetic fascism" of beauty in the service of a baffled "wider audience." Conceptual art is, in short, Danto's institutional theory minus all the fancy philosophical footwork, an economy of reputation plain and simple. Or rather, not plain and simple but complex and sly: somewhere in there, the high priests of the art world still insist that it is all about the purity of the art, even if they cannot say what art is.

David Summers's massive work, *Real Spaces*, arrives on this enervating scene with a blast of air, a loud flourish.[2] Its ambition is nothing less than a comprehensive theory of art that will, among other things, dethrone the modern West's habitual assumption of cultural superiority. That superiority has many forms, but the central expression here is the foursquare "virtual plane" of the canvas, wall or page: the flat pale surface on which any image can be inked, painted, penciled, projected. Summers's method has many moving parts but is best described as galloping aesthetic anthropology, a linked globe-trotting exercise in vast erudition and dizzy equivalencies. Aztec temples in Central America illustrate the same points as artifacts from ancient Sumeria; twentieth-century abstracts are pushed up against prehistoric cave paintings. The book, sprawling and undisciplined at almost seven hundred dense pages of history and analysis, offers a conceptual repositioning of the very idea of art. Piece of cake.

But is it the new philosophy of art, what Summers calls "postformalist art history," we have been waiting for? Much of his analysis will be familiar from debates both inside and outside the art-history academy. For instance, the modern art museum or gallery, cornerstone of the art world, is not only of very recent vintage but a particular and skewed temple dedicated to the isolation and display of works. It is the warehouse of the singular genius, dominated by the local and still novel oddity of painting scenes or figures on rectilinear flat surfaces. Objects and creations predating this weird institution may be brought into it but only by submitting to its insistence on "aesthetic" appreciation independent of other values. Religious and cultural artifacts that might once have signaled the presence of the sacred or shared are now themselves subjected to isolation in the secular church of art. We remove them from the "real spaces" of their making and display and insert them into an arid space of isolation—real in its own way, but strange and local and decidedly not superior.

Like his distinguished forebear Erwin Panofsky, pioneer of the art-historical approach known as iconology—accessibly glossed in Michael Frayn's 2001 novel, *Headlong*—Summers wants to read back the deeper significance that fashioned objects and structures offered to their contemporaries. These things, he argues, created spaces of focused attention, where relationships to land, history, divinity and destiny were sketched and contemplated. The facts of their making—materials, placement, style, duration—were essential to this function. In the deep connection between makers and made a dimension of human existence is exposed, a "second nature" that typifies the way a local community or culture understood its relationship to earth, mortality, the human body and consciousness. First nature is invariable, but second nature is realized in multiple forms throughout space and time. Indeed, different notions of space and time are crucial aspects of that variation—the ticking clock and biaxial geometry of the modern West once more merely particular examples from a large range.

Such a notion of art takes the wind out of progressive and antiprogressive sails alike. Art history is not a long narrative of movement from lesser forms to greater ones; that is just the whiggish arrogance of hindsight. But neither can we just declare art history over and the bubble of the contemporary art world a self-contained, ahistorical realm. The virtual spaces typical of the modern world's art (not to be confused with modern art) are themselves attempts to create new real spaces, typically in the rather unwelcoming precinct of a Metropolitan Museum of Art show so crowded it reduces "contemplation" to a quick hip-to-hip shuffle past works obscured by bad haircuts and worse conversation. Still, our pilgrimage is not exactly optional. We go to the Louvre ostensibly to "look at" the *Mona Lisa*, but really so we can say we didn't, to have the experience precisely of *not* enjoying its aesthetic qualities while feeling first-hand the impossibility of doing so: burping, farting crowds, the thick pane of security glass, the long waits on line in I. M. Pei's hothouse-pyramid additions. This, too, is a real space.

The trouble with dismantling Western arrogance, about art or anything, is that it must always be done from the inside, and thus risks a fatal circularity: the philosophical assumptions of the West are affirmed in the very act of questioning the validity of the West. Modernity's reach is hard to elude, perhaps especially in rational criticism of it, which makes it the cultural equivalent of the New American Century, a weird amalgam of exceptionalism and imperialism. What if the nature of our moment in cultural time is precisely the assertion that we will now, finally, understand the nature of cultural time? You can run but you can't hide.

Summers's historicism offers no escape from this logical snare but it does offer some brilliant slashes of insight, particularly on the ideas of style and innovation. The best sections of *Real Spaces* are the final two chapters, where Summers traces the West's creation of single-point perspective and resulting notional space of infinite coordinate extension, or "metaopticality." (The book is marred by neologisms of this sort, also by self-indulgent technical flourishes and an ever more irritating fondness for etymological back stories, not all of them apposite. These are the tics of the academic mind, all best ignored.) Perspective doesn't merely revolutionize painting, it opens up a whole new world, creating radically new notions of space, subject, object, location, even identity. So it is no exaggeration to say that the spatiotemporal universe we now inhabit was born in the studios of a few exceptionally talented Italian painters, mathematicians and lens-grinders who laid down the conceptual possibility of everything from reliable navigation to the high-precision ballistics of the cruise missile.

This story deserves a book of its own, perhaps many of them. Summers has bigger fish to fry and can only dwell briefly on the genius of Filippo Brunelleschi, Leon Battista Alberti and their followers as they sketch, then realize, the advantages of coordinate space and infinite perspective. Brunelleschi, the Florentine goldsmith and engineer now once again rightly famous for his restoration of the ancient orders of architecture, was a master of the science of optics, crucial enabling knowledge for the rendering of sight- and light-lines on plane surfaces. Right angles, foreshortening and bisecting orthogonals had all existed before, to be sure, but now, attempting the ancient goal of accurate representation of reality, these pioneers stumble on a new world where any rectangle can be made to suggest not just depth within the frame but infinite spatial extensions beyond the frame. From Leonardo da Vinci's reckless, astonishing frescoes in the Sistine Chapel it is a small step to the frame-flooding moodiness of Caspar David Friedrich and then, in stages of ever more clever reaction, the cubist fractures of Georges Braque and Pablo Picasso, the playful geometric forms of Piet Mondrian, Jackson Pollock's drips, Ad Reinhardt's eye-filling blackness . . .

But it is more than just art, since this new fascination with the foursquare surface also conditions every other aspect of modern experience. Consider, for example, the panoptical grid plans of new-world cities like Manhattan, where, as Rem Koolhaas and Michel de Certeau have both noted, new combinations of determinacy and freedom are catalyzed on the notional Cartesian plane of the city. You are always locatable on the urban grid, occupying an intersection of coordinates like the ones offered habitually— by second nature!—to cab drivers; and yet you are always moving, a node of potential resisting the implication of surveillance carried by the grid. Modern notions of infinite space and time likewise encourage incipient projects of twinned creation and annihilation: speed. The space-time grid plots distances between points, at once showing separation and demanding its instantaneous elimination. Velocity begins by seeking to destroy time and ends by trying to destroy space. We shorten the time between locations until, at speed's vanishing point, time collapses into a single spatial point where all locations are potentially identical.

Or, closer still, consider the pages on which these words appear, trailing themselves from top to bottom and left to right, using a version of the planar paper surface and the saddle-stitched technology we call the codex—another rectilinear space essential to the modern world's dominance. In Chip Kidd's novel *The Cheese Monkeys*, an imperious graphic design instructor clarifies the stakes for his young pupils: "The page, the poster, the surface you are working on—THAT's your territory, and they are going to invade. Fine, let them. That's what you want anyway. But be ready. They are coming from the left. Always, always, always, always!!... We are the Western world. We read, see, think. Left. To. Right. You have few givens in this life, in this class. That is one of them. Use it."

All of this is wonderful, if again familiar. But does it deliver the goods we seek? Could a theory of real spaces aid us in the age-old task of distinguishing art from nonart? (Not to be confused with the equally ancient task of telling bad art from good.) Could it explain why art seems to matter to us, though we cannot always say why or how? Here it seems the idea of "real spaces" is not wrong, merely unhelpful. Art history alone, no matter how rarefied, cannot resolve the uncomfortable question of what art means.

In part this is a function of generality. Summers suggests at great length that art is about the peculiar role that made things have in our lives, the way creativity, skill and gorgeous materials can, in virtuoso combination, establish centers and peripheries. They help establish the ordered cardinal spaces of embodied consciousness—that is, you and I as we experience a structured world of up and down, left and right, inside and outside. But the more widely this notion of art is applied, the less critical purchase it seems to have in our world. We live in times of unprecedented image-profusion, a great trans-historical spasm of pictures and visual stimulus that is one meaning to the so-last-year word "globalization." "The entire human environment [has become] a work of art," Marshall McLuhan and Quentin Fiore said as far back as 1967's *The Medium Is the Massage*. And yet less and less can we say, with any confidence or happiness, *this* image, this one created thing, is laden with the special sort of meaning we seek from art. General scope, for so long the goal of theory, may combine with wide diffusion to become its own worst enemy: The result is the night in which all cows are black.

Maybe this is just a nonproblem and any general aesthetic theory a nonsolution to it. Maybe we all need to relax and just surf. If there is no ontological distinction belonging to art, as the institutional theory says, maybe there's no logical distinction either: art is whatever anyone says it is. The conceptual artists of the 1960s, Alberro shows, met the condition of profusion by collapsing the distinction between art and advertising from both sides, making the art world a realm of anti-aesthetic intellectual play, where cognition overruled experience, even while constructing themselves as artful objects of marketing savvy, the artist as brand. They could not quite complete that collapse, since that would have spelled the end of their special status in chains of social-capital exchange. Nor could they entirely follow through on the antimaterial logic of conceptualism, which finally renders the artwork, no matter how detached from a beautiful object or document, dispensable.

Unfortunately, the endpoint of conceptual art, namely the nonobject nonevent, is reached too quickly and too finally: once there, there is literally nothing left to say. This horizon is what Jean Baudrillard called "the xerox degree of art," a conceptual vanishing point where conceptual art's attempted critique of modernist art institutions and their "aesthetic fascism" simply ends up blurring any distinction between art and publicity, art and mass culture, art and everything else. Instead, then, these artists continued (and continue) to show their works either in traditional galleries or in installation spaces (parks, traffic intersections, streets), which soon become equally traditional. Paradoxically, and predictably, these attempted anti-elitist moves only sharpen the art world's privileged boundaries, and without giving art anything much to say except the banal tautology—still all too common—that art is art. Conceptual art isn't so much about ideas as it is about the idea of ideas.

In a way quite different from the institutional theory and its conceptual beneficiaries, Summers ends up arguing a similarly empty conclusion. Anything can be, indeed has been, art. But with this claim, anthropological universalism collapses under its own weight. This overarching historicizing denies what might be the remaining grain of truth in old-fashioned aesthetic philosophy, namely that there is something particular in artworks that makes them artworks. Like most critics of his antihegemonic persuasion, Summers wants to break the Western prejudice that things are only art when viewed for their aesthetic qualities alone: that confines art to the austere precinct of the museum or gallery. It's true that this insistence on disinterest robs sacred objects of their original functionality and placement, also true that it can lead to a dominance by what Danto once called "arrogant Kantians." But so what? Maybe there is a defensible narrative in artistic endeavor after all, whereby the creation of things simply for their interesting play of beauty, ideas and resonances is what we've been struggling towards all along.

That is precisely the sort of thing a respectable academic art historian does not say these days, but every now and then his desires, like our own when wandering the galleries and streets, surface nonetheless. To my ear, the strongest echo in Summers's notion of real spaces is Heidegger, the Nazi flirter and critic of technology whose gnomic essay on "The Origin of the Work of Art" is worth considering again in the bleak dawn of this new century.

Heidegger sees the work of art first of all in its materiality, its having-been-made: what Summers would call its "facture." But this connection to the "earth" is extended by the artwork's ability to force a clearing in the everyday exchanges of existence. The artwork presents no particular propositional truth—it does not mean something or other. Rather, it offers the deeper truth of Being, a moment of reflection on the fact that there is something rather than nothing. This is what Heidegger means by art's ability to open up the world, to illuminate the fourfold structure of earth, sky, mortals and gods. "By the opening up of a world, all things gain their lingering and hastening, their remoteness and nearness, their scope and limits," Heidegger says of art. "A work, by being a work, makes space for that spaciousness." Uselessness is not the artwork's essence, but is an important aspect of its otherness, its ability to arrest our attention. Art is not ready-to-hand but present-at-hand: not a piece of equipment but a slab of existence. The authentic work therefore *obtrudes* in our field of experience, somehow forcing a confrontation with wonder. Instead of the curiosity and marvel of the spectacle-soaked everyday world, the play of cheap novelty and distracting images, we confront an existential insistence on the question of *what it means to be here*.

Summers distances himself from Heidegger, citing the German philosopher's "primitivism" and unpleasant politics. He might also have mentioned the overly negative view of technology. But he should not be so hasty, or so ungrateful. Heidegger offers, in just a few pages, what Summers tries and fails to provide, a sustained thought about the wonder of art. We seek wonder fitfully and with misgiving, frequently disappointed and even more frequently distracted by the nattering of critics and theorists, but we still somehow know it when we feel it: the staggered attention, the clearing of thought, the shock of recognition that a work of art alone makes possible. Historical comprehensiveness, analytic precision and conceptual shenanigans all fail to illuminate this fully. They can, at best, weave a discursive web around it, outlining the mysterious space of art's work. Only art itself can open up that space from within. Only art is a thing that, like consciousness itself, cannot be translated into any terms other than its own.

Notes

1.   Alexander Alberro, *Conceptual Art and the Politics of Publicity* (MIT Press, 2003).

2.   David Summer, *Real Spaces: World Art History and the Rise of Western Modernism* (Phaidon, 2003).

2. Monumental-Conceptual Architecture

The architect Daniel Libeskind, now in the public eye for his World Trade Center (WTC) reconstruction, is also the muse behind a less spectacular project, the three-year, $150-million renovation—or "renaissance"—of the Royal Ontario Museum (ROM) in Toronto. In both designs Libeskind has shown himself a master of high-profile success in the current architectural market. The ROM project especially, a striking crystalline outline, is a good example of the sort of mutation a recent vogue for distinctive, high-profile architecture, often for museums, has created. These projects—Frank Gehry's Bilbao Guggenheim; Peter Eisenman's Wexner Center for the Arts at Ohio State University and City of Culture of Galicia in Santiago de Compostela; Libeskind's Jewish Museum in Berlin—have an influence disproportionate to their number, becoming the focus of most recent nonacademic (and much academic) debate about architecture.

This is not surprising. Their position astride major public spaces makes such projects highly visible, usually through public money and major municipal cooperation. Like all urban architecture, they belong to everyone, including future generations. In many cases, they are driven by form rather than content. The Bilbao Guggenheim, for example, was not built to house or display an existing collection—there was none—but as a $100-million, 256,000-square-foot end in itself. The City of Culture of Galicia, with a projected cost of $125 million and 810,000 square feet, also has no existing collection, selling itself instead on the 173-acre mountaintop site and Eisenman's thrusting stone walls that one commentator describes as looking "as if they were pushed right up through the earth."[1] All these projects, and others of even more recent vintage—Diller and Scofidio's Institute of Contemporary Art in Boston and, still more, their Blur Building on Lake Neuchâtel at Yverdon-les-Bains, Switzerland, a "structure" that exists only as a man-made fog mass suspended above a ramped bridge—share a penchant for what we might agree to call the monumental-conceptual. Many of the now-familiar architectural stars were first celebrated in a 1988 show at the MoMA in New York, assembled by Philip Johnson and guided by Eisenman, which marked a development of modernism from within its own radical wings. Gehry, Libeskind and Eisenman were joined in the show by Koolhaas, Zaha Hadid, Bernard Tschumi and Wolf Prix of Coop Himmelb(l)au.

Monumental-conceptual architecture, as I shall use the term, is not to be confused with simple theoretical architecture. Waves of theory-driven architecture are hardly new, with ideas borrowed liberally from fashionable philosophical works emanating mainly from Paris, Bologna and Berlin—Eisenman's use of Noam Chomsky, Jacques Derrida and Gianni Vattimo; Tschumi's debt to Debord and the situationists; Diller and Scofidio's Lacanian probes; everyone's use of Heidegger and Walter Benjamin.[2] From the admittedly judgmental perspective of professional philosophy, such "theory" architects and, especially, their lesser acolytes, appear to be intellectual magpies, distracted by anything shiny and new. But at least their debts were, in most cases, openly stated; and if, in practice, a deconstructionist building or Deleuzian blob-and-fold structure was less interesting in reality than in theory, well, so what? We could note the theory, judge the building, move on.

The newest large-scale works pose a somewhat different problem. Though Johnson's show grouped Gehry, Koolhaas, Libeskind and the rest under the banner of deconstructionist literary theory, in fact the group is united only in their facility with ideas and subsequent success, especially in highly contested museum commissions. With open theory-debts now somewhat out of fashion, architects of the first order have taken to selling their game in terms of concepts rather than theories—a sketch or simulacrum of theory, a theory of theory, where ideas are often unmoored and scattered (also, to be fair, sometimes brilliant and bold). Theory/concept is a fine distinction, yes, but in effect it is a matter of responsibility. Theory, whatever else it does, makes demands: of coherence, of consistency in application. Concepts, as I shall use the term, and the monumental-conceptual architecture they allow, are free-floating and undemanding, such that the mere play of ideas, the juggling of concepts, is seen as a sufficient justification, an end in itself.

The question then becomes: are the monumental-conceptual works living up to the responsibility of public money and public attention, or are they large-scale con games feeding the self-indulgence of a new breed of installation artists, the architect as seer? To answer that question we must not only examine current architecture, but also continue our retrospective stroll through the early days of conceptual art, an important enabling condition for the latest generation of big-name architects.

I must immediately confess a complicated interest in the topic, especially as it relates to Libeskind and his ROM reconstruction in Toronto. From 2001 to 2004 I was chair of the ROM's Institute for Contemporary Culture (ICC), a semiautonomous body within the museum. The ROM, founded from a private collection in 1912 and first opened to the public in 1914, is one of Canada's most important cultural institutions, roughly equivalent to the Metropolitan

Museum's eminent position in New York. Its two neo-classical wings, built of warm Ontario sandstone and yellow brick, adorned by grandly optimistic slogans and friezes, occupy an enviable corner of downtown real estate. Libeskind's design will remove the undistinguished stack of 1970s-vintage pebbledash slabs that currently sit uneasily between the two original buildings, which lie parallel to each other on a north-south orientation. The resulting middle space was the focus of all the submissions, since the original wings are to be preserved. Proposed solutions ranged from a huge cantilevered roof with gallery space actually inside it, to a kind of domed-shed design that would have made the ROM resemble the world's largest Quonset hut.

The ROM is both a fine art and a natural history museum, a twinned mandate that over the years has proven tricky, to say the least, in terms of allocation of space and curatorial resources. Navigating the internal politics of the ROM is work of mandarin complexity, and the choice of Libeskind as the architect of its largest-ever renovation (I was only peripherally involved in this choice) was naturally rife with controversy both inside and outside the museum. The new ICC, meant to be a link between the old ROM and the wider reaches of contemporary culture, including art, film, fashion, architecture and design, secured some prime real estate in the scramble for space in the museum's upcoming construction. It will have a dedicated gallery, its first ever, in one of Libeskind's sprouting crystal excrescences. These massive shards of glass and steel will hang out over the museum's currently neglected frontage on Bloor Street, Toronto's main upscale shopping district. Our gallery is a soaring cathedral space with no vertical walls and potential acoustic dead zones in the high corners; but it will be a beautiful room and a foundation for the ICC's future growth. The plans also show that it is right next to a projected split-level bar and restaurant that will look out over the University of Toronto's neo-gothic spires and the little ravine known as Philosopher's Walk, which is very nice.

The process by which this design came into being has become

notorious and, while in some sense distinct from the result, nevertheless indicates the intellectual space of the monumental-conceptual. Libeskind settled on the crystalline entity in what has become a legendary act of bravura design. Unlike the other short-listed firms—which included Italy's Andrea Bruno and the Vancouver-based local favorite, Bing Thom—Libeskind offered no plans or models. Instead, he briefly toured the museum, went to the in-house restaurant, grabbed a handful of large paper napkins, and swiftly produced six rough charcoal sketches of his design. These were displayed, in Lucite frames, alongside the elaborate elevations and table-sized models of the other, less inspired—and eventually less successful—submissions.

Libeskind later said that the crystal idea came to him suddenly, prompted by a case containing geodes that he passed in the ROM's geology displays, though cynics have pointed out that his design for the renovation of the Victoria and Albert Museum in London is remarkably similar. Perhaps lightning does strike twice, but that evident sloppiness at once exposes and weakens the conceptual basis for the design. Libeskind's practice is to find an idea rooted in the local site and expand it to building dimensions. The zig-zagging walls and grim steel cladding of the Jewish Museum are modeled on the barbed-wire fences of concentration camps, for example. The ROM concept attempts to link the building with its collections, crystal to crystal, but the idea is both conceptually weak (the museum's geology holdings are but a small part of its character) and creatively suspect (does the V&A also have geodes prominently displayed between its entrance and restaurant?).

Since then, the design has also been severely modified. The project engineers, a group of stolid Manchester problem-solvers, announced that the original glass design was impressive but unfortunately in violation of the laws of physics. Glass was anyway a poor choice to withstand the nasty Toronto winters, and it would also expose rare artifacts to excessive sunlight. The crystals were reduced in size, simplified significantly. They are now clad in dull metal with prominent slashes of inset windows. Meanwhile, overall

gallery footage did not exceed the formerly cramped interior allocation, has in fact been both reduced and chopped into awkward
small chunks, leaving the museum's curatorial staff understandably
disgruntled. Architectural savants may consider them philistines,
but the curators have problems with nonvertical walls and exposure to variable humidity. These issues have not disappeared in the
flurry of publicity over the new building, any more than they have
at Libeskind's other monumental museums—his only two completed buildings at the time—the Jewish Museum and the Imperial
War Museum North in Manchester. The former, especially, a zinc-
clad series of forms, offers lightning bolt window slashes and disturbing, sharp, dead-end spaces. It is not a house of artifacts or
even of memory, but rather what one critic calls "an abstract cham-
ber of horrors," including a thirteen-foot-wide void in its center to
symbolize the Jews snuffed out by Nazi genocide.[3]

In both his buildings and his methods, then, Libeskind—like
Gehry, Koolhaas, Tschumi and Hadid—is emblematic of recent
monumental-conceptual architecture's tendency to fuse personal
style with distinctive silhouettes. (Or, in the case of Koolhaas, distinctive books and interiors.) Personality is almost as important as
the buildings or spaces it creates, perhaps even more so. We have
been told that the latest generation of celebrity architects are the
new rock stars, but in fact they are more like the first generation
of conceptual artists. They are not theorists, exactly, yet they have
apparently observed the influence of theory and absorbed its useful bafflegab. (Gehry, vocally antitheory, is an exception; but such
hostility is a conceptual artist's habitual move, too.) They know
massive public buildings can no longer be sold on solid technical
principles alone; there must also be a frisson of Bright Ideas, architecture as a dashing intellectual exercise, with a twist of self-
promotion thrown in.

To say this is decidedly not to cast down any and all theoretical architecture, of course. There is ever a balance to be struck
between theory and practice. It used to be that the highest expression
of architectural purity was drawing a building that would never be

built, say in Neil Denari's mode of "visionary" works of unbuilt architecture, almost a form of pure mathematics that illustrate ideas from (as it might be) Gilles Deleuze and Félix Guattari, Werner Heisenberg or Kurt Gödel.[4] Not surprisingly, such moves proved influential with the most impressionable members of any profession, its students. The popsicle-cool architecture majors I knew during graduate school at Yale designed underground shopping malls with a single door or houses accessible only from the roof. These drawings might be published, but that was as much as the rising young architects desired. Building was for the crude, a ham-fisted exercise in compromise, and Howard Roark would never have been forced to dynamite anything if he'd just stuck to making drawings.

It's easy to mock such self-important purism, or excuse it as a forgivable tic of the young. After all, we all know architecture is about building things, and drawings are tools, not ends in themselves. But of course it is never that simple. A drawing may embody as many revolutionary notions, and prompt as much significant reaction, as a built form—indeed, may do far more, given how many merely banal buildings we are forced to live in and work around. Intellectual purism, meanwhile, may also take many forms, not all of them so forgivable as youthful excess or as limited in effect as a drawing published in a scholarly journal. The hallmark of monumental-conceptual architecture is that its ideas are realized at full scale and huge public expense, often buttressed by some gifted fast talking.

This can be hard to resist. In a talk on "The Architecture of Meaning," sponsored by the ICC, Libeskind addressed an audience of more than five hundred at the ROM and spun a weird extemporaneous web of words and theories, rambling and vivid, which had the effect of thaumaturgy. He mentioned Paul Celan, Emily Dickinson, William Shakespeare, Derrida, and the Marx Brothers— but not, for all his evident debts to him, Heidegger. He compared architecture to music, to fire, to time, to human consciousness. He rejected the idea of a unified theory of meaning and also a unified theory of architecture. His presentation was literally mesmerizing in that one felt held, then released, by a sort of hypnotic intellectual gaze, and emerged with no clear sense of what had transpired.

There were some good stories, indicative of how monumental-conceptual architecture secures commissions and works in practice. Bidding for the World Trade Center commission, Libeskind asked to be taken down into the excavated ground zero site—something he says no other architect did—and looked up. Immediately he called his studio in Berlin and told them to tear up all their preliminary drawings: the entire project would have to be reconceived from this subterranean perspective. In Switzerland, competing for a shopping mall contract, Libeskind recalled watching *Room Service*, the 1938 Marx Brothers romp in which Groucho and company take over a department store and make it their combined home and club, subverting the logic of shopping. The clients, he says, gave him the job without further ado, without a single drawing being created, even on a napkin. They knew that, thinking this way, Libeskind would produce a place people would want to visit; the shopping would look after itself. So, for that matter, would the building. The Bright Idea is everything.

But here's the trouble with bright ideas: sometimes they're not flashes of insight or challenging sallies, just high-wire waffling, often in the service of the current arrangement. The shopping mall commission provides an excellent example. The Marx Brothers would be dismayed to know they were enlisted in a project to facilitate shopping, not mock it. Instead of undermining consumerism's dominance, Libeskind's scheme merely gives it new gloss, supplying a sheen of cleverness to the most pervasive fact of life in the first world. The only subversion here is the subversion of satirical energy entailed by borrowing, then reversing the polarity, of a much more hard-won and authentic comic genius. Disconnected ideas may impress the clients, but they are not honest if their awkward implications are left unpursued, if their critical effect is neutralized by glibness. The discipline of linear thinking, following the demands of logic, isn't just hard work one might or might not care for; it's a political responsibility, especially when there are obvious public consequences, so that (at a minimum) subversion isn't sold back to us as commodity, or mere plausible facility taken as genius. In fact, another name for those sly moves is propaganda, once wisely defined by the classicist Francis Cornford as "that branch of the art of lying which consists in very nearly deceiving your friends without quite deceiving your enemies."[5] But now we can never be quite sure who is a friend and who an enemy, because distinctions tend to run together when mere cleverness is sufficient to secure the job.

Toronto audiences, though usually polite, can also be hardheaded. In the question-and-answer period following his talk, Libeskind faced various challenges over the crystal design. (Because I was selecting the questions from submitted index cards, I was able to weed out a few outright hostile ones, such as "How did you get so good at fooling your clients?") It was clear that many people in the city were less than thrilled about the design, though often enough intrigued and provoked by it, too. But provoked how? The design is neither revolutionary nor witty. It sits oddly in the current urban fabric but without really challenging or recasting the surrounding skyline. It's just there, already something of a mere novelty, whose value will wear off more quickly than its remaining windows will be scored by winter salt and acid snow. There is nothing truly shocking here, none of the invigorating disdain of a theorist such as Eisenman, say, who refused to alter dangerous, ankle-breaking staircases in one building so that people "would never take stairs for granted again."[6] In a familiar paradox of recent monumental-conceptual architecture, like Gehry's "Bilbao-Lite" projects in Seattle and Cleveland, the building risks being difficult without being interesting. Or, more charitably, these buildings *are* interesting—but just for a novel moment, a high-octane honeymoon of passing originality.

I dwell on Libeskind here because his project is close to my interests, but also because he exposes most clearly the intellectual tendencies of current public building on a grand scale. And the ROM project shows, more than any other current major building, how monumental-conceptual architecture shares the problem of evanescent novelty with conceptual art. Indeed, you might say that conceptual art is an important enabling condition of the current architectural scene. As we saw in the previous essay, without the pioneering slyness and precedent of clever self-promotion in the Seth Siegelaub stable of 1960s New York postpop artists, today's architectural high-wire artists would probably not exist or function in the global limelight. Siegelaub successfully packaged the likes of Weiner, Graham, LeWitt, Kosuth, Douglas Huebler, Carl Andre, and Robert Barry, and sold them as a new art world brand.[7] Their group shows at Windham College in upstate New York and at Manhattan venues, from Siegelaub's downtown galleries to the School of Visual Arts, established new norms of intellectual playfulness in an art scene at once moribund and confused.

The various tendencies of these early conceptual gestures resist easy generalization, but certain common (and now familiar) themes emerge: irreproducibility, occasionality, immateriality, resistance to the "aesthetic fascism" of beauty, the ascending importance of titles for understanding artists' intentions. Titles and descriptions take on new importance, overshadowing, even contradicting, the "works" themselves. Often elaborate imperative or passive-voice instructions—"A can of aerosol paint is sprayed for exactly two minutes six inches from the floor"—define the works, making their actual execution more and more irrelevant. Indeed, the primary information of the object or piece is not just supplemented but eventually dominated by the secondary information of the concept suggested, allowed, by the object. Art sheds its bonds to beauty or even the visual. First it becomes text (Tom Wolfe's "painted word"), then eschews even text, real or implied, to become pure idea: a free-floating, nonmaterial concept in theory available to anyone and everyone, anywhere and everywhere. In theory and as theory.

Artists in the Siegelaub stable indulged in much self-conscious play, again now familiar, with logical contradictions and visual paradoxes. Perhaps the most immediately emblematic works are the well-known series by Kosuth called "Titled (Art as Idea as Idea)," which comprises a series of wall-mounted black slabs inscribed with dictionary definitions of key words ("water," "painting"); also of the word "nothing" as given by various dictionaries. Kosuth here mixes everyday experiences (the dictionary definition) with the expectations of the arid traditional gallery space, where we expect to see not definitions of "water" but representations of it, not the word "painting" but paintings. In the array of "nothing" slabs, the thought is deepened: we can define "nothing" but only at the cost of tangling ourselves in paradox. (As the entry of "nothing" in the *Encyclopedia of Philosophy* has it, "Nobody has a lot to say about nothing; but then, he would.") Kosuth's visual flirtation with self-reference and revealing paradox is typical of this first generation of conceptual art—unfortunately typical, we might say, since "Titled (Art as Idea as Idea)" soon collapses under its own weight, such that the little joke at its center is too quickly "got," and so the air of intelligence too quickly dispersed. It becomes pretentious, not provocative.

The celebrated Xerox Book show, which Siegelaub organized in 1968, presents a similar series of logical tangles, one of the main routes of exploration for this generation of conceptual artists. Each of the seven artists in the show, including Weiner, LeWitt and Andre, was allowed a series of 8½ by 11–inch sheets of paper. Whatever they produced would be xeroxed and displayed in intentionally cheesy plastic-sleeve binders, the whole show intended to exhibit a democratic and antielitist accessibility. Xerox was chosen precisely for its then-novel combination of cutting-edge technology and in practice poor reproductive quality: an intoxicating duality for these antiestablishment aristocrats of the art world. An attendant irony was that the cost of xeroxing the Xerox Book was prohibitively high, and so the mechanical reproduction that was supposed to undermine the auratic uniqueness of the displayed works was carried out by old-fashioned offset printing. The casual reproduction techniques of xeroxing created works that looked casual but were, in practice, as unique and irreproducible as any art object of the traditional fetishized sort.

More than that, though the works are as self-consciously down-market as the presentation, "aesthetic fascism" nevertheless creeps back into the binders in the form of great incidental beauty. Andre's sheets in the book, for example, are xeroxes of wooden blocks dropped semi-randomly onto the machine's glass surface, and are casually gorgeous, their power a result of a virtuoso combination of material and talent. Weiner's graph-paper maps and scribbles, by the same token, though accompanied by his usual explicit codes and instructions, rise above words and overtake them, reasserting the primary information of the visual object. They are, quite simply, beautiful—and not because of the ideas set out in the accompanying text, but rather almost despite them. In both cases, very traditional norms of composition, balance and significant form are decidedly involved. We see the play of possibility within constraint that is a hallmark of all art, and in addition feel the compulsion of art that both uses and reflects on its medium—without falling into the trap of other contributors to this project, who make reflection on the medium their sole concern. Conceptual art can be strong but only when the concepts are married to material expression. "What makes [something] an artwork," Danto observes, "is the fact that it embodies, as a human action gives embodiment to a thought, something we could not form a concept of without the material objects which convey its soul."[8]

Hence the central paradox of all conceptual art, a far more important one than the usual problems of self-imposed exile, wherein artists cast themselves out of one art establishment simply by taking up residence in another part of it, and elitism, whereby works intended to break the monopoly of art end up being far more forbidding and inaccessible than any mainstream museum show. No, the fundamental paradox is that conceptual art fails just to the extent that it succeeds, and vice versa. If the works are visually beautiful and compelling, if they excite a prehensile wonder that cannot be translated into or reduced to words, they reward our interest but violate the artist's intentions. If the work fades and the ideas obtrude, on the other hand, then the work risks self-annihilation, disappearing in a puff of zero-degree smoke. Or, as Baudrillard nicely put it, "xerox-degree" smoke.[9] The work is no longer necessary, and the only logical outcome of this line of thinking is a series of nonshows in nonlocations featuring nonworks. Serious conceptualists, of course, would embrace that endgame, but then their work (and the work) is done—art is over. But art is not over, and conceptual art embraced by the art world loses its original critical purchase, which was anyway never very large, and becomes the mainstream. Works continue to be shown, naturally, but they are no longer comprehensible or interesting without the backing ideas of the catalog essay and critical intervention. The Canadian artist Ian Carr-Harris, for example, a darling of contemporary art, offers works such as a table of old books, all stamped with the title "Index," that surrender their meaning (the variability of meaning—what else?) only in the accompanying text.

We might dismiss the first generation of conceptual artists as silly sixties-style rebels, more angry than bright, but their influence is too pervasive to bracket so easily, and their original ideas too apposite. The cult of the beautiful and the institutional pathologies of the big-gallery art world are ever in need of critical tweaking. But the succeeding generations have not improved on the original thoughts, or resolved the ongoing paradox of presentation. The contemporary art world is still dominated by their nostrums of immateriality, and antiestablishment posturing. Jenny Holzer or Barbara Krueger, still more Emin or the Chapman brothers, are celebrated for presenting ideas neither unsettling nor new. In some cases, as with Emin, provocation itself is made empty, since she (unlike a genuinely disturbing artist such as Damien Hirst or Mark Prent) merely rides a wave of critical dismay: in a way, she is provocative not for being outrageous but for being outrageous in her claims to provocation.

In a sense, this continuing influence of banalized conceptualism is a problem of level-jumping, Hegelian dialectics run riot: instead of remaining at the level of sensuous realization of The Idea, as Hegel argued art must, these artists are trying to become philosophers, getting their art not only to embody ideas but also to speak them. While understandable—even in Hegel's terms, previous realizations of the truth tend to push upward, aiming at purer manifestation—philosophizing art is a mug's game, because it is precisely the concrete sensuousness of the work that makes it art. Art may *point to* philosophy, but it cannot *become* it—not, at least, without sailing close to the wind of irrelevancy, since the work would thereby destroy itself in the act of being itself. One can either follow through on the logic of conceptualism and become a philosopher, or one can ignore it and remain an artist. But one cannot do both. There is, to be sure, a continuum of human expression about what it means to be here that embraces both artistic and philosophical efforts.

There are even interesting figures at the margins, whose work enacts an ongoing debate about the demarcation and even validity of this distinction: we might think here of the later Heidegger, say, whose thoughts about art and poetry acquire, through a hard search for reiterable philosophical truth, a unique artistic and poetic quality; or the raging incandescence of Nietzsche or Henry David Thoreau, who write with their feelings burning and images unbridled. (It is perhaps no surprise that all three figures, plus others of the same proclivity, are not considered "serious" philosophers by the mandarins of the academic world.) From the other side, with an artist such as Rilke we observe a thrilling marriage of images and ideas, the unimprovable expression of ideas that trouble as well as move us. No philosopher, no matter how talented, could hope to delve any deeper into the human condition. But of course poetry is text and therefore avoids the hard cases of visual-textual combat that the term "conceptual art" usually evokes. And in conceptual art, the distinction between art and philosophy reasserts itself despite all forms of play attempting to undermine it. Art without concrete sensuous presentation is merely text. And art whose concrete sensuous presentation is baffling without text is juggling ideas without really confronting them.

You may be thinking: just another turf war between art and philosophy, more of what Danto calls "Platonic aggression" against makers of images.[10] You make the pretty pictures, and leave the thinking to us! But I am not a Hegelian, confident that philosophy has higher *geistlich* truths to communicate; nor would I, like Plato, confine art to the exercise of mimesis. Plato himself, as is well known, appeared to fall into performative contradiction, offering masterpieces of imaginative art that argue the inferiority of imaginative art—a contradiction acknowledged implicitly in the palinodic discussion of the *Phaedrus* and openly in the deathbed dialogue, *Phaedo*. In the former, the Socratic arguments against the emotional appeal of rhetoric and poetry, deployed in the first half, are subtly undermined by an extended poetical appeal to love in the second half. In the latter, the condemned cobbler-turned-philosopher Socrates allows, apparently as an afterthought, that he would have enjoyed making music instead of just making shoes and arguments. Nietzsche seizes on this stray remark with typical ferocity, saying that what we really need is not the arid rationalism of the Socratic method, dedicated to truth, but the lightness of "a music-making Socrates," dedicated, presumably, to Truth.

And yet, and yet—there is a grain of truth here, in that art's power to excite wonder is, and should be, qualitatively different from philosophy's. They may often be related, as when a powerful work calls forth a train of thought impossible otherwise or situates me suddenly in a world of meaning, "lifting a corner of the veil," as Albert Einstein said of numbers. Wonder has many sources and occasions, including natural ones. But the special status enjoyed by art, much disputed though it is, rests finally on its artificial and sensuous arousal of "rapt attention," to use Heidegger's phrase. It opens a clearing of thought. The mistake at the heart of too much conceptual art is its lack of openness, the implicit project of intellectual control, as if ideas could always be prethought and precaptured. The work is not allowed to be simply the work, and the result is not an act of philosophical aggression against art, but rather an act of aesthetic aggression against us—not playfulness but its simulacrum, not possibility but manipulation.

Naturally, even this claim is a little too crude, for it does not account for the important exceptions to these somewhat sweeping generalizations. Everyone has their own lists of these. For what it's worth, and as suggested in the previous chapter, mine would include the Fluxus Movement colleagues, funny and moving pieces from Reinhardt, John Cage and Joseph Beuys, contemporary works by Liz Magor, Walter de Maria or James Turrell. A Cage video included in the Whitney's American Century show of early 2000, for example, was a deceptively simple success: an extended "talk show" sequence, complete with cheesy set and back-and-forth camera cuts, in which the "host" and "guest" did nothing but stare thoughtfully into space. Over the course of thirty minutes, this becomes first hilarious and then unnerving, the grammar and ingest-ed assumptions of televisual "debate" exposed with deft precision and silence. Contrast that with, say, Jeff Koons's giant metal sculp-ture of an inflatable rabbit or Matthew Barney's Cremaster videos, both included in the same show, which seem to have little point beyond their surface cleverness and some impressive technical skill. It is not that one work "translates" well and the others don't; but rather that one has something to say that could not be said otherwise, and the others are showy and "smart" even while being empty.

Such lists could go on and on, not least because good art of ideas (to use a phrase decisively distinct from conceptual art), which enlarges thought through the sensuous excitation of wonder, is to be found in many places, almost despite the influence of crude conceptualism. Such claims, when particular, are inherently con-troversial, as most aesthetic judgments are. I find Fluxus boxes of mislabeled ephemera and strange functionless tools compelling and somehow emotional, as evocative as a Joseph Cornell box; others will see only pretension and obscurity. Jeff Wall's photo-graphs of unkempt bedrooms or bestrewn workspaces offer a subtle commentary on the banality of appearances; others think they are themselves banal rubbish. The making of such lists, and debates about which works belong on them and why, is a matter for criticism and appreciation, not for philosophy. The main philosophical point, and the only valid one that can be made in general, is that aesthetic success hinges on how much the work opens up, rather than closes down, the spaces of thought and wonder.

Which brings us, finally, back to architecture and its peculiar tensions at the level of the concept. Here the stakes are higher (buildings obtrude on everyday life more than most artworks) and the conceptual tangles more complicated. As with conceptual art, there is always a creeping danger that a bright idea is really just a piece of fleeting self-importance, that apparently virtuoso intellectual play, which seemed diverting at first, will come to seem mediocre at last.

More than this, though, the economy of reputation that has developed around architecture in its high-profile monumental realizations means that simple excellence in design is no longer, in itself, sufficient to fetch the public imagination. Even an architect of surpassing aesthetic gifts like Richard Meier begins to seem too simple, too easily appreciated—or maybe too familiarly modernist. (His lovely $1-billion, 360,000-square-foot design for the Getty Center in Los Angeles, which opened at the same time as Gehry's Bilbao Guggenheim and was much admired by visitors, did not create nearly the same international sensation.) Architects, as Witold Rybczynski argues in *The Look of Architecture*, dislike the notion of style, thinking it exposes a fatal susceptibility to fashion or sensation.[11] In fact, style is inescapable in architecture as in much else, and, in the current atmosphere of public scrutiny, defined architectural style is not just inevitable but essential. Indeed, we must go further: to be truly successful, one's style must be grand and singular, a result of conviction or revelation. It must convey a big idea. It must be monumental-conceptual.

This need, which in a sense we all feed, creates new problems the conceptual artists did not face. As a profession, and as a matter of practical reality, architecture is an applied art and therefore, necessarily, a crucible of compromise: compromise not only with the laws of physics and materials science, but also with competing aesthetic visions, client desires, municipal bureaucracies, and a host of imponderables gathered under the vague but powerful notion of "future use." It is even the case, as Koolhaas and others have long argued, that architecture cannot even be conceived except as collaboration. Buildings are never built alone, and the tortured romantic genius of Ayn Rand's febrile imagination is little more than a bugbear of the B. Arch. graduating class. So much is obvious.

At the same time, the current vogue for monumental buildings, destination buildings—especially museums like the Bilbao Guggenheim, Gehry's Rock and Roll Museum in Hollywood, Libeskind's Jewish Museum, James Ingo Freed's Holocaust Memorial Museum, or even Santiago Calatrava's soaring addition to the Milwaukee Art Museum or cathedral vault in Toronto's BCE Place—highlights the opposite pole, the impetuous visionary who clambers down into the Lower Manhattan pit of slurry walls or boldly sketches a melted-down mound of swooping metal shapes. We need to enliven and elevate such singular figures, to raise them up in our own gaze. Even Koolhaas, so prominent in his recognition of architectural collaboration, owes much of his prominence precisely to cultivation of his individual image, a cult of personality. The same phenomenon may be observed in the well-known studios of other designers and architects in the highest reaches of the contemporary pantheon, people like Norman Foster and Tschumi. (Gehry, offbeat in his early Santa Monica semi-obscurity, used to consort with the likes of Jasper Johns and Robert Rauschenberg; now famous, he is unable to avoid the pressures of the celebrity round.) Once more, this is hardly new, not at least since the transcendental arrogance of Le Corbusier or the glowering genius of Ludwig Mies van der Rohe, but these name-brand figures now seem to consort almost exclusively with one another, at least as a function of their public image, the way Hollywood celebrities do. Or they cloak themselves in a necromantic isolation, like Greta Garbo. They exist on a higher plane than the rest of us.

The reasons for this duality of collective and individual are obvious. There is no zip—though there may be good design—in a broad studio collaboration. Clients, and still more the wider public, are simple creatures: they need a face, a name, and a personality to humanize and animate their interest in design. It is not very alluring to learn that Studio Daniel Libeskind is actually a team of twenty-seven architects and designers, all working with various project engineers, landscape architects, contractors and materials specialists who will go nameless as the ROM, the new WTC and that shopping mall in Switzerland all rise from the ground. As with the art studios of old, the brass tacks workshops of Michelangelo or Brunelleschi, here Daniel Libeskind the man is merely the head of a sprawling creative corporation known as Daniel Libeskind the studio.

If the studio model is the reality, then, the dominant myth remains that of a lone aesthetic genius, the isolated visionary. We are somehow uncomfortable with the fact of collaboration in creative endeavors, even ones as obviously multihanded as architecture. The reasons for this are not hard to unearth. Western culture has too recently passed through the excesses of Romanticism, Impressionism and Modernism, all of which cultivated and encouraged the single-genius model, sometimes beyond all reasonable proportion. One might even, in a censorious mood, indict Wilde for his particular contributions to this mythology of the self, especially the much quoted line, "I put my talent into my works; I put my *genius* into my life." Add that swath of history to the culture of publicity exploited so avidly by that first generation of conceptual artists analyzed by Alberro and you have a potent combination and a familiar contemporary figure: the architect or designer as conceptual artist.

Gehry, Libeskind, Eisenman, Koolhaas, Tschumi are thus, in effect, the Idea Men, designated hitters of concepts, impresarios of inspiration, who sprout their notions faster than 1980s-vintage comparative literature grad students. They don't build; they muse. They don't design; they imagine. And no self-respecting city can now afford not to have a museum or gallery or other monumental building designed by one of them. Asked by a member of that audience in Toronto whether he considers himself "a visionary," Libeskind displayed a becoming modesty. "That is something only a madman is prepared to claim," he said. But even while playing down his status as seer, and playing up his responsibilities as builder, he somehow made it clear that vision is exactly what he trades in, big ideas that result in big buildings.

And you know what? Good for them. Good for them that they can be the guys who descend into the WTC pit and say, "No no no, tear up all the drawings." Good for them that they can get multimillion dollar commissions on the strength of a Marx Brothers movie or a few sketches on paper napkins. Good for them that this goes over so well with people—perhaps you admit, as I will, that you are occasionally one of them—who crave a little pizzazz in their architectural lives. Conceptualism and collaboration are a linked tension, the first playing down the second in order to satisfy our collective desires for what Libeskind rightly called an "architecture of meaning."

Good for them, but perhaps not always so good for the rest of us. In his talk, Libeskind recalled a conversation in which Derrida acknowledged the small stakes in his own brand of theoretical gambling. "If he publishes an obscure article, it does no harm," Libeskind said. "If I build a bad building, it stands there in public view for some time." Admitting this responsibility doesn't always mean living up to it. When the circus leaves town for the next show, and the excitement dies down, when the first blush of romance has faded, we still have to live and work in the idea buildings. We have to hang things on walls and clean windows and preserve brittle artifacts. Above all, we have to walk by and around the building, look at it, accept it, try to bring it into the fabric of everyday life. Monumental-conceptual architecture, though compelling and inescapable as it often is, can be a form of prestidigitation. A fleeting feeling of wonder, a big idea; but then, like the joke we've heard before or the trick we already know... poof.

Notes

1. See Jayne Merkel, "The Museum as Artifact," *Wilson Quarterly* (Winter 2002), p. 67.

2. For the details of these appropriations, see Neil Leach, ed., *Rethinking Architecture: A Reader in Cultural Theory* (Routledge, 1997), passim.

3. Merkel, *op. cit.*, p. 78.

4. See Neil Denari, *Gyroscopic Horizons* (Princeton Architectural, 1999).

5. Francis Cornford, *Microcosmographia Academica* (Bowes & Bowes, 1922), preface.

6. Quoted by Geoffrey Harpham at the Tulane Symposium on Ethics in Architecture, 1999.

7. Alexander Alberro, *Conceptual Art and the Politics of Publicity* (MIT, 2003).

8. Arthur Danto, "Art and Artifact in Africa," in *Beyond the Brillo Box: The Visual Arts in Post-Historical Perspective* (University of California, 1992), p. 110.

9. Quoted in Alberro, *op. cit.*, p. 120.

10. Arthur Danto, "Dangerous Art," in *Beyond the Brillo Box*, p. 185 *et seq.*

11. Witold Rybczynski, *The Look of Architecture* (Oxford, 2001), *passim.*, but esp. ch. 2, "In and Out of Fashion." Compare this discussion to my analysis of fashion as a trope in ch. 14 of the present volume.

3. Modernism à la Mode

In 1967, Ideal Toy Company of New York introduced a building kit called Super City. Intended as a high-end rival to Meccano or Lego, Super City offered ABS-plastic modules and triangular struts, plus bubble skylights and sleek cladding, to create miniature towers and slabs. "The best building kit ever made," the writer and artist Douglas Coupland enthused in 2005, "Super City was the first purely modernist building kit. Anything made from Super City looked like a Craig Elwood or Richard Neutra or Wallace K. Harrison." Riffing on what he saw as the kit's space-age, high-modern coolness, Coupland added annotations that mocked the sophisticated style of the designs. "Karen Carpenter's apartment," he suggested in one corner of a Super City ad. Opposite that, "[Robert] Jarvik heart transplant centre." Nearby, "Henry Kissinger and Jill St. John having sex," and "Parking lots that only accept vehicles with gull-wing doors."[1]

When a style of architecture is so familiar as to be rendered in toy blocks, a sort of loopy apotheosis has been realized. Mark 1967 as the year modern architecture reached the pinnacle of its pervasive influence: now even the world's kids were being indoctrinated into its program of modular construction, uniform steel-and-glass structure, and straight unadorned lines. In a few short years some of those kids would surely be in a position to shift from representation to reality and commission full-scale versions of the same for that new corporate headquarters project in Berlin or Shanghai, that new capital city planned for somewhere in the jungles of the developing world.

This style of building was, to be sure, a very particular version of modern architecture, and one with a specific devolution: what sociologist Nathan Glazer calls a move "from a cause to a style."[2] The standard story, a narrative Glazer accepts uncritically, goes something like this. In the beginning, a beginning dated more or less to the start of the twentieth century, a handful of visionary architects, inspired by the potential of new materials like concrete and steel, imagined a world of urban living free from spurious ornament, cluttered *gemütlich* interiors, and status-defining stylistic tropes. Built forms, always the bedrock of social interaction, could be planned and executed not in the haphazard, follow-the-money manner of yesteryear, but in progressive waves of ever-improving, even utopian, design. New buildings for a new age! And behind it all, a heroic commitment to social justice via the building art. The architect emerges not as a mere purveyor of commodity, firmness and delight, to cite the ancient Vitruvian desiderata as translated by Sir Henry Wotton in 1624, but as a social revolutionary par excellence: philosopher, critic, activist, craftsman and artist all rolled into one egomaniacal package. "We are in a diseased state," Corbusier wrote in 1923, "because we mix up art with a respectful attitude towards mere decoration." The received styles are dead, and the "great epoch" and "new spirit" of the age demand innovation. His singular masterpieces, the Villa Savoye and the chapel at Ronchamp, plus ambitious workers' housing schemes and city plans, show what could be done with such a bold vision.

In the event—so the second act goes—reality proved, as ever, a super-resistant medium. The grand schemes and social visions are dashed by the exigencies of financing and construction, the dirty-hands business of actual clients, not to mention the wider influence of economic downturns, war and technological innovation. In a small but telling irony, Corbusier, perhaps the most exemplary of modernist architects under this standard narrative, had to improvise expensive handmade components for his early buildings and give them the machined look that mass production was not yet capable of achieving—a sort of reverse techno-effect, foreshadowing the faux authenticity of more recent machine nostalgia, with the current proliferation of false rivets in a sports car interior or exposed, load-free girders in a restaurant. When large projects, or even specific buildings, were realized, there was a visible declension of modernist dreams into dismal reality. Corbusier's notorious "Radiant City" design, with its lithe residential towers surrounded by parkland and curving superhighways, became the model of dead-zone tower-block projects of the 1950s and 1960s, many of them now either abandoned to vertical-slum anarchy or torn down in favor of low-rise new urbanist alternatives.

The exemplary form of the modernist movement, meanwhile, the glass-curtain slab skyscraper, moved effortlessly from bravura gesture—Mies's Seagram Building in Manhattan, a masterpiece of matte black volume and generous public space—to the favored building block of corporate globalization. Imitation becomes the sincerest, because cheapest, form of theft. As Martin Filler insists in his entertaining and informative survey of modern masters, *Makers of Modern Architecture*,[3] Mies cannot be held responsible for the bad iterations of his style any more than Andrea Palladio can be indicted for all the hideous neoclassical arches and pedimented columns that festoon everything from skyscrapers in Shanghai to pitched-roof monster homes in the suburbs of Dallas. Nevertheless, it is at least disheartening and at most scandalous that what began as a revolutionary movement for social change should expire, within the span of four decades, into a mere style. Which style, moreover, now appears smoothly to serve the interests of the very forces, capital and class that it claimed to oppose. "We showed them what to do," Mies complained to his friend Arthur Drexler. "What the hell went wrong?"

As usual, the official story is far too simple, but making it more complex forces a series of tendentious choices. One can, like Filler, refuse to define a single modernism and simply lay down firm historical parentheses that embrace more than twelve decades of building practice and link the nineteenth century to the twenty-first. His list of makers of modern architecture begins with Louis Sullivan, the *fons et origo* (not Frank Lloyd Wright, as many think), of the much-abused dictum that "form ever follows function," and ends with Gehry and Calatrava, two disparate practitioners with only an attenuated kinship to what most people consider modernism. This capaciousness then allows Filler to pick and choose idiosyncratically from a wide swath of builders for his raves and pans. Along the way, the classic statements of Corbusier and Mies are acknowledged, but so are various forms of organicism (Wright, Alvar Aalto), techno-modernism (Norman Foster), and postmodernism (Robert Venturi, Renzo Piano). Charles Rennie Mackintosh and Charles and Ray Eames, designers known for furniture rather than buildings, earn respectful full chapters. At no point is a larger narrative of modernism offered; Filler resolves the definition issue by ignoring it.

This approach has its virtues. Filler is right to blast the rhetoric of -ism and counter-ism that has vexed architecture since the Second World War, with new stylistic trends set up every few years to oppose whatever has become fashionable: postmodern succeeding modern, deconstruction succeeding that, and so on. He challenges the superficial theoretical pretensions of the various after-modern "schools," with their cheap philosophical pronouncements cribbed from works of philosophy or literary theory. Architecture, like art, enjoys an oedipal energy where creation is always destruction, usually of one's most proximate influences. But its story is really one of repetition, not progress. New materials,

new styles and new techniques arise, but the problems of rendering built forms in a physical universe remain ever the same. There
may be dialectic conflict in architecture's forward march, but there
is no absolute standpoint at its end.

Nevertheless, Filler's inclusiveness creates as many problems
as it solves. If we abandon the standard progress-of-styles narrative, what arises in its place? Despite some effort to remain cool
and focused on the work itself, Filler cannot resist a bit of alternative myth making and some of the insider's arrogance unfortunately typical of the architectural profession (though as a critic he
already occupies an outer circle). For him, the chief fallacy in
laypersons' talk about architecture is the identification of modernism *tout court* with one of its less fortunate spur lines, the
familiar International Style—the very identification Glazer
accepts as a premise of social critique.

The term "International Style" was coined by MoMA founder
Alfred Barr but made popular, and eventually canonical, by a 1932
exhibition at MoMA organized by Johnson and Henry-Russell
Hitchcock. The exhibition proved as influential in architectural
circles as the Exposition Internationale des Arts Décoratifs et
Industriels Modernes of 1925 or the Armory Show of 1913 did in
the realms of design and fine art. More than just the talk of the
town, the show established the agenda of modern architecture for
decades to come, including both masterworks and disasters. Mies,
Corbusier and Wright were all included, and because there was little attempt to reconcile the differences between the European
vision, especially Corbusier's expansive social conscience, and the
American emphasis on practicality, the emergent style was a
volatile distillate of divergent programs. Outside and a dozen
blocks downtown, the deco-inflected Empire State Building had
opened its doors just a year before; inside the museum, deco was
done and the clean-slab future was on the march.

Style has always been a bad word in architecture, suggesting
either a lack of imagination or a susceptibility to replication, or
both. In the MoMA, exhibition style was boldly celebrated as the

essence of the art, and modern architecture was instantly reduced
to a single branch of its family tree. It might have taken decades
for the ravages of the International Style to be felt worldwide,
but the decisive move came at or near the beginning.
Revolutionary modernism was born in 1923 with the publication
of Corbusier's *Vers une architecture* (Toward a New Architecture),
the most innovative book on the subject since the Renaissance. It
defined a humane Cartesianism far more subtle than the boxy
sameness to come, deftly defending the idea of the "regulating
line" in all great building, ancient and modern. Corbusier praised
the timeless geometric beauty of the golden section, the same proportions that had excited everyone from Vitruvius to the realist
landscape painters of the Italian Renaissance. "There exists one
thing which can ravish us, and that is measure or scale," Corbusier
gushed. "To achieve scale! To map out in rhythmical quantities,
animated by an even impulse, to bring life into the whole by
means of a unifying and subtle relationship, to balance, to *resolve
the equation*." But thanks to Johnson and his opportunistic
cronies, this beautiful vision died its theoretical death less than a
decade later—indeed, just a year after the English translation was
published—reduced from grand longing to mere template.

To be fair, Corbusier himself remains somewhat vague about
style. He at once declared it dead and demanded it be reborn along
the functional lines of the airplanes, automobiles and steam liners
he so admired. But with the International Style now conflated
with modernism, soon set to colonize the planet's urban spaces,
confusion reigned among architects: they could either jump on
the bandwagon and do worse, because it could not be done better,
what Mies and Corbusier had taught; or they could seek new and
ever more desperate reactions to the dominant ideology of steel
framing, tinted glass, orthogonal construction and rigid minimalism. Thus, instead of a teleological model of creative progress,
Filler offers a chaotic mind-map view of modernism, with the
International Style an immovable blob (or slab) at the center and,
around it, a constellation of reactive satellites—biomorphism,

neo-ornamental kitsch, computer-generated antibuilding, sculptural overstatement, and so on—fighting for the recognition, and the money, that allows the architect to practice his art. Where Glazer is concerned with a political narrative, Filler is a devoted aesthete in search of creative heroes and copycat knaves.

Johnson emerges as the arch-villain of the drama, an unrepentant scoundrel with early ties to Father Charles Coughlin and the Nazis ("all those blond boys in black leather," to quote one of Johnson's letters home), followed by a stint coattailing the far more talented Mies, and then a long toxic endgame in which he naughtily championed whatever style or counterstyle seemed to have the biggest wind behind it. MoMA is, moreover, the wicked pavilion in which Johnson was able to exert his poisonous influence, first as a curator and later as an influential trustee. The 1932 exhibition was just the beginning of a series of group shows and retrospectives that, in Filler's view, allowed Johnson to continue defining the trajectory of American architecture through the rest of the twentieth century. Johnson died in 2005 at age ninety-eight, a master necromancer finally brought down by a neglectful reaper, who, Filler almost suggests, ought to have attended to the business sooner.

According to Filler, Johnson was "a born salesman and glib improviser," "deeply superficial" and "bored easily," produced designs that were, variously, "sorry," "hollow," "offensive," "appalling" and "bordering on outright thievery." His "undisguised pleasure in perversity" is the one constant in a fad-following life spent switching styles at whim, making him "the magpie of Modernism," a man "symptomatic of the poverty of American civic culture in the late twentieth century." A few others get similar, smoothly phrased drubbings: Meier ("limited powers of invention"), WTC designer Minoru Yamasaki ("fleetingly fashionable"), MoMA renovator Yoshio Taniguchi ("much-disparaged"), not to mention *New Yorker* architecture critic Paul Goldberger, whose 2004 book on the ground zero reconstruction, *Up from Zero*, like all of his writing, lacks "a discernible moral character," continuing the "maddening equivocation" of his reviews and revealing his "essential complicity" with the financial heavyweight dominating the project.

Beneath the demonizing and score settling, Filler wants ardently to avoid the reductionism so typical of discussions of modern architecture. His refusal to endorse the standard view that modernism is synonymous with the brief moment of the International Style, as if modern art were reducible to abstract expressionism, immediately disarms common criticisms, such as Glazer's, that modernist architecture is cold and inhumane. More importantly, it invites a larger aesthetic embrace of the past century's building innovations. And yet, the refusal fails to account for the loss of political charge in architecture, which is a main concern even of friends of modernism. How did style—of whatever kind, by whatever name—become so important, to the detriment of the reformist principles that had animated the movement at the beginning?

The current stars of architecture, whether they or we call them modern, appear far more interested in signature gestures and exalted status as conceptual artists than in the passé social engineering of a century ago. Indeed, probably never before in the history of what Filler likes to call "the building art" have its leading lights seen themselves so emphatically as artists first and builders second. This is not always a bad thing: Gehry's Bilbao Guggenheim Museum has survived both a massive hype-storm and a predictable backlash to secure its position as perhaps the only genuine masterpiece of late-century architecture. Lesser talents, often with bigger egos, have fared more poorly. As discussed earlier, Libeskind's Jewish Museum in Berlin, a notable success, was followed by lackluster projects in Denver and Toronto, plus an embarrassing failure as part of the WTC reconstruction, where he was outmaneuvered by David Childs, a slick operator whom Filler likens to the feckless Peter Keating in Rand's *The Fountainhead*. Calatrava, despite his formidable command of structural beauty, has yet to produce a work as stunning as Eero Saarinen's TWA terminal at JFK in New York or the Dulles International Airport in Chantilly, Virginia. (A planned Calatrava spire for the Chicago waterfront is delayed and in any event disappointing, being little more than a twisted version of a standard pyramidal tower.) The architect-as-sculptor may be the logical outcome of one reaction to modernism's doldrums, but it is not at all clear who the beneficiaries are, apart from the architects themselves.

Whom should architecture serve? In *The Human Condition*, Hannah Arendt, rare among political theorists for her interest in the built environment, called architecture "the space of appearances" and argued plausibly that, because it provided the canvas for all social life, it was essentially political. Certainly no other fact of everyday life is as inescapable. You can turn off a television or a computer, avoid cash transactions, even stifle advertising's constant blare; but you cannot avoid being in the fabric of your place. Architecture, alone among the arts, is inescapable. It is also persistent, existing in time more than space. And yet, most of us have little, if any, influence on how it is made. It is no wonder that the most common pejorative verb used about architecture is "foist." People's choice awards and community review boards aside, as citizens, we get most architecture whether we like it or not.

The artist Frank Stella has famously rejected the idea that architecture is an art form, since it includes functionality among its aims, but it is hard to maintain that position when so much of the movement of architecture precisely mirrors that of the art world. Styles and stars come and go, trends are announced and denounced, sometimes simultaneously, and the aesthetic logic of creation is everywhere celebrated. The upside is a potential for great civic beauty and even, sometimes, the social change craved by the early modernist reformers. The downside is ugliness, clutter, enervation, and heedless destruction of the old in favor of the novel. Great cities, opponents of planning like to say, are grown rather than built, implying that there is a kind of mystery in the process; certainly it is true that big plans have often done more harm than good.

Glazer wrings his hands about these issues, touching down here and there to denounce the elitism of modern architecture and modern art, which he tends to lump together. Richard Serra's controversial work *Tilted Arc*, which dominated a plaza among federal buildings in Lower Manhattan, comes in for particularly heavy fire, presumably because it is a fusion of the two: installation art as a kind of architecture. Glazer favors the adjectives "far out," "wild" and "radical" for schemes that seem to him to defy human scale or the accepted urban vernacular. He would surely be baffled by the warm reception given to Serra's recent MOMA retrospective, which shows the artist to possess a command of space and materials that any classical architect would envy. Like Jane Jacobs before him, Glazer has a thoroughly normative position about city life that masquerades as mere common sense; it is not so much defended as revealed through counterpunching. What he likes is what the people like, whether the people know it or not, and what the people don't like is modern architecture.

Glazer is a sociologist, not an architect or even an architecture critic, so his aesthetic judgments will provide easy targets for the sort of trigger-happy architect likely to review it for an intramural audience. But that fact is actually part of the problem he is trying, gamely if awkwardly, to address. When arrogant architects insulate themselves from criticism by adopting the refined disdain of conceptual artists, what hope is there for an architecture of social change? The trouble is that neither Filler, with his quasi-academic combination of detachment and critical savagery, nor Glazer, with his activist's righteous anger and bluff lack of architectural pretension, can resolve the complex of paradoxes that wreathe the issue.

Why is it, Glazer wonders, that it took Prince Charles, the very embodiment of elitism by birth, to speak up for the people of England against the depredations of modern architecture? But this is not a mystery to anyone who has lived in Britain and felt the deep consonance between "ordinary" subjects and the Barbour-and-wellies banality of the Windsors. High and low alike fear the intellectual challenge of genuine innovation, especially anything demanding or experimental. Verdict: the familiar (neo-gothic, Victorian red brick) is good, the unfamiliar (aggressive modernism) is bad.

On occasion, however, it does take a prince. Many if not most of the world's best buildings have been erected, not through popular choice, but by central power, sometimes concentrated in a single man. Architecture is the most collaborative of the applied arts, but it cannot be done, or done well, by committee: witness the ongoing fiasco of the WTC reconstruction. Success often comes from ignoring the public desires in favor of a singular vision that might just benefit the public. The people, meanwhile, simply want what they want. That is, their desires are just their desires; in themselves they mean nothing, and mostly they cannot be predicted or, still less likely, programmed. Great architecture educates desire, it does not pander to existing ones. Of course this claim risks being paternalistic and insulting, as well as elitist, but the truth is, in architecture, you do not serve the common good by consulting the common man.

Thus the vision trap. Even modestly talented practitioners such as Libeskind can, with a few lucky commissions, find themselves on top of the media world—only to be dropped just as fast. Filler notes that Libeskind's 2004 autobiography, *Breaking Ground*, with its "unmitigated self-regard coupled with a stunning lack of self-awareness," is likely to be "an enduring camp classic." Koolhaas, the most mercurial of the current star crop, has repeatedly denounced the West, in particular New York, for its petty constraints on his vision. He prefers to build in the hyper-capitalist hothouse of China, where a combination of central authority, deep pockets, and no regard for environmental niceties made possible his arresting CCTV Building in Beijing, a structure impossible to imagine in North America. Perhaps the resolution of this issue is simply to note that China is the only place on earth big enough to house Koolhaas's ego.

The more urgent question is whether architecture should be part of a larger urban vision. Early modernist planners thought they could, and should, create whole neighborhoods, even whole cities, in order to hasten democratic change and improve the quality of life. The results, when attempted, often had the opposite effect, especially in roiling cities: for every park created by Robert Moses, that much-derided draconian master planner of New York, there is a brutal concrete overpass. And planners are frequently just wrong. The ambitious 1969 La Guardia city plan, with its laudable hatred of car traffic and machined-slab office towers, now reads like an old issue of *Amazing Stories*: "It is assumed that new technology will be enlisted in this improved transportation system, including transit powered by gravity and vacuum and mechanical aids to pedestrian movement, such as moving belts or quick-access shuttle vehicles. These devices almost surely will become available by the end of the century to meet the demands of the most influential business center in the world." While we're at it, where the hell is my jetpack? Nor are planners always on the people's side. Baron Haussmann's beloved redesign of Paris, with the spiraling arrondissement system and broad boulevards, was also a comprehensive military plan to level guerrilla-friendly warrens in favor of the state's cavalry. He could not have predicted that, thanks to a hundred years of de facto racial segregation, the expansive *banlieues* at the edge of the same city would prove the best place to riot in 2005.

Glazer, like many citizens, wants architecture to enhance urban life and, ultimately, the democratic practices of the nation. Grand public buildings, restful and lively public spaces, a balance of privacy and the common good—architecture can provide all of these. But the more it tries, the greater the risk that the project will backfire. Architects, moved by innovative design and the new liberty of materials, lose the social ambitions of their forebears and become ensnared in thickets of individual self-expression and competing styles. They strive for signature buildings, the kind that elevates a modest practitioner from mere servant of his clients' wishes into an international celebrity and Pritzker laureate. At that point, the architect really is an artist—everyone tells him so—and the notion of social service is unthinkable because it is directly contradicted by the outsider ambitions and tortured-genius mythology of all modern art. The affairs, alcoholism and trademark clothing all follow, with Issey Miyake black and kooky eyeglasses "as carefully thought out," to use Filler's words, "as Wright's anachronistic presentation of himself as a caped Aesthetic Movement dandy or Corbusier's droll impersonation of a Magrittian bourgeois."

In this sense, Glazer is right to link modernism in architecture with modernism in art, though his insights on the subject are clunky. He laments the decline "from meaning to muteness" in public monuments, noting sadly that Lewis Mumford's pronouncement has come true: "If it is a monument it is not modern, and if it is modern, it cannot be a monument." Mocking Serra's far-out desire to "subvert the context" of a public installation, he denounces the tendency of modern art to become self-referential, elitist, theoretical, rebarbative and antisocial. "This is an understandable point of view," Glazer writes, clearly thinking the opposite, "but it is not, I would argue, legitimate for public art, whose very point is to symbolize common values, common concerns, yes, a common political vision. From this point of view much public art today fails, but there is little of it that is as direct and aggressive an attack on the common values as Serra's." Late modern architecture, taking its cue from the art world and the academy, retains the alienation effect of Marxist theory but loses the commitment to social reform. "The theories in favor today among advanced architectural theorists and students are those that emphasize, indeed celebrate, breakdown in society and meaning, often in obscure and contradictory language." Glazer, lonely co-author of *The Lonely Crowd*, is pained that failures in urban planning should have driven architects into this cul-de-sac. Stay the course, form makers! The people's utopia still beckons!

For better or worse, that is a call that will likely go unheeded. These writers ultimately agree, Filler with qualified aesthetic admiration and Glazer with dismay, that recent architecture has become both a star-making machine and a forum for massive signature sculptures: tourist-friendly architectural monuments, which too often leach funds away from other, less spectacular projects such as public housing. Both trends will pass, if they haven't already, but the utopian imaginings of early modernism seem decisively lost. Those desires were always overblown, however attractive. Architecture can only ever be the occasion for thought, not thought itself. It is political, as all public things are, but it is not itself politics. We citizens have the business of sifting among our built forms and public spaces for the ideas and interactions that may make for a thriving society. Nobody can do the work of democracy for us.

"A plan proceeds from within to without, for a house or a palace is an organism comparable to a living being," Corbusier concluded in *Vers une architecture*. He used an even more delicate metaphor in the next paragraph: "A building is like a soap bubble. This bubble is perfect and harmonious if the breath has been evenly distributed and regulated from the inside. The exterior is the result of an interior." A living being, a soap bubble: these are not the images we expect from the machine-for-living man. More seriously, many of the most successful contemporary architects no longer seem to take such claims to heart. Monumental-conceptual architecture is designed from the outside in, with bravura sketches on napkins or flashy computer imaging systems. At its far end, modernism has realized one ambition of its most aggressive proponents: finally, people are an afterthought. The world is the ultimate Super City toy kit, and we, like batteries, are not included.

Every age gets the architecture it deserves, and ours is an age of transnational capital, steep inequalities in wealth and runaway narcissism. But perhaps it is not too much to hope that, in the generation currently at study, there can be found new prophets of design, architects who combine classical norms with sustainable energy, an organic materials palette, who knows, maybe inflatable or underwater housing. The possibilities of environmental architecture are just as shattering as the dreams inspired by concrete and steel. Modern architecture does not end, it mutates; it does not change the world, it reveals it. At their best, these mutations are humane, useful, and beautiful. Commodity, firmness, and delight may be the old answer; ever reconsidered and repurposed, it is still the right one.

Notes

1. Douglas Coupland, *Super City* (Canadian Centre for Architecture, 2005), passim.

2. Nathan Glazer, *From a Cause to a Style: Modernist Architecture's Encounter with the American City* (Princeton University Press, 2007).

3. Martin Filler, *Makers of Modern Architecture* (New York Review Books, 2007).

4. Earth and World in James Lahey's Index Abstractions

"World and earth are always intrinsically and essentially in conflict,
belligerent by nature. Only as such do they enter into the conflict of
clearing and concealing. Earth juts through the world and world
grounds itself on the earth only so far as truth happens as the primal
conflict between clearing and concealing."
—Heidegger, "The Origin of the Work of Art"

Not every work of art resonates with earth/world strife the way
Heidegger suggests it ought to do, but the work of James Lahey
presents vivid examples of how this "belligerence" might lie at the
heart of artistic truth. Traditional in method, orthodox in technique and yet powerfully unstable in meaning, Lahey's paintings,
especially as they have progressed from figurative to abstract, offer
a series of insights on representation, image, proportion, color and
ultimately paint itself. Like the work of Richter, to which it bears
some kinship, Lahey's painting interrogates the very idea of art by
probing the medium of which it is ostensibly composed.
"Ostensibly" because the medium is never simply the work, and

the struggle between the medium as an earthly fact—that is, pigment drawn from the soil's own chemicals—and the world opened up by the deployment of that medium is what makes the work *true* in Heidegger's sense. True not as a proposition whose truth-value could be determined by comparison to an alleged pre-existing external reality; but as a simultaneous clearing and concealing—as a revelation that hides as much as it exposes.

This process begins in the taken-for-granted structures of the artwork: the foursquare, two-dimensional surface on which is projected a scene or object; and the medium of paint, which, applied there, resists and constrains the act of creation. Indeed, canvas and paint together constitute the medium, the site of struggle, where intention is not so much exercised as revealed, the way I come to see what I mean not by pre-forming a sentence in "mentalese" then translating it into, say, English; but rather by finding out what I mean to say when the intricacies of vocabulary, semantics and syntax *push back* on me even as I push forward on them. This, surely, is part—if only part—of what Heidegger means when he says elsewhere, "language speaks us." But a more accurate (if that is the word) assessment of the struggle comes in the thinking of J. L. Austin and Derrida, where language is always escaping intention, recalling lost voices, acting like an unruly stranger. *Je veux dire*, Derrida likes to write—"I want to say"—a discursive tic shared, albeit mostly unconsciously, by Wittgenstein. (A second-language user of English, the latter did not form an attachment to the more common but less poignant "I mean to say.") I want to say: the habitual burr of language is revealed now as a plangent voicing of desire, a sense of thwarted urgency. We say many things, none of them precisely what we want because "precisely" is precisely what we cannot realize!

How is this tragicomic dynamic enacted in painting? Significantly, Lahey's favorite motifs within painterly representation are the landscape and the still life. Significant because both forms offer what appear to be straightforward views of the external world, in one case by framing, according to traditional golden mean proportions, a chunk of viewed nature, the other by isolating and intensifying the presence of a single object: an orchid branch, say. (The celebrated cloud paintings, Lahey's signature works to this point, might be viewed as a compromise, or compression, of these two linked techniques: still-life skyscape.) These works are meticulous and luminous, an inner glow achieved via painstaking layering of pigment in tiny brushstrokes or via application of paint over a photographic pentimento. As with other masters of realist representation, Lahey's figurative works begin, when viewed consistently, to exceed their edges, flooding the eye and the frame. The images become almost too vivid, throbbing with an unearthly luster and aura.

As if aware of this, Lahey then begins to deconstruct the painting from beneath and below. The flower image is allowed to distort and waver, sometimes apparently scraped or defaced or showing parts of the photographic pentimento (the Eric's Garden series from 2001, the floating glowing orchids and peonies from 2004). Or the blurring of the camera lens is itself precisely rendered in paint (see, for example, *Tulip, May 20 16:30 53.1* and similar works). Or the paint drips and disintegrates towards the bottom of the large square frame of mixed-media works, such as the 2004 work *Atlantic Ocean, Vero Beach, FL (Dec 3 AM)* and its kin, and 2003's *Atlantic Ocean, Watch Hill, Rhode Island (2001 Aug 26 6:44.12.2)*. Indeed, like the Vero Beach works, the whole series of canvases from Watch Hill, dating from as early as 2000, both vertically and horizontally oriented, work this same magic; as do the brilliant La Jolla and Brasilito works from 2001 and the Pacific Ocean series of 1999. Even some of Lahey's most traditional landscapes, the long series of *Field from Highway 115* works, occasionally show the same bottom-of-frame blurring.

This willed decomposition, the falling apart of representational illusion at the base of composition itself, is arguably the point towards which all of Lahey's remarkable technique has over the years been pointing. We are reminded of the basic insight that, as Gadamer puts it, it is not the frame that holds the picture, but rather the picture that secures the frame. But now the traditional illusion of representation is both maintained and broken, revealed and concealed, and the elegant dimensions of the frame are queried or perhaps mocked by a self-referential confidence that would, with a different artist, risk arrogance. The sometimes absurdly precise documentations of the image reflect their origins in Lahey's vast photographic practice, but also suggest a kind of satire: the crashing waves of the ocean scene are caught in a time-split moment of image making, then carefully and lovingly rendered in paint—only to have the project undermined by its own decomposition as paint moves from stunning realism to deliberately sloppy runs and drips, a suggestion of decay or even refuse.

There is retained, nevertheless, a sense of charm, one might say wonder, that at once revels in and ironizes the superb technical skill otherwise made invisible. These paintings manage to establish what we might think of as a visual analogue of Wittgenstein's remark that, while philosophy is thinking devoted to clarity, astonishment too is a form of thinking—a form admittedly as yet unlinked to precision or propositions (still less precise proposition), but thinking nevertheless, and not merely the "broken knowledge" that Francis Bacon considered wonder to be. Like the playful trompe l'oeil works of the bravura early Dutch masters, Jacques de Gheyn and Samuel van Hoogstraten, who tried to follow the way of the "empty eye" and merely realize sight as such—a doomed enterprise, of course, because all looking is some kind of seeing, however partial, and so never empty—these works revel in their presumptive ability to render three dimensions into two. Also like those earlier works, they likewise take obvious pleasure in performing and disclaiming the trick at the same moment, with the same image.

The paintings open up a world of meaning in the depicted natural scene or reverently observed object, the crashing waves or too-bright tulip; but that world—achieved by close application of pigment—is immediately dismantled by exposing the struggle implicit in all works, between the materials of their existence and the meanings they are able to embody. The thingly nature of the work, as Heidegger reminds us, is not explained by the traditional philosophical accounts. It is not a bearer of traits or properties, as in René Descartes; nor a unified manifold of sensations, as in John Locke; nor even an amalgamation of matter and form, as in Aristotle. Its thingliness is more mysterious, and more deeply embedded in a larger world of things, than these abstracted accounts would suggest. The larger world includes the equipment which the work of art resolutely refuses to be, but to which it cannot help but relate—either directly, as in Heidegger's celebrated example of Vincent van Gogh's *A Pair of Shoes*, an earthly capture of a whole world of labor; or indirectly, as when the work of art is a labor without use-value.

From here it is a short step to the square canvases and bright abstractions of Lahey's other recent work, once again large (some 30 by 30 inches, but most 60 by 60 inches) canvases mostly in vibrant red, orange, yellow and blue. Viewing these works in context suggests they are natural extensions of the more abstract examples of the ongoing cloud series, since some of the latter— three 2003 18 by 18-inch tokens, for example—are already almost abstracted studies of blue swirled with wisps of white. In the abstracts proper, once more deep effects are achieved by careful application of color in repeated layers, the revelation now coming not from superb details but in the form of scraped surfaces that reveal cognate relations and internal disharmonies of hue, small patches or streaks of underpaint showing through the "master" color on the surface. Deep orange reveals an undercurrent of indigo, teal is haunted by dark olive, blue turns black at the edges of the square. Some of the earlier examples, such as *Abstraction No. 5* and *Abstraction No. 4*, from 2001, and some examples from the years before—see *Abstraction No. 3* from 1999, say—show an even greater range of color, but the later works suggest a preference for a single dominant note rendered more powerful by what lies beneath. These works are brilliant and striking, but despite the vivid colors, they lack a sense of the struggle that brought them into being. They may be considered intermediate works, indicators of something else still to come—as long, that is, as we are allowed to see and approve the further development to which they might be seen to point. The *Buried Ocean* works, for example, diptychs that link abstraction with representation, are too didactic to engage the dialectical energy implied by Lahey's practice.

Which brings us, finally, to the *Index* or *Salvage* abstractions. (One is inclined to speak of a temporal progression here, but in fact the works discussed all come from the same intensely productive period beginning in 2000 and running to the present.) The first of these new-style abstractions were small works, 18 by 18 inches, drawn from a series of rather somber traditional figurative paintings of the Great Lakes, mostly with stormy skies and troubled waters. Three of them are dated 2003 and show Lahey already beginning to experiment with the possibilities of rescued paint. The tones are mainly gray, white and blue, indicating their origin in the Great Lakes works, and already we see what will become a key feature of the later, larger works, the working of texture into surprising focal points, thick encrustations that make the eye play between edge and center. One slightly larger (30 by 30-inch) work from 2005, now labeled *Abstraction (Index Series)*, shows the future direction—indeed, various larger works had already been attempted. This example is a kind of unnerving thesis in the language of suggestive formlessness, constantly setting up expectations of figurative success—a hint of a skyscape, a gesture towards representation—that are then immediately dashed. The paint swirls in the square frame, but so does the eye, seeking and not finding the sort of resolution somehow hinted at, or presupposed, by the fact of a painting. Three more small *Index* or *Salvage* works were completed in 2004, one from the Great Lakes paintings, another from flowers (and hence a somewhat bloody combination of dark red and green), and a third called *February Landscape*. These are gritty and thick, less nuanced and more insistent, bolder, than the earlier ones. The idea is gathering strength.

In the past few years, Lahey's *Index* paintings have become bolder, larger and more vibrant. Now square canvases typically of the 60 by 60–inch dimensions he favors in the slicker "intended" abstracts, the latest *Index* works are big swaths of color, with bright chemical greens joining violet, crimson, lush blues that all echo, and reference, the oceans, skies and open fields of the source works. But in addition to color, the basic earth/world truth of these works is enabled by texture, especially big clumps of exuberant impasto. The paint clots and gathers in thick tactile nodes, or is cut into runnels and patterns of risen spots or blotches. Light and dark play across the square surfaces, creating lines of flight for the eye, the same suggestive possible resolutions—really, nonresolutions—opened up in the earlier, smaller examples. The result is a series of works that are chthonic and tough in feeling even as they are etiolated, almost ethereal, in color tone. The combination is intoxicating; but the larger argument—about the place of pigment in a painter's practice, the struggle of earth to jut through the very world that is grounded in it—is all the more so.

Indeed, these works are, like the Greek temple described by Heidegger in "The Origin of the Work of Art," a conjunction of transcendence and groundedness. "The Greeks early called this emergence and rising in itself and all things *phusis*," Heidegger notes, giving the Greek word that we now limit and constrain as physics or the physical. His suggestion is that *phusis* had, originally, a deeper meaning. *Phusis*, says Heidegger, "clears and illuminates, also, that on which and in which man bases his dwelling. We call this ground *earth*. What this word says is not to be associated with the idea of a mass of matter deposited somewhere, or with the merely astronomical idea of a planet. Earth is that whence the arising brings back and shelters everything that arises without violation. In the things that arise, earth is present as the sheltering agent. The temple-work, standing there, opens up a world and at the same time sets this world back again on earth, which itself only thus emerges as native ground."

The temple is an aspiration and a foundation; it is able to soar precisely because it sits, because its feet remain on the ground and gather a world of meaning to a singular site. (Heidegger makes the same point, perhaps even more vividly, about the bridge at Heidelberg: a bridge creates a world by joining two separated earths, sitting firmly on each bank.) And then, because it is both soaring and site, the temple also shelters the meaning that mortals desire for the sky, the divine. It is a happy apposite irony that Lahey's earth/world struggles are drawn, in some cases, from paintings precisely of sky—one corner of Heidegger's fourfold, earth/sky, mortals/gods structure of all worlds. Without traditional intention, instead via the poignant process of discard and rescue, scraping and working, these works gather up all the careful depictions of Lahey's practice, all the paint and technique, into surprising, moving and, finally, unsettling meetings of material forces and spiritual ones.

At the same time, these are Lahey's most challenging works, not least because they are not beautiful—from a painter whose reputation and success hitherto have been largely a matter of beauty. The risks for the painter are obvious, and in themselves a good illustration of the intimate strife that runs beneath the surface of all true artwork. Critics who disdained the supposedly too-easy haptic qualities of earlier works are now replaced by critics who cannot see past the disturbing ugliness, the thick materiality, of the *Index* works. They are formed by paint that has been scraped and palette-knifed off other canvases, then worked and layered as new conjunctions of earth and world. They refer back to the origins in pigment, the characteristic colors of other series showing up in blue-gray ranges, red-yellow ranges and so on. And yet, they also, when they succeed (for not all of them do; one or two are incomplete or off-kilter, failing to achieve the special alchemy of the best) open up new worlds of their own, a kind of metacommentary on the act of painting that is also a revelatory work in its own right.

The installation conceived for these works includes nine 60 by 60–inch *Index* pieces and a single large cloud painting—an eye-filling 60 by 120 inches—and thereby creates, in effect, a single work. The conjunction with the clouds realizes the painterly origin, but also opens up the moving dualities of the series: *prima materia* and heavenly sky, profane and sacred, earthly and transcendent. Source and result are both necessary to complete the implied argument, the revealing urgency of dazzling representation surrounded by bright, tough, almost loamy surfaces. The studio, the site of work and play and rescue, is captured and displayed in a nine-plus-one metawork, a narrative of truth into which the viewer can both enter and gaze.

The *Index Abstractions* are a distillate of aesthetic practice, literally and metaphorically. They are the compressed and sometimes intoxicating remainders of other works, other visions, other worlds, worked from paint scraped and gathered together almost as refuse, as the sloughed-off. Unlike the self-conscious gorgeousness of his representational works, especially the prized orchid and peony still lifes, where the paint-extended natural detail glows so bright it becomes quivering and almost surreal, the *Index* canvases are earthy, muted, even ugly. They seem determined to refuse the beauty so characteristic of Lahey's earlier signature works (the flowers, the clouds) and opt instead for a challenging counter-position, a necessary resistance.

Their swirling abstraction, meanwhile, achieved with paint massaged and reworked, offers a complex statement on creative energy. An indexical, in philosophy of language, is a pointer word (or, sometimes, gesture): "this," "that" or the stylized finger that may, in public signage, point to an exit or seating area. But an indexical sign is also, as in C. S. Peirce's semiotic analysis, a sign that points to the conditions of its own origin: a weathervane is an indexical sign, pointing to the source of wind by pointing away from it, where the wind blows; but so is a fingerprint, which "points" to its owner and the fact, so crucial in murder mysteries and criminal investigations of the old sort, that that owner was somewhere in particular, namely here, where the print is found. The *Index Abstractions* capture these layered meanings of index. The individual works point back, as indexical signs, to the conditions of their own possibility, namely the rescued earthly pigment and the *ur*-paintings from which it has been gathered. But because of this relationship to other works, other occasions, the works are indexical in another sense too. The series as a whole serves to order Lahey's entire artistic output, to index it, by gathering the world of the studio into imposing yet intimate blocks, squares of tactile color that, however teasing and suggestive, finally refuse to resolve or focus. You get lost in these works precisely because they are, in the best sense, found.

5. David Bierk and Appropriate Beauty

i. Enframing

Not all the works of David Bierk are, or even feature, landscape, but landscape is nevertheless the operative sign of the works, as indeed it was of Bierk's later career. We may think of this development as a rational culmination of concern with the act of painting, creating the rectilinear artifact of the picture. Just as the frame of a picture works to delimit but also to gather the range of the world—the edges that shut out the totality of what we don't see, and so focus on this part that we do—so landscape as a genre enables Bierk to frame and recontextualize his earlier preoccupations. His concern is with appropriation, quotation, juxtaposition and diptych; likewise with still life, palette, technique and materials: here we see all of these themes or issues reworked and refigured, literally, in light of the land. Whether rendered on canvas, board, photograph or copper, whether large or small, these landscapes at once bind and liberate the aesthetic practice of Bierk.

The whole and its parts are intimately related. As Stephen Daedalus observes in James Joyce's *Portrait of the Artist as a Young*

Man, paraphrasing Longinus as it happens, what is distinctive about beauty is that we see the relation *between* part and whole as a third dimension of appreciation. We confront here beautifully realized borrowings from the likes of Johannes Vermeer, da Vinci, Claude Monet, Edgar Degas, Édouard Manet and Giorgio de Chirico—about which more will be said. We see an ironic (or anyway unstable) didacticism in the invocation of "truth" and "memory," vestiges of the thorough devotion to the play of image and word in other Bierk works. And we see, everywhere around and between these, the distinctive deployment of brushed-steel paneling, itself a material with a palette that ranges in color from dark gunmetal to almost flannel—even, memorably, in *Locked in Migration, River Plain*, a remarkable play of billowing clouds and weeping runnels of rust.

But we see, too, a concern, almost an obsession, with arrangement. The recurring gesture of enframing to be found within many of these works—"locked in migration"—suggests a tension between movement and stasis. The frame within the frame, sometimes as wide as the painted component of the work, makes the image float and lift out of the main frame; at the same time, it works to deepen and tighten the image, so that the eye seems to fall into it, working the perspective back and ever back. Paradoxically, these works become reflections on the act of enframing, in short, as much as on image—the violence of constraint that is also a moment of release. In "The Question Concerning Technology," Heidegger suggests that the inner logic of the technological is *Gestell*, or "enframing," by which he means the way technology makes the world disposable, ready for consumption in its entirety. The forest ceases to be a forest and becomes a potential source of fuel.[1]

This is not without pleasure or benefit, to be sure, and enframing is not to be simply resisted or denounced, being an act of making-ready that can also uncover a truth beyond itself; but a keen danger lies in our falling into enframing as the only, or dominant, sense of revealing, a picture of the world as what Heidegger calls "standing reserve," made ready for use. The German is instructive, since while the ordinary word *Gestell* means, literally, a frame or stand, the related root *Stellung* means "position or place." Enframing may thus be understood as the mode of truth that entails a setting in place, a making available, or positionality: the very goal promised by the laying out of a grid according to the Cartesian model, the total surveillance picture that will act continuously to fix each one of us in *coordinate location*.

The literal enframing performed in and by these works by Bierk is not quite like Heidegger's enframing, of course, except in sharing a revelatory doubleness, working to stress both limit and transcendence. But there is also a usefully unstable hint of the technological. It is a nice touch that the enframing material is so often the burnished steel reminiscent of a familiar and admittedly appealing techno-aesthetic: the surface of high-tech appliance, the facing panels of a space-program console, the smooth unfinished flank of a prototype performance vehicle. Bierk's images do not seek to flood the frame, and so to break it, as, for instance, Karsten Harries has suggested Caspar David Friedrich's do; instead they increase the pressure of the frame, compressing and intensifying the image.

"Frames re-present what they frame," Harries notes. "Such re-presentation invites us to take a second look, bids us take leave of our usual interests and concerns and attend to what is thus re-presented... [T]hey call for and serve that disinterested attitude in which Kant sought the key to aesthetic appreciation. Frames may be understood as objectifications of the aesthetic attitude." Despite this powerful objectification, or indeed really because of it, the frame comes into question, such that, as Harries goes on to observe, "part of the evolution of modern painting has been the progressive elimination of the frame ... transform[ing] paintings from representations into self-sufficient aesthetic presences."[2] Frames, holding beauty in so that it may be presented aesthetically, are nevertheless meant to be broken, or simply abandoned. But a picture without a frame is still enframed by its edges, and so the breaking is never completed; we might say, even better, that no *frame* is ever completed, because even when apparently sound, it is, in its frozen artificiality, always already broken.

In these terms, Bierk could be read superficially as a kind of antimodernist, a painter who reverses the polarity again, returning to the solidity of the frame. But this reversal is only apparent, because, as Harries notes of another artist who worked frames into his works rather than employing them ornamentally, Gustav Klimt, "when the frame becomes an integral part of the painting it no longer functions as frame meant to re-present the painting. It has itself become an integral element of the aesthetic object and helps to liberate it from the rule of representation."[3] In fact Bierk's practice is more complicated still, because he doubles the frame even as he reverses the abandonment of representation; he quotes early modern images even as he reaffirms the objectifying power of framing. And then he holds the pieces of the work together with a material, steel, whose presence, as well as being aesthetically repurposed in surprising and appealing ways, continues to act as a paradigmatic signifier of superstrength. Steel! Thus the recurrence of *locked* migration. In the diptychs, the migration moves between and around the juxtaposed images, one framed and one not. In the single images, the square of mimetic intensity takes its place within the established logic of the work as a whole. In all cases, migration is locked, but not really, only momentarily; or rather, the migration is a matter precisely of being locked, of rocking in place within the foursquare field of the frame.

ii. Landscape

The landscape in play here exerts an interest of its own, as a component. Many of Bierk's later masterpieces were large realizations of this sort of landscape, marvels of palette and varnish that blasted themselves onto walls and offered viewers an astonishing spectrum of visual experience. Depending on ambient light, the world depicted might be bathed in melancholy shadow or lit up by a strong hint of heavenly redemption. The trademark blue that Bierk developed in these works, a lovely teal that is forever finding itself shading into dark yellows and umbers of cloud, makes these works instantly recognizable as well as beautiful. The proportions, which vary somewhat from work to work, tend to cleave to the Dutch classical norm of big sky composition, such that the horizon is established in the lower quarter, or even lower sixth, of the frame. The result is a landscape of possibility but also with hints of menace. The mounting cumulus volume of clouds can seem to overwhelm the earth beneath, which frequently has a watery or blasted-heath appearance, an earth denuded of structure or figure, a river basin suggestive of hard going.

Though several of the works included here are labeled as to location—*Kawartha Vista (Locked in Migration)*, 1993; *Kawartha Stream, Dark Hills*, 1993; *Kawartha Landscape, Copper Sky*, 1998— Bierk's concern with landscape quickly transcends particularity. Or, to be more precise, the inspiration of the actual skies and plains of the Kawartha Hills near his home in Peterborough, Ontario, transforms the painting practice in a direction that takes on a life of its own. The landscapes become notional, otherworldly, almost mythical, while still being anchored in the pigments and contours of the specific region. At the same time, Bierk's technique for rendering landscape itself becomes more gestural and pure. At its fullest extension, this purity paradoxically flirts with, or deconstructs, the sort of machine logic implied by the enframing of technology, specifically in the form of the assembly line. Completing a series of copperplate versions of one late image, for example, he had reduced, or rationalized, production such that a single brushwork component could be repeated, time after time, across an array of plates held in a large frame. The resulting works, each unique and varied, were not tokens of a dominant type, nor even simulacral copies lacking an original, but miniature works that at once copied and defied the larger matrix image, a new logic of representation enacted by means of performance itself.

These landscapes, then, freed from the bonds of mere representation, seek to make larger statements than the visual. Thus the rather hopeful titles of so many of the works in this group, which combine landscape with an appropriated detail from another artist: *To Gauguin and Mankind*, 1991–92; *Save the Planet, to de Chirico*, 1992–2001; *Requiem for a Planet, Pompeii Man 11*, 1994–2001; *Requiem for a Planet, to Earth & de Chirico*, 1996–2001; *Eulogy for Mankind, to Degas*, 1992–93; and *Eulogy for a Planet, to Leonardo*, 1992–94. The dates on these works are suggestive, raising the thought that the joinings observed here might be, in some cases at least, *post facto* achievements, with earlier studies repurposed or repositioned in this fashion. True or not, the pairings serve to throw both aspects of Bierk's practice into sharper relief. The landscapes acquire a new resonance, now presented as, or as components of, a message, a requiem, or a eulogy.

A funereal tone is thus indicated, if not always visually established. The eulogy works are quietly beautiful, not mournful; though perhaps the best eulogies are likewise. We are asked to take note of a passing, to hear the lament of the earth, or the planet, or mankind. Death, it appears, is in the air. This is no simple environmental plea, however, despite the importance of the natural field in the landscape images. That is, the earth and the planet indicated here are not, it would seem, simply the earth of Earth Day or the literal planet referenced in urgings to save the planet. They are, instead, the world of signification itself, the lived earth as it becomes conscious of itself through us, the word- and image-wielding creatures who dwell upon it. As such, these works take us back into the heart of art making, and hence of appropriation as an aesthetic tactic.

iii. Beauty

There is no need to rehearse, here, the details of argument about aesthetic appropriation. Some critics find the practice as reprehensible, or possibly as banal, as mere plagiarism; others, sensing a deeper engagement, understand that immersion in the history of art, especially the history of painting, is an essential component of any post-historical practice. Appropriation is motivated by a sense of the inevitability of the past, the art-historical storehouse of

imagery that cannot be ignored or evaded—such that any attempt
to do so is, in effect, to forget oneself in a pre-defeated attempt at
novelty. Pre-defeated, that is, because novelty, despite its published
sentiments, is not so much a striking out, as in a voyage of adven-
ture, but rather a crossing out, a willful erasure, of what always lies
beneath the surface of the canvas.

Aware of this conundrum, Bierk does not negotiate his relationship to painting by ringing bravura changes on the medium's
possibilities, as Richter does (famously depicting his wife in a gorgeous homage to Vermeer, for example); nor does he play much
with the movement from abstraction to figuration that occupies
other talents. Instead he raises to visibility the always already
scored palimpsest of painting, tracing lines of anxious influence
from work to work, master to master, honing a technique of precise imitation that both reproduces and alters the beauty of the
originals. The real concern reveals itself to be not merely painting,
but painting as a seeking after beauty, that much abused notion.

In some cases, that tracing entails a literal recreation of lines
and imperfections in the inspiring canvas: the smudges of brushwork and even the tiny fissures of craquelure are rendered with fine
accuracy. Beautiful command of palette and brush thus serves to
establish, or makes reappear, the beauty of the originals. But because
this beauty is now placed before us *with intent*, and not merely by
the way, it raises questions about itself that the original cannot. This
is most successful when the appropriated element is further dis-
placed from its original frame by placement within a landscape
work. The best examples of this here are the works featuring details
from Vermeer, da Vinci, Degas, Gauguin and de Chirico.

The somber empty spaces of the natural setting, often small
and always locked in the steel plates of the signature style, open up
the human figures found on the other side of the work. Food and
structure, the individual face, all absent from the landscapes, make
an insistent and complicated call across the seam of the works, setting up an endless, oblique and suggestive dialogue of the human
and the natural. *Requiem for Life, Passage, after Vermeer,* 1994–

2000, *Eulogy for a Planet, to Leonardo*, 1992–94, and *Eulogy for Mankind, to Degas*, 1992–93 are particularly dynamic. The de Chirico and Pompeii Man images fare less well, perhaps because there is too much movement in the original images already; and the works that do not feature a Bierk landscape partner—the works with central appropriated images from Manet, Pierre Bonnard, Monet, and Paul Cézanne—are revealed as static by contrast, though the Cézanne still life, locked in migration again, has obvious appeal for its beauty alone.

Yet, taken together, there is a larger movement, and sentiment, about the nature of beauty, such that we end where we began, with the framed and gridded bit of the world we call a landscape. The individual works talk back and forth, but also converse among themselves. And it seems that, over and over, they gesture towards and reference the stand-alone landscapes, both the studies and the finished works. Of these, two are triumphant celebrations of every part of Bierk's aesthetic gift. *Kawartha Vista (Locked in Migration), Red Cloud*, 1993, offers an experience at once tough and gorgeous, a haptic magic that swallows the viewer's expectations and desires in a sort of foursquare visual *Wunderkammer*.

Even better, indeed the best work in this group, is *Locked in Migration, River Plain*, from five years later, with its complex bath of rust opening up the classically proportioned rectangle even as the square one closes it in. Here, the artificiality of the landscape, the artifice of the natural, is made deliberately, and permanently, unstable. The rust, so tactile and rich in hue, is a reminder of corruption more powerful than any symbolic memento mori, the inevitability of oxygen's toxic effect. The element that allows us to breathe, and so to live, is also, in the same instant, an active agent of chemical decay and degradation, breaking down strong materials in their natural exposure—and incidentally creating beauty.

To offer one further qualification in a scene that is full of them, we should rather say that the beauty is not incidental but essential. Found beauty, appropriated beauty, fractured and imperfect beauty: the achievement of Bierk's painting is his complex and enduring engagement with the central preoccupation, even in rejection, of all art making; indeed, of all human experience beyond the level of mere utility. In these earthly landscapes, beauty finds its appropriate home.

Notes

1. Martin Heidegger, "The Question Concerning Technology," in *The Question Concerning Technology and Other Essays*, William Lovitt, trans. (Harper & Row, 1977); orig. "Die Frage nach der Technik," in *Die Technik und die Kehre* (Pfullingen: Günther Neske, 1962). The lectures that form the basis of this essay were first delivered in 1949 and 1950.

2. Karsten Harries, *The Broken Frame: Three Lectures* (Catholic University Press, 1988), p. 67.

3. *Ibid.*, p. 84.

6. The Truth in Photographs: Edward Burtynsky's Revelations of Excess

"Art is not truth. Art is a lie that enables us to recognize truth."
—Picasso

i. Truth

The first truth about the truth in photographs is this: truth in photographs is like the truth more generally, only harder.

Start at the beginning. "Truth" is an abstract noun, and an escalator noun at that—one of those words whose uses go forth and multiply, usually into some vast metaphysical theory. The truth won't just sit there, merely useful for proximate purposes. As soon as you say something is true, in other words, someone somewhere wants to know what you mean by truth. Contemporary philosophers may want to restrict this demand, pushing instead what are known as deflationary or disquotational theories of truth—to say "snow is white" is true is just to say snow is white—but run-of-the-mill humans find that rather thin soup. They want to beef it up with more metaphysical protein.

One could even sketch a broad scheme of these big truth

ideas—just four of them, in fact—that have dominated the ongoing human obsession with *getting things right*. They are, in rough order of historical priority: (1) the truth you feel, (2) the truth you are told, (3) the truth of reason itself and (4) the truth you perceive through the senses. All of these have had various names in their different contexts, but for present purposes let us call them inspiration, authority, rationalism and empiricism. In each case, the theory posits not the truth of this or that proposition or experience, but an idea of Truth overall.

The trouble with these big ideas about Truth is, first, these rival theories seem irreconcilable with one another, forcing a choice—or, if you prefer, a story of progress, itself a controversial choice. Second, though, any dominance by one tends to lead, often by its very own efforts, to self-destruction. Success breeds its own counterintuitive failure: the more we try to establish *once and for all* the final authority of our minds and senses, the more the attempt backfires. Inspiration fails. Authorities are deposed. Reason distorts, and the senses themselves can be doubted. The paradox of all foundational truth is thus that it invites the very questions that will, sooner or later, make it crumble.

Even if we abandon the search for a general theory of truth, however, we still need the word "true." That is, we want to be able to say whether—or perhaps the better issue is how—this or that specific thing is, or might be, true. And the more we press that question that arises from practical needs to decide, to judge, the more complicated matters once more become. Consider what happens when we shift from propositions to pictures. Can an image be true? How or when? What would it mean to make the claim? Are photographs propositions about the world, chunks of empirically verifiable fact? Or are they interpretations, filterings, fictions? If so, what sorts of intent—documentary, social activist, "merely" aesthetic—must we associate with their making?

We are, I think, well past the first, unhelpful stages of this debate. I mean the stage where photography was thought guilty of a sort of double-distortion about truth. The criticism was based on a faulty original conception of the medium of photography, and went roughly this way: photography, while purporting to be a clear-paned window on reality—a simple snapshot, an *image*— was actually a fiction framed by choices, lighting and artifice. It distorts reality and then, worse, denies the distortion. Photography isn't merely subjectivity, but subjectivity masquerading as objectivity. The critic Alexander Cockburn sums up the view as part of a general indictment of photojournalism. "A photograph is by definition a moment seized from time, and the seizure can remove context in a way that might not be exactly unethical, but does damage the truth," he writes. "Photography is almost always manipulative."

Despite its basic appeal, this view is rather naive, largely because it is based on a crude understanding of both truth and photography: one truth, photography as manipulation thereof. At a more sophisticated philosophical level, we might want to say something rather different. Photography is a medium, we say, and therefore not a window on the world, nor even a mirror of it. It does not simply capture what is there, light held prisoner by the technological magic of shutter speed, exposure and photosensitive chemicals. Rather, like all media, photography is a symbolic system, a game of signification. The image is made, not found, and the making is inherently personal, rooted in prejudice. The important truth is to recognize and acknowledge bias openly, not least in the essential decisions around framing the image. "When a photograph is cropped," says the philosopher Stanley Cavell, "the rest of the world is cut *out*. The implied presence of the rest of the world, and its explicit rejection, are as essential in the experience of a photograph as what it explicitly presents."

This second-order view of photographic truth is compelling (and partially true) but it, too, is naive, and ultimately misleading. The thinking in play here still relies on an unspoken, and unjustified, presupposition that there is a world out there, just one. This world is now not merely shown but interpreted in various subjective ways, yes; but its *ante facto* consistency—its reality outside the frame—is still assumed. Cavell claims, mistakenly, that a painting *is* a world, whereas a photograph *is of* the world. It makes sense, he says, to ask what is behind something in a photograph, but not in a painting.

No. Once the photograph is taken, there is no more something behind the photograph than there is something behind a painting. In other words, the deeper lesson about the truth in photographs, even or especially in documentary form, is that there is no single world, indeed no world at all, absent this particular image. Photographs are not multiple depictions of some single reality, waiting out there to be cornered and cropped, and somehow regulating, even in the cornering and cropping, what the image means. Rather, photographs offer multiple makings. The presented image is not a reflection, or even an interpretation, of singular reality. It is, instead, the creation of a world.

ii. World

Since the object of the photograph is never merely "waiting there" for the image to be made, but rather comes to be what it is partly via the image, photographic meaning is never simple or, a fortiori, reducible to propositions. We make a mistake if we understand photography as coding of information, as a document that reports rather than reveals—even as a coding about the subjective intentions or prejudices of its maker. A picture isn't worth a thousand words; it's not even for sale in the word market.

That is why the best way to consider the truth in images is to see images not as documents but as gestures within a larger play of signs; that is, as tokens of semiotic exchange. Meaning, not truth, is actually the compelling question here, but we cannot see that except as an investigation of our desires about truth.

Images are not mere visual signs in a simple economy of exchanged representations, then; nor are they even simple symbols in the way that a red rose conventionally symbolizes love. Rather, they are moves in a supercharged visual-cultural system of layered meanings, the surrounding welter of eye-filling noise with bits of now-and-then resolving signal, offering their powerful (and often

misleading) stories about "how things are" or "what makes sense."
In many cases, these visual mythologies of the cultural surround
are also self-erasing, in that their visual power simultaneously
amplifies and obscures the clusters of meanings they support.

This play of figure and ground, of signal and noise, is part of
any image's existence. An image needs to find its meaning in a field
that is, categorically, unstable. We might wish there were an overarching theory of truth to sort the valid from the twisted, but there
is—and can be—no such theory. Every image has to take its
chances in the visual culture. Any images styled as "documentary"—a mere factual image, to use the old language—is particularly susceptible to this layered distortion, because it allows a range
of meanings without acknowledging that it does so. And so documentary images present, as in the case of Edward Burtynsky's
work, an especially acute problem of meaning investigation. They
are never merely informative, like a newspaper illustration, and
yet their rootedness in real states of affairs is essential to their
meaning. How can we ask after their truth without falling back
into exploded truth ideas and bankrupt epistemology?

A symbolic sign is one that signifies its object without resem-
bling it in any way. Most natural languages are symbolic in this
sense, as are, even more clearly, mathematical and logical languages.
Twenty-six letters or nine digits and zero suffice to generate a
potentially infinite number of meaningful moves in the symbolic-
sign system. Iconic signs entail some resemblance of signifier to
signified, but they do not reduce to any simple logic of correspondence. A figurative painting is iconic in this sense. So is a graph,
whereby growth or velocity is indicated by an upward vector or
implied volume. Hexagonal stop signs or green lights are symbolic signs in Peirce's sense but the red hand and walking man used
in many pedestrian signals are iconic. Visual icons, including documentary images that compel attention beyond a newspaper
spread, are both iconic and indexical: they exploit resemblance,
and a trace of connection to the "original" object, in order to celebrate that object, or to reinforce its meanings.

Since the object found in the finished image is never merely "waiting there" for the image to be made, but rather comes to be what it is partly via the images, these meanings cannot be simple. We make a mistake if we understand iconography as the routine decoding of information. To think that way is to succumb to the very naturalization of images, the general tangled field of visual culture we must analyze. Image icons must be investigated, instead, as nodes in a complex system of cultural self-regard and self-understanding: iconology, in other words, rather than just iconography.

And perhaps "self-understanding" is also the wrong word here, since much of what fascinates us about the image is *not understood*, is relegated precisely to the level of taken-for-granted, "how things are." Iconography can, all too easily, become ideology. In consequence, our investigation must entail a special kind of refusal: a refusal to take the taken-for-granted for granted.

It follows that the responsible image is the one that makes that refusal necessary, unavoidable, insistent. *That* is the truth in the image—though perhaps not the truth we thought to find.

iii. Document

It follows, too, that the best documentary photographs, which is to say the most compelling and arresting ones, are therefore ontologically unstable. They seem, at first glance, to offer simply a record of "what was there." But they also manage to indicate just how contingent, and constructed, their revelation is. Though clearly the residue of choice and subjectivity, they spill beyond the chosen frame, indicating a series of relations with what lies outside the image: time, circumstance, events. The documentary is a special kind of fiction, a fiction predicated on an exploded concept of truth.

Burtynsky's China photographs illustrate this instability vividly, and at scale. Earlier Burtynsky works were often more painterly in composition, using landscape conventions in composition, capturing "natural" images of mountainside railway cuts or toxic-waste spills that were structured according to the golden section and classical disappearing-point perspective. In contrast, the newer works are less polished, rawer—and more unsettling. They retain the depth of aesthetic awareness that guides all of Burtynsky's work, but appear to have a more straightforward, even insistent, intentionality. The viewer is swallowed up by them, no matter what dimension they employ, and there is always a small detail (a lone figure, a dab of color from a parked truck) that the eye finds, then cannot discard. Awareness revolves around the structuring power of the detail, and the works teeter back and forth between a pure aesthetic formalism and the informing realistic ends of photojournalism.

This instability in turn generates a familiar moral dilemma, itself a residue of larger truth seeking, found in still darker forms in the work of Sebastião Salgado, James Nachtwey or Larry Clark. The moral issue is more and more central to Burtynsky's work. How can we "see" the social or political truth of the image when we are drawn to it primarily by its aesthetic power, its beauty? Are we distracted by gorgeousness, or seduced by it, such that the reality of the depicted scene is lost in transfiguration?

In the case of earlier documentary masters, the issue was often raised as one of personal responsibility. Evidence suggests that Henri Cartier-Bresson staged his scenes of spontaneous emotion, that Walker Evans left on his contact sheets the images of smiling or laughing Okies and sharecroppers, preferring to highlight their grim visages instead. In war photography, the issues become even more pointed, extreme cases of what Cockburn calls "psychic hardening." Can the image maker stand by and record images of genocide or famine and not intervene, distanced by the lens and intentional concerns about light and composition? In a word, yes. Cockburn himself tells a story of a photojournalist in Northern Ireland, apprised of a hidden time bomb in a public place, waiting, camera poised, for the detonation—and the resulting shots.

Can a photographer, furthermore, simply capture images of evil and use them as a personal canvas, transforming tragedy into celebrity? Neither Nachtwey nor Salgado, in particular, resolved these questions satisfactorily, leaving viewers adrift in a pool of contradictory justifications and half-baked rationalizations even as they rose to celebrity-icon status themselves, riding a wave of documented human misery. (Salgado has lately explored a less troubling, or at least less clearly moral, subject: the Antarctic landscape.) Rivers's participant-observer aesthetic sociology, meanwhile, while arguably more consistent and honorable in the treatment of drug addicts or delinquent teenagers, ultimately elides its own fragile distinctions, so that advocate or recorder is indistinguishable from voyeur or fetishist.

For viewers, the pressing question remains one of response. What do we *do* when confronted by arresting images of profound human suffering? Can we enjoy the beauty of the image when the scene offered is one of disaster or violence? The second-order argument that our discomfort with ourselves as we aestheticize human depravity is somehow instructive begins to ring hollow when that discomfort has no outcome, generates no action. Photographer and viewer are soon joined in a complicity of stimulated inaction that is at best grotesque and at worst actively evil.

iv. Ecosystem

Burtynsky has, of course, faced similar charges. Even sympathetic critics have wondered, with some reason, whether his overwhelmingly haptic images are critiques of landscape degradation and the costs of technological fetishism, or merely glossy celebrations. Is he a crusader for sustainability or an unwitting purveyor of eco-porn?

When we look at his celebrated images of industrial waste poisoning water supplies, for example, or the landscape rapes of Italian quarrying and Indian ship-breaking, and are fetched by the unearthly colors of oxidized steel or toxic effluent, are we letting ourselves off the hook, entering into a kind of desecration, in its way just as bad as those offered by beautiful silver-gelatin faces of hunger or mangled limbs of genocide? What impact remains if, let us say—in what is in fact a true instance—a large image of environmental disaster is used as artistic decoration in the business-class departure lounge of a major North American airport? (It is in the new Terminal 1 of Toronto Pearson International Airport.)

At this point, though not via direct intention, the work has become inert or even disreputable in either or both of two senses: as mere wallpaper, the sort of well-meaning neutering liable to overtake any work via fashionable appropriation (a problem, let it be said, hardly unique to Burtynsky's work); or also, and worse, as slyly doubled avoidance ritual, such that a sop to environmental awareness is offered and then as quickly withdrawn, or set aside, by the work's surrender to an existing logic of aesthetic appreciation.

These ethical tangles were already obvious in the gallery showings of Burtynsky's pre-China work. One thinks here of the varied responses to the large, and moving, retrospective at the Art Gallery of Ontario in 2003, where viewers were often divided, and sometimes stangely conjoined, by activist approval and aesthetic appreciation. But they are exacerbated by the dissemination, and assimilation, of the work into the larger world. Outside the gallery setting, the works can slide too easily into the background visual culture, lose their impact, become mere ghosts of themselves.

There are no simple resolutions to these dilemmas; but some partial judgments can be offered, and some complicated truth responsibilities outlined. Salgado in particular was guilty of what we might call "the paradox of the generic real." In capturing images of misery drawn from various times and places, looking for common features or conditions, he managed instead to reduce them all to the same level of generality, and hence banality. Trying to go universal—if that is indeed the intent; it is not always clear— in this case only created useless particularity, divorced from its time and place. These were mere images, we might say, rather than world-making ones. Truth disappeared in the subjectivity of the wielded camera, rather than being opened up by it.

There is no doubt that Burtynsky himself, though never a mere journalist of extremity, has grappled with these questions all along, and in recent years has shifted his position, or at least his emphasis. His newest works, and the discourse offered alongside them, strike a much more obvious political note; he has put his environmental-activist cards on the table. But the background instability has not been removed, only renewed. Indeed, the China works present new ways of grabbing our attention and unsettling our assumptions, in part because we are forced to confront the fact that we sometimes miss the obvious beauty of precedent works! In the images from the *Three Gorges Dam Project*, for example, there is less sense of clear formal composition and more apparently straightforward documentary intent. And yet, the overall impact is still one of alchemical mixture, with aesthetic power and political awareness permeating and negotiating with each other—witness, in this regard, the eloquent play of color and scale in shots of a human river during a shift change at the Yuyuan Shoe Factory or the pink and white bleakness of a factory worker dormitory in Dongguan.

The result is a fascinating confusion. We cannot finally decide what the image is up to, what its purpose is. We can't decide, perhaps, what we want from the image! And this is not necessarily a failing, not because mere confusion is somehow independently interesting, an end in itself, as those earlier celebrity documentarians suggested, but because it generates, let us say dialectically, new insights about our relations to technology, to beauty, to production and consumption. To the logic of excess.

I think here, inevitably, of the first work of Burtynsky's I ever saw, an image of an automotive tire graveyard that dates from 2002, and which, when I saw it, I did not know was his work. From the first, your eye is drawn by principles of classical composition—here deployed by a master photographer's framing skill—to a point roughly in the lower center left. There it focuses on individual tires. You think: what is a tire? A circle, a ring, a sort of automotive platelet or wafer. A token.

But then the background crowds in, the rest of the tires flow together and now swim around the focal point and beyond, flooding the frame. Your eye saccades up and to the left, up and to the left, to the weird diamond oasis of color and detail in the tractor trailer, but there is no relief there. So many tires! So many wheels! The number-less cars and suvs that bore them form up in a mental convoy, suck-ing back their discarded rings of rubber, plotting the arc from use to discard. They are all here by implication, the vehicles, their rubber shoes now worn and tossed aside, replaced by new galoshes of the road. But not tossed aside just anywhere: gathered together here, concentrated, in a landscape of depletion and rejection. The pleni-tude of discard, these vast concentrated remnants of wear.

And now the too-muchness floods not just the frame but also the mind: *excess*, to go beyond, always beyond. The ceaseless cycles of production and consumption, the never-ending movement of the vehicles along their ribbons of highway, rolling their tires as the rubber meets the road and combustion becomes friction and we *move*. It does not stop, the never-ending cycle, it just deposits its black rings of waste here in this eerie meadow of steel-belted, galvanized nothingness. Use and discard, use and discard. You might set the world aflame here and it would burn, slowly and noxiously, for weeks and months. You might take one circle and, filled with another petroleum by-product, use it as an especially nasty means of torture and execution.

What you cannot do is return these circles, these sooty tokens, to the earth from which they came. They create their own world, our world, our rolling global machine of use. Our abundant wasteland.

The China photographs, labeled scenes of the next industrial revolution, actually reveal the latent truths of the first one, our past by way of the future. I mean the underlying logic of decay, the way things break down. At their best, these are essays in entropy, at once beautiful and harrowing. We confront, over and over, the truth of technology that technology typically keeps hidden, or ignores, namely the twinned logic of possibility and negation. Here we are made to see the internal necessity of waste, the mechanical body sloughing off its dead skin cells and inert hair in the form of obsolete diodes and printed circuit boards.

Megaproject-blocking cities are erased, scrubbed from the earth. Old concrete, breathing noxious carbon dioxide, is crumbled and piled into archaeological mantles of disuse. This is not experienced as a narrative of justified progress, of the dangerous or useless old supplanted by the new; rather, it is enacted as a kind of Sisyphean farce, brutal and meaningless, constant repetition of theme with a change only in the specific materials, like a bleak version of Theseus' ship, planks and gunwales constantly replaced without altering the basic template.

At the same time as the destruction and waste, then, there are impressive and unnerving scenes of production, the sleek and sometimes oppressive order of vast factory spaces and assembly floors, the ranged and serried ranks of workers, worker housing, work stations, work clothes. The vast engine of the Chinese labor force, the billion-strong population that keeps this economy booming at a rate that, during the first part of the new century, regularly topped 10 percent annual growth rates—in turn prompting worries that the Chinese economic machine was overheated and needed cooling. Though there are an estimated one hundred thousand millionaires in China, the strange new superelite of what can only be called command-structure hypercapitalism, personal income levels across the population are only where Japan was in the 1950s.

If Chinese production taps into Chinese consumption, creating a new middle-class market for goods and services now mostly offered for sale offshore, another two decades of two-figure growth is possible. At the same time, many analysts both in China and elsewhere caution, in the mixed metaphors so typical of economic punditry, that the country's economy must at all costs avoid a hard landing: the big crash that always follows inflation, in what is as close to an iron law of determinism as the latter-day theology of markets will produce. This outcome has not yet arrived, but neither has growth significantly slowed. Burtynsky's treatment of China is therefore poised at a moment of alarming perplexity: how high can it all go before something comes crashing down?

This inescapable trajectory of production and decay finds ample illustration everywhere in the unnerving techno-feudalism of twenty-first century China. Shanghai's sci-fi skyline, for example, with its overwhelming jumble of architectural styles and scales, is particularly resonant. The mix-and-match stylistic exuberance of Shanghai's architectural boom sits on a foundation of routine human suffering and poverty, the stink and dirt of its always-crowded streets. Beijing's newly favored showcase to the West, the city is a palimpsest of histories and self-images, an exhausting exercise in central-command economics and the open-secret capitalism of Red China. Meanwhile, as Burtynsky's extensively documented travels show, there is an unearthly infrastructural economy of obliteration: outmoded industrial-age factories are swiftly abandoned and dismantled, their sites leveled and the old enterprises immediately replaced by new apartment buildings or cutting-edge production facilities. The new economic realities obvious here are hinted at, sometimes lamented, sometimes admired, in the range of this work.

v. Judgment

Every photographer, indeed every photograph, creates singular conditions of judgment. Not multiple relative truths, but specific demands of what truths will be seen *here*. That is one reason there is never enough space to say everything that needs saying about photography's truth.

We might say this little more, though. The truth of the image is the truth of time: not its metaphysical essence, whatever that may be, but its presence; its inescapability. A photograph is a machine for making worlds. The background lie in play here—the belief that the image delivers to me a captured slice of the world "as it really is"—actually works to open up a different, foreground truth: that time and light are how we make our worlds.

Responsible work is in the service of the world a photograph creates. Documentary photographers, at their best, unfold both the truth of a time and place *and* the truth that there is no general truth, and hence no single world, out there. The alleged double distortion of before becomes, on more careful analysis, a double revelation: of circumstance, and of our troubled relationship to circumstance. Otherwise known as mortality.

To be sure, some documentary photographs have, historically, demanded an active response, not just (though it is never really "just") the contemplation of the image. Indeed, the value of certain celebrated works of photographic revelation—Evans's Appalachian families, Lewis Hine's underage workers—lies to some large degree in the social awareness they create, even the political changes they have wrought in housing relief or improved labor conditions. Burtynsky's images of ship breaking in India and Bangladesh have prompted, or anyway supplemented, similar environmental interventions. And yet, in a kind of post-social moment, a sort of neo-aesthetic loop, these images are often swallowed up by the forces of general cultural mythology, and so rendered inert. The same process afflicts Robert Mapplethorpe's work, so relentlessly celebrated for its formal beauty—as if the subject matter were of no importance, to him or us. Whether reduced to postcard fodder or elevated by high-level art exhibition, such images perversely become, we might say, mere icons, romanticized and nostalgic, empty gestures of "noble labor" or "sturdy poverty."

These layered effects cannot be predicted, and so the positive ones cannot be guaranteed. Indeed, we must go further: they cannot be actively sought. That, after all, is propaganda. Aesthetic integrity is not a superfluous addition to the document but an a priori function, a condition of possibility. The final truth of the responsible image—the specific rather than generic real—is that it can serve no purpose other than being. After that, it is up to us. Who else?

7. Unlearned: Losing Your Way, Finding Yourself

"Not to find one's way in a city may well be uninteresting and banal. It requires ignorance—nothing more. But to lose oneself in a city—as one loses oneself in a forest—that calls for quite a different schooling."
—Walter Benjamin

The Latin root of the word education—*educare,* from *e* + *ducere,* "to lead"—reminds us that learning is always leading, here a leading out, but elsewhere, as in the cognates of deduction, induction and seduction, a driving out or pressing on or leading in. Education can be seductive, and sometimes so can deduction (the sweet, certain allure of logic must be acknowledged); pregnancies and conclusions can be induced, the latter by that strange contingent reasoning that depends on examples and prior experience: the sun will rise tomorrow. But what kind of schooling allows us, per Walter Benjamin's dictum, to lose ourselves? How do we abandon not just the routine way-finding of a specific route or map, but the entire logic of how we find ourselves? The various works gathered together in the large 2006 group show *Unlearn*

point the way by—among other subversive *détourneau* tactics—
reversing the field, disrupting the line, deracinating the sign, and
humanizing the icon. The result is a poignant, witty meditation on
the usual arrangements of didactic visual culture, rendered by
means of derangement.

The familiar made strange is always illuminating. Here, the
familiar approaches and recedes in an unnerving succession of
strange and not strange. We are disoriented, but in a manner
somehow welcome or inviting. The suddenly living and conflicted
presence of the ubiquitous sphere-headed human figure offers a
complex commentary in Lars Arrhenius's works. The generalized
abstraction of the bathroom or fire-exit sign takes on particular
form and we make out, in a large field, not just mostly identical
workers toiling before cubicle computers, but also a man apparently undergoing psychoanalysis. Another panhandles on the
street outside. A third drives heedlessly by, his car invisible.
Elsewhere there are what appear to be arguments, sad lovers,
active copulation, administered CPR and even a poster of the
Hindu deity Vishnu—the first time, it would seem, that a sphere-
head has enjoyed more than two arms. The joke is obvious but the
result surprisingly moving, the figures denuded of their symbolic
function—their standard way-pointing employment—and
reduced (or maybe elevated) to the workaday challenges of the
human condition. Who would have predicted that little black circles could, in these many different scenes and confrontations,
express so much human emotion?

Of course, it is not so much expressed as projected, and this is
surely the deeper message: messages of everydayness are sent more
than they are received. Or rather, they are received in the manner
that wisdom is said to be received—which is to say, making it not
wisdom but rather the taken-for-granted. Kelly Mark's broken line
photographs work in a similar manner, detailing the minute and
apparently meaningless ruptures of the street's routine lines. A
manhole cover replaced without thought breaks the street's conven-
tional division, a small breach in the contingent but authoritative

plotting of the circulatory system. The city could not function without this authority, but it rests on unexamined presuppositions about movement and control. The street's lines are a kind of hygiene system, a linked mesh of *cordons sanitaires* serving to regulate the direction and flow of people, vehicles and thought. They discipline the street, and hence the users of the street, in leading ways.

In the end, the small observed breaks and splits of these images, the way lines are gashed and burst, only serve to reinforce an awareness of their usually strict power. The fact that the breaks are, in almost every case, the result of covers shifting pulls the insight deeper—indeed, deep underground. The line's dominance is revealed by the fact that the skin of the street is itself permeable, and the manhole cover reminds us that we can, should we wish to risk it, abandon one circulatory system for another, less conscious one. The sewers beckon by, in this sly fashion, interrupting the smooth flow of the acknowledged city. Containment is bought at a price, namely unease about what has to be contained. The street doesn't just regulate traffic; it regulates, as its opposite, the drift of waste.

David Foster Wallace called popular culture "the symbolic representation of what people already believe," and that—more than its endless reproducibility or even its relentless consumer dissemination—is what makes popular culture a system of thought. Or rather, of nonthought, since it functions to render unthinkable anything that does not already fit. In this manner, popular culture is best read as the structural antithesis of poetry, or art generally, understood (perhaps romantically) as the creation of boundary-stretching innovations of form and content. The strong poet, as Harold Bloom calls the resister of this cultural presupposition, is a master of invention. But more than this, the strong poet is a movement delinquent, a jaywalker. Benjamin senses this possibility with his combined dwelling on the Parisian *flâneur* and the fact of the one-way street, but he is still too enamored of the *flâneur's* exquisite attention, his connoisseurship of the everyday. In a culture dominated by the signs and directions of the popular, *flânerie* must be replaced by moments of playful anarchy: repurposing public spaces, reversing or tangling lanes, blocking and subverting circulation.

Thus, for example, Michel de Broin's superbly cheerful *Entrelacement* installation, with its ball-of-string pavement plan and bicycle-route signage leading us down a garden path of madness; or Ken Lum's *Untitled (Language Painting)*, with its bold public assertions of nonsense, somehow hinting at meaning (the exclamation point!). Johannes Wohnseifer rebrands a dominant icon of the consumer universe, the high-end running shoe, with *The Wohnseifer*, a handcrafted, absurdly low-tech simulacrum of the Nike or Adidas article. Louis Cameron's *Puzzle Series—Visa, Staples Inkjet Paper, Newport*—appropriates the color schemes of familiar marketed objects and reveals the beauty that lingers in those hues and combinations. More beautiful still is *Corona Extra*, from the *Colour Bar Series*, which repositions the brand's trademark shades in an arrangement of pigment squares deliberately reminiscent of Kelly, Joseph Albers or Richter.

That piece hints, finally, at the real aesthetic possibility in these unlearnings and unstitchings of the familiar signs and their systems. The small leverage of critique offered by this kind of knowing play with the assumptions and hidden norms of the popular means very little by itself. If critique is expanded into full-dimension cultural theory, on the other hand, such critique rapidly grows flabby and loose. There is no shortage of bad cultural theory; indeed, it is an economy of sewage circulation all its own, running parallel to the very thing it wishes to challenge: dreck about dreck. The trick of unlearning lies in what can be learned in the doing, what revelations of self can be prompted by getting lost. There is no point in replacing one normative map with another, as if *now*, only now, we know where we are going.

Germaine Koh's installations show the way by not knowing the way. With their deftly redacted signs—themselves mass produced, available at a hardware store near you—the banal messages of disappointment are at once blunted and enhanced. *Sorry*, a closed door says in sprightly white script, generalizing regret to encompass everything, and nothing. No message of return, and no claim about being closed—which would logically imply the possibility, and time, of being open. Meanwhile, in the companion work that is reminiscent of Michael Elmgreen and Ingar Dragset's *Welfare Show* installations, the architecture of government aid stalled and broken (as when, for example, the stairs leading to the "Administration" department are shattered), the desk of an exchange or complaint department lies abandoned, a study in banal absence. *Help*, the sign behind says, eliding the usual offer of aid into a sad appeal that lacks origin, target, sense and referent. *Sorry* the other one echoes back again, just as empty.

Lost. *Sorry.*

Help. *Me too.*

8. Imaging the Artist: Going to Eleven and The Legacies of Joseph Wagenbach

i.   Philosophy

I have recently come across two striking appropriations of the idea of the artist, both from *The Simpsons*. I mention them not just to steal their jokes, although they're good jokes, but also to indicate what happens in cultural constructions of the artist under current conditions of mass culture.

There are two separate episodes from two different seasons; the latter refers back to the first. And they offer an illuminating twinning of artist images. In the first episode, Marge, the long-suffering housewife holding together this benighted all-American family, resuscitates a desire to be an artist that has lain dormant for some years. It has to do in part with a fan letter she sent to Ringo Starr, a portrait she did of him, and his enthusiastic reply being lost in the mail for decades.

To resuscitate her aesthetic ambitions, Marge takes a commission to do a portrait of Montgomery Burns, tyrannical overseer of the nuclear power plant and reigning billionaire of Springfield. Mr. Burns, sitting for Marge, says, "Can you make me beautiful?"

(If you've seen the cartoon, you know how absurd this is.) Marge says, "I think so," to which Mr. Burns replies, "I'm no matinee idol, you know." Marge tells him she has "the gift of revealing inner beauty."

Clearly this shows one kind of construction of what the artist is and can do; that is to say, he or she can, via a special gift, transfigure not only the commonplace, but also the ugly. The artist as seer. After various plot devices, the portrait is done. It is a nude—which, if you've ever seen Mr. Burns, you'll find rather appalling. When the painting is premiered, the curtain is flipped back, there are many gasps of appropriate shock. Burns is stooped and scaly, his hands hanging claw-like in front of his shrunken, evil frame. Marge says, "I guess I wanted to show that beneath all the cruelty, Mr. Burns is as beautiful and vulnerable as any of God's creatures." A viewer, hearing this, then looking at the painting, says, "He's bad. But he'll die. So I like it." Which is perhaps not exactly what Marge had in mind.

I mention this to set up the second instance of *The Simpsons* appropriating this idea of the artist, in a now-famous episode where Homer Simpson attempts to build a barbecue pit in his backyard, with predictably disastrous results. There's a great scene where Homer takes a run at his failed attempt to construct this barbecue pit with a patio umbrella, which lodges in the side of it and flings him backwards violently.

Homer tries to dump the mangled barbecue as garbage, and thus it is somehow brought to the attention of an art dealer in Springfield. She comes to the door of the Simpson home and wants to buy it. Homer tells her, "This isn't art. It's just a barbecue that pushed me over the edge." The art dealer, rendered here with a pedantic, sophisticated Boris-and-Natasha voice, says, "Mister Simpson, art isn't just pretty pictures. It's also the expression of raw human emotion. In your case, rage." She instructs Homer in the new doctrine of outsider art: "This is art that could be done by anyone: a mental patient, a hillbilly or a chimpanzee, for example." Homer is enthusiastic. "In high school, I was voted most likely to

be a mental patient, hillbilly or chimpanzee!" The artist not as seer
but as wacko.

At this point Homer becomes an instant art-world celebrity,
and among other things takes over Marge's memories of aesthetic
aspiration, so that he thinks he's the one in the family who's always
wanted to be an artist. "I've always had an interest in art," he tells
the furious Marge, "dating back to my schoolgirl days, when I
painted portrait after portrait of Ringo Starr." I can't help noting
here one of my all-time favorite scenes in *The Simpsons*. The art
dealer's friends descend on Moe's Tavern, the local watering hole,
and Moe, its famously ugly bartender, sidles up to some of them
at the bar. "So...you guys are Eurotrash, huh? How's that workin'
out for ya?" One of them responds, "To be honest, we are adrift on
a sea of decadent luxury and meaningless sex." Moe looks at him
and says, "And where is this sea located exactly?"

Homer's show with the barbecue is advertised in *Art in America*.
But he finds that something has changed in his accommodation
by the art world. His attempt to replicate the initial success is met
with stunned disapproval. New works that join the barbecue, like
Attempted Birdhouse, and *Failed Shelving Unit With Chainsaw and
Applesauce*, are not as celebrated as the first. The very same
Eurotrash art fan says, "You've gone from hip to boring. Why don't
you call us when you get to kitsch?"

Homer lies on the floor and says, "I don't get it, why don't people like my art anymore?" Marge takes Homer on a kind of lickety-
split tour of contemporary art and the history of art, searching for
new inspiration. He finds it in Christo. Marge points out that,
among other projects, Christo had put up umbrellas along the
shore in California. "Unfortunately," she admits, "some of them
fell and killed people." Homer says, looking into the middle distance, "Killer umbrellas, of course. Exquisite." His final artwork
involves flooding the entire town of Springfield. The artist as
transformer of the everyday world.

Now, my suggestion here is not just that this is a playful,
maybe sarcastic, comment from mass culture to, let's call it, elitist

or nonmass culture; but also that it plays with, and puts into question, the very idea of what an artist is. As so often, the multivalent effects of layered irony prompt deeper questions about the very idea of culture. How have images of the artist changed over time? I want to give you, very briefly, my list of ten, more or less historically ordered, notions of the artist. And then leave you with a suggestion for the future.

Over the course of the Western tradition at least, artists have been rooted in the first conception, which is to say, merely artisans of a particular kind. In Plato's day, for example, there was an understanding that artists were, by and large, to be seen as part of a continuum of workaday creation that included furniture makers and other kinds of artisans. Given this, insofar as artists declared themselves different, they were dangerous. So in the second book of Plato's *Republic*, we get the notorious denunciation of the "inspired" artist as a politically disruptive figure. This moralistic denunciation of the artist means that political art will not come to fruition for some centuries.

The second important conception of the artist, therefore, is the toiler in the workshop, the dutiful apprentice attempting to acquire mastery. This is really just an extension of the first, such that the artist who painted a given portion of a so-called masterwork might in fact be an anonymous workman who was hacking out an arduous apprenticeship in somebody else's studio. The studio was the genius, not the individual.

We move from this to the third, which is the first significant image of the artist for contemporary purposes, namely the artist as disinterested genius. I don't mean uninterested, but rather disinterested, in the Kantian sense of genius in pursuit of the use-free beautiful. The disinterested genius is a source of much influence, not least in disseminating the concept of autonomous art; but, even here, we don't quite get a sense of the individual as the crucial fact. That is, this artist remains largely anonymous, if singular, acting as a kind of servant of beauty itself.

Only in the fourth image of the artist, historically speaking, do we begin to appreciate our own, present difficulties. This is not just the disinterested genius but also the romantic genius. That is, the artist as someone different from other people: able to feel things more deeply, perhaps; certainly able to translate feelings more effectively into some kind of making. Modest though she remains, Marge Simpson appeals to the romantic genius notion when she speaks of her art as "revealing inner beauty."

The fifth category we can isolate is the dandy or, later, the gutter dandy—one of the favored modes of modernism. Here, in contrast to the Enlightenment disinterested genius or nineteenth-century romantic genius, we get an interesting distinction—in its way, a logical extension of Romanticism. Life itself, as Nietzsche suggested, becomes the work of art. The creation of works is considered, in some ways, secondary to the occupation and living out of a certain kind of life. Because the dandy refuses conformity, his life becomes an extended essay in resistance and self-creation.

That leads almost directly to the sixth category: the artist as social rebel. We might think of this as modernism without the art. Whatever the forms of his or her making, the artist is now understood to be a nonconformist, a "bad-boy artist" indeed. The artist as outsider, not in the sense of creating outsider art, but rather as someone who stands against the mainstream or dominant culture. This image, to be sure, is still with us.

It is not a long step from that sixth image to a seventh, namely, the artist as political agitator. The difference between them is simply that the generalized social rebel or nonconformist, role six, has no particular political agenda. The political artist-agitator does.

Eight represents a swing against the dangers inherent in seven: the artist as philosopher. Here we witness, among other things, the influential rise of conceptualism. I was struck by the recent news item that Marcel Duchamp's urinal had been chosen as the most significant work of the twentieth century, because it is the most philosophical of works, in that it draws to our attention the contours of the art world itself, the present circumstance where anything can be the work of art. The artist who absorbs this lesson, or repeats it, is engaged in philosophical argument—though often, as I argued earlier, at a rather sophomoric level.

Unfortunately, from that point, things get rapidly worse in the field of artist self-regard, not least because conceptualism too often backfires in the form of jejune philosophy. The ninth category I would isolate, therefore, is a combination of the previous three: the artist as charlatan. I mean the person who is, and cheerfully sees himself or herself as, a manipulator of the art world's bankrupt economies—on the make, cynical, blithely fraudulent.

Finally, though, and happily, we witness a return to the idea of the disinterested genius, but in a kind of new form: somebody who is fully aware of these various modalities of the artist's life but isn't trying simply to recapture an earlier moment. Who is trying to push traditional forms of making in directions that are consonant both with the history and the cutting edge. Not a servant of beauty, then, since art needn't be beautiful, but of a medium (Reinhardt, Mark Rothko), of ideas (Fluxus, Holzer), or, at best, both (Cornell, Serra, Richter).

Now, paradoxically, the image economy of the artist collapses, and the artist actually disappears. We are back where we belong, focused not on the artist but on the work: not on the work as "mere object," as Heidegger reminds us, but as experience. Art's postmodern revolution lies not in bringing outsiders into galleries, but, reversing the polarity, in extending the art world to every corner of existence. The right question then is not the pointless *who is the artist*, or even the traditional *what is art*; but rather, *when is art*.

Turn the knob up to eleven: the best image of the artist is the nonexistent one. The artist has disappeared; long live art.

ii. Art

What is a hoax? A gag, a goof, a blindfold; a spoof, a jape, a deceit; deliberate equivocation, fakery, impersonation, infiltration. Pretending what is not the case. The triumph of appearance over reality. A joke that functions by way of deception.

The English word *hoax* has a suitably cloudy etymology. It is, authorities aver, probably a contraction of "hocus," as in "hocus-pocus"—the traditional utterance, as any child could inform you, of witches over their infernal cauldrons. A spell, a trick, a magical confusion. Probably. But *hocus-pocus* itself traces a necromantic origin, for it is—probably—a corruption of the priestly Latin pronounced over the bread and wine, rendering them into flesh and blood, *hoc est corpus meum; hic est enim sanguis meus.* Reenacting the drama of the Last Supper, the priest quotes Christ: *Here is my body, here is my blood.* With the corruption, the words, which perform the holy Roman Catholic doctrine of transubstantiation, are mocked as magic.

The body of Wagenbach, by contrast with Christ's regular reappearance at the mass, was never found. Visitors to the house he was thought to inhabit saw every trace of him, from clothing and food to the very depressions his form would have made in the couch and bed—not to mention the stacks of drawings and jumbles of sculpture. But his body was absent, removed, they were told, to a local nursing home when his neighbors finally noticed the old man was even less visible than usual in the surrounding streets. We can investigate the corpus of his work only because his flesh has been removed.

As a work of art, Iris Häussler's *Legacy of Joseph Wagenbach* joins a lineage of hoaxes that surely includes everything from elaborate fakes and impersonations to the infiltrated readymades favored by that mutt Duchamp. Though *The Legacy* alludes to them, it is not really concerned with issues of authenticity or uniqueness—standard preoccupations of the art world skewered by some hoaxes. There is no concern here for the visual puzzles of representation tricks of trompe l'oeil, nor even with the now familiar gesture of puncturing the art world itself, in its institutional forms, as a collective delusion of corporate approval. Offering a layered experience of engagement, disillusion, and confusion, it goes well beyond these, and sets up a work—a network—of meaning whose reality lies neither in the house nor in the fiction.

It is an example of what we might label *haptic conceptual* art: the art of ideas that functions by way of immersion, even ravishment.

Immersion was essential to the work. Visitors to the house, located on a quiet residential street in Toronto, were greeted by an archival agent, dressed in a white lab coat, who issued warnings and latex gloves. They were made to sign a release form. Entry was by way of a narrative frame in the form of the "field office," which had been hastily constructed to include reassuring objects of investigative authority: the office coffeemaker, a fire extinguisher, notices and signs of warning. The exterior sign, in an inspired touch, was a sly modification of the City of Toronto municipal logo, rendering its usual form, a graphic representation of architect Viljo Revell's famous City Hall design, instead as an open book: one of many incidental jokes within the main frame of the work.

The house itself had been elaborately and meticulously filled with ephemera, not just artworks. Drawers were stuffed with old matchbooks and takeout menus, culled from garage sales and basements. Out-of-print books and obsolete hygiene products crowded the shelves and tabletops. The small house was jammed, stacked, piled, entirely claustrophobic. The final stop on the standard tour involved climbing a small ladder and placing one's head in an enclosure that allowed a view of the top of one large sculpture that dominated the living room—an obscure homage to Constantin Brâncusi from Häussler via her creation, Joseph.[1] The archival agent, sometimes the artist herself and sometimes various associates, took visitors through the house while unfolding a narrative of mystery and disappearance.[2] The artist who never was, Joseph, was reconstructed in a *post facto* psychic autopsy. Details and hints were highlighted: the recurrence of a certain female form in the sketches, the rabbit ears that would indicate a subsequent obsession, the tiny pencil mark on an ordnance survey map that indicates the location of the German concentration camp Bergen Belsen.

The main intention of *The Legacy* was never mere deception. Nevertheless, many people were taken with (or taken in by) the narrative contained by the house. The will to believe is strong, and small doubts were frequently squelched by visitors when faced with the overwhelming facticity of the work: the physical presence of all that material, not limited to the works themselves, plus the sense of sadness that pervaded the poky little house and its bizarre dirty rooms. Some visitors claimed to guess that the work involved a fiction, but this was hard to verify.[3] Certainly by the time the work had been available to visit for some weeks, many people were wondering how to bring Joseph's work into the "official" art world, how to comfort him at his nursing home, even to send music or flowers.

The artist had planned a formal reveal of the work's frame but she was anticipated, against an embargo, by an article that appeared in the *National Post* on September 12, 2006, with the headline "Reclusive downtown artist a hoax." This breach of the embargo deprived the newspaper's own readers, among others, of the chance to experience the work in full—not to mention bolstering a sense among journalists that they need not take artists' wishes seriously. When I called this action "unethical" (though perfectly legal since embargoes are not binding), one newspaper writer sent me a hostile e-mail demanding to know why this "bullshitting" art project was worth respecting in the first place. Where are the ethical obligations in fooling your audience?

It is a valid question. The answer, it seems to me, is that the project is a sustained, unnerving and moving meditation on the importance of art, and of life, which can only achieve its ends by means of the basic deception *plus the reveal*—like magic, only more so, hocus-pocus with punch. Or, if you like, a mystery story with the ending retroactively conferring sense on what has gone before. The philosopher Harry Frankfurt has famously defined bullshit as a lack of regard for the norm of truth. The bullshitter is not deceptive; he does not care, one way or the other, whether what he says is true. In this sense, *The Legacy* is, if anything, the antithesis of bullshit: its deception is in the service of truth, since the reveal allows for, indeed forces, a confrontation with the power of deception. Some visitors were amused, some shocked or even outraged, by the revelation, but all were united in finding the experience compelling. Why had they been taken in? What did it mean to forge an attitude or a relation to someone gone, only to find that he had never been there in the first place?

In "The Origin of the Work of Art," Heidegger notes, "the mere object is not the work of art." What is the work of art in Häussler's *Legacy of Joseph Wagenbach*? I suggest it is not the house, still less the contents thereof: the "works" of the "artist" Wagenbach. It is not even the experience of visiting the house. It is, rather, the entire field of meaning opened up by the installation plus the reveal.

That field can be surveyed along the following five vectors that I can do no more than sketch:

Narrative. The story of the reclusive melancholy artist was fetching to visitors, not least because it conformed to an available norm. Further, it heightened a sense of the anonymity of the urban, especially in a city like Toronto with its layerings of immigration and polyglot districts. How many millions of complex stories lurk behind the doors of our neighbors?

The *National Post* story, meanwhile, which ran on page one, was itself a miniature narrative of outrage. How often does installation art constitute front-page news in a national newspaper? Only when it involves a hoax, the story carrying an implicit journalistic judgment that this is just the sort of tomfoolery we might expect from the jape-happy modern art world. The hint is offered that all modern art partakes, to a greater or lesser degree, in a confidence game. The very phrase "reclusive downtown artist" is a condensed narrative of exposure—a "recluse" is not known to be a "downtown artist" unless and until discovered, his reclusion made known as a matter of righteous interest. That was one reason why the newspaper, to save its self-image, had to break the story first rather than cooperate with the intentions of the work.

Narrative and its conventions are thus embedded in the work at many levels: the narrative of Joseph's life, the narrative of our tour through that life's detritus, the narrative of our experience that the mystery of his absence not only has been solved, but was, in a sense, never a mystery at all.

Archiving. The frame was, importantly, established by the fiction of the archive: establish an artist's legacy by picking over and cataloging his works. The joke at the heart of *The Legacy* is a wry commentary on this archival impulse: to rescue the unknown artist by sorting the jumble of his life into secure categories of sense—the jumble having been created for just that purpose!

The insight is crystallized in the old-fashioned cardboard tags that were tied to each piece of sculpture. A rubber stamp had been applied to them, reading "Municipal Archives—Legacy Assessment Joseph Wagenbach." The stamped image included a rendering of Joseph's signature and a line fronted by the phrase "Testified by _____." These were already, like the assessment office, a clue in the form of a joke: archivists do not use such tags anymore, nor are they likely to use a phrase like "legacy assessment." The tags are thus a kind of kitsch. Even more, the rubber-stamped version of the "artist" signature had, of course, been fashioned by the artist Häussler (writing left-handed). Her scrawl was then added, in the character of the archivist assessing the legacy, in ink on the blank line below, "testifying" to the authenticity of the works assessed—all of which had been created by her. Assessment, testimony, authenticity, all collapsed under the sign, the trace, of the signature, both the work of one person and both "false," but at different levels of the work.[4]

Mediation. The art world is always a function of mediations, throughputs and frames of interpretation. Likewise the world established by the archival impulse. Both forms of mediation are investigated here, sometimes mocked or deconstructed. This art world is outside the usual walls—it has its own walls—but nevertheless, perhaps because of that, offers a rich meditation on art and its worlds. It refuses, finally, the Hegelian completeness effect of mediation, whereby all tensions are eventually resolved by the absoluteness of the idea, insisting instead on remainders and unassimilated pieces. The legacy of Joseph Wagenbach is unstable, in part because fictional, but *The Legacy of Joseph Wagenbach* takes this instability, which it has itself created, as a starting point, not a conclusion. Or rather, it folds beginning and ending together. The work begins anew with each visitor, each tour, each moment of the reveal.

Time. And so time, too, is part of the legacy. The work lingers, and does so in part because of its method of temporal excavation. The archivists, laboring in the present, are trying to reconstruct the past of the man's life, even as the "artist" is apparently trying, in his practice, to confront and maybe work through events from his own past. The three timelines are intertwined by the work, deliberately warped together and collapsed. And the effect does not stop as we exit the frame, since the largest part of the work's effect is still to come: the moment, in some near future, when we find out this experience has not been what it seemed to be.

Threshold. The final layer of meaning of the work was constituted, or excavated, by the line between the work and the world, between the experience and its aftermath. We crossed the threshold of the house and so entered the frame, were immersed in the world of the absent, fictional creator. But the frame was broken by the reveal, forcing an awareness of how frames of meaning are always presupposed. After the reveal we are, as it were, suspended on both sides of the threshold, inside and out at once.[5]

Taken together, *The Legacy* thus offered visitors a way of dwelling in thought for a sustained, indeed recurring, period. Again and again, they would recall the first impressions of the house; then the moment they learned it was a framed fiction. What to do with the feelings associated with the first experience when placed under the sign of the second? Häussler's work radiates its significance ever outward. It is conceptual art—art not just of ideas, but art about the idea of art—but it functions only because of the viscerality of its experience. In this final sense it is, to use Hegel's phrase but shorn of the dialectical arrogance, "the sensuous presentation of the idea."

It was Nelson Goodman, noting the open-ended nature of the post-Duchamp, post-Warhol art world, where anything may be a work of art, who said that the important question was no longer "what is art?" but instead "when is art?" At what point does a soup can or urinal shift, in its meaning, from mundane piece of equipment to object of our rapt attention? It is not merely when they enter the gallery or museum, as some suppose. The multiple legacies of *The Legacy of Joseph Wagenbach* demonstrate this, offering a work entirely outside institutional boundaries, a work that continues to resonate over time, expanding its meanings.

The fact of its fiction is essential to that effect. *The Legacy of Joseph Wagenbach* is therefore a hoax, of an elaborate kind, but only as long as we recall the magic transformations, the transfigurations of the world and ourselves, effected by the incantatory power of hocus-pocus. Not bread into flesh, perhaps, but memory into meaning—and vice versa.

Notes

1. One impulse for the work was a feeling on the part of the artist that the work she was producing seemed to be in a form unrelated to her own training. "When I got to the studio and worked in sculpture and drawing I noticed that the out-coming pieces relate to Art Brut," she has written. "But I am not an Art Brut artist. I can't be, because I got the education that disqualifies me. The consciousness and frustration sits in this corner." (Private correspondence, February 14, 2007.) The frame of Joseph Wagenbach's legacy gave her a kind of masked license to create as she wished. At the same time, these works were not exactly hers, since she created them under the sign of his (imagined) identity. Like any vivid fictional character, he becomes more real in her imagination as time goes on. The same can be said for those who visited the house: Joseph Wagenbach is a man they will never forget.

2. Iris Häussler told me it was a talk I had given on "Disappearing the

Artist" in 2005, reproduced here as the first part of the essay, that prompted her to get in touch with me about *The Legacy*. As a consequence, I was not able to visit the house except under conditions of prior knowledge, obliterating the opportunity to experience the work fully.

3. As someone seeing the house from outside the frame, I noted a certain lack of plausibility in the very perfection of detail that makes the work so technically remarkable. It is unlikely that someone would, for example, have so many different matchbooks from businesses that disappeared at exactly the moment Joseph decided to become reclusive. But this feature, ostensibly a flaw, was neatly folded back into the work. Häussler notes: "After a while I included into the tours a sentence like: 'Often we think during our archiving process that we find something hintful, just to discover in the next moment that it is probably an item Joseph had collected at a garage-sale or found in the garbage and is not a personal private object'." (Private correspondence, February 14, 2007.)

4. I asked the artist for one of these tags, which is the single artifact from the overall artwork that captures all elements of the ideas it deploys. The house, meanwhile, remained untouched, if no longer visited, as late as the spring of 2007. A documentary film, directed by Anthony Gratl, will assess the work, while a fictional film based on the reception, *The Archivist's Handbook*, is planned by director Peter Lynch (*The Herd*, *Arrowhead*, *Project Grizzly*, etc.).

5. I dwell further on thresholds and the idea that meaning is a function of liminality in a series of three articles published under the general title "Crossing the Threshold: Towards a Philosophy of the Interior" (*Queen's Quarterly*, Spring 2006, pp. 91-104; Summer 2006, pp. 275-89; and Fall 2006, pp. 443-59). This material in turn forms chapters 6 and 7 of *Concrete Reveries: Consciousness and the City* (Viking, 2008).

9. Five Stops: Homesick and Wanting in the Blue Republic

i. Nostalgia

The Greek roots of the word "nostalgia" contain a doubleness that is lost, or concealed, in standard usage of the term to denote a yearning for some earlier time (often enough, to be sure, an illusory one). *Nostos algos* is, literally, the pain associated with returning home—homesickness, we might say, thinking at the level of a disease. But nostalgia is future as well as present pain because, lurking behind my longing to return home there is the additional pain of what returning home actually entails. As that most famous of Greek nostalgists, Odysseus, reminds us, home is no longer home by the time we return. And, moreover, we are no longer ourselves. Odysseus comes in disguise, cloaked against his strandedness in time, having yearned for what was gone the moment he left. Just as the past is never a dwelling place, much as we strive for it, home is not the place we thought we knew. Not all scars are visible, or physical, and not all desires are subject to sense.

Thus does pain double, and ultimately triple, itself, becoming finally the anxiety we feel for losing the lack that nostalgia allows.

We secretly wish to dwell in nostalgia itself, not in home or past, and so what we wish for is not the return but the continuation. Nostalgia makes pathology into a mode, a delicious strandedness.

The two-person art collective Blue Republic has, over recent years, given concrete shape and expression to this nest of insights about desire, dwelling and time. In works that are deliberately unstable, witty and beautiful, they both acknowledge and dismantle the yearnings that are characteristic of a cultural moment whose predominant narrative is that it has no narrative.[1] Here "the future," once considered a debatable category, a site of (possibly rational) plan and project, dissolves in layers of confused aspiration drawn from utopian politics and architecture. Technology evolves from tool to threat, semi-organic and uncanny rather than calmly useful. Garbage configures itself into shapes suggestive of personal space or urban dreams, not rescued and recycled so much as reorganized into revelations of situatedness. Beneath it all one hears a thrum of play and possibility that may be the one and only valid meaning of that much abused notion, utopia.

A retrospective of recent Blue Republic work is timely in both, or at least two, senses: at once well-timed and time-conscious. The three parts of their practice from which these works are drawn— *Limited Activities, Simulations,* and *Alterations*—present distinct aspects of reflection on everydayness that, together and apart, rise to a thrilling if unsettling climax. The omnibus show called *Nostalgia for the Present* thus takes us into its world of hyperconscious engagement with materials, forms, found objects, structure and measurement; and then returns us, *expels* us we might even say, back into the other world, the world of our "normal" engagements, with a heightened awareness of all things urban and real. Thus "present," too, opens up a double meaning, twining the usual sense of present as the now with the metaphysically missed present of *presence.*

By mirroring, miniaturizing and reconfiguring the tools and garbage of daily experience—maps and paint rollers, injection molding and broomsticks, discarded toys and tools—Blue Republic ruptures any smooth assumption of a world simply waiting for our perception or, still more, consumption of it. The in-progress status of some of the best works here, especially *Speeding* from the *Beautiful Infections* series, the exhibition's astonishing magnum opus, testifies to this ongoing destabilization. There is always more to add because, by the very logic of order and control, the projects of order and control can never be completed.

This larger insight is composed of smaller ones, each wedded closely to the works presented here, such that the overall effect is refracted and reinforced with every step. Our exit from the land constructed as and by Blue Republic is itself a "blue" journey, one that leads to a city in which maps no longer calmly indicate route and destination, where buildings are revealed as impaired Erector Set dreams of a banal imagination, where dust and refuse signal new meanings and beauties.

ii. Contamination

Many of these pieces force us to reconsider the assumed liminal relationship of use and disuse, the firm line between stuff and garbage. *Beautiful Infections (urban)* and *Speeding*, the two largest installations, sprout as complex installations of found objects, readymades, drawings on paper, wood and wall, and shredded bits of magazine and book. Paint cans, tin cans, balloons and old bread are discernible in the latter; the former includes bits of Styrofoam, toy soldiers, a plastic model of an airliner and elaborate structural achievements rendered in corrugated cardboard. Both works create miniature cities of deliberately confused scale, with branching electrical tape fractal patterns creeping along the floor and up the wall to induce a vertiginous pullback of consciousness similar to those scalar films and books that rush from nanonomical to astronomical in the span of seconds or pages.

In these quasi-urban sites, with their echoes of Cornell and Adams—the whimsy of the latter deepened by the pathos of the former—composition becomes a reflection on materials, as indeed it always is despite our ability to overlook it in familiar or "successful" versions, where materials efface their presence in the service of form. There are echoes, too, of Kurt Schwitters's melancholy Dada collages, or the intricate toolkits and equipmental joking of Fluxus installations, with their slight inflections on use value and deployability. No such effacement is possible here, and so we confront, again and again, the garbage of everyday life resuscitated as the stuff of building. Indeed, the usual *cordon sanitaire* between safe and contaminated, between useable and used-up, is that which in these installations gets erased. We see, even as we traverse, the threshold that holds the modern city together, an internalization of contamination in an extended, but always failed, attempt at hygienic control.

Sewers, dumps and cemeteries now perform the function once reserved, more simply, for the city walls. Instead of merely (and literally) ejecting foreign and rotting matter, the corpses and garbage of routine urban sloughing off, defending the boundary as indeed a military necessity, we attempt to manage garbage, and so make it vanish, from the inside out. In a graphic and relevant parallel, especially given the predominance of readymades here, the toilet bowl famously rendered aesthetic by R. Mutt is a symbol of the modern inside-outness of sanitation-as-control. Bodily waste will be disposed of inside the house, not in an out building; garbage will be removed from sight but not from site.

Thus do we attempt to manage a necessary threshold by making it, in effect, no longer a simple line but a kind of Möbius strip.[2] And thus, too, our horror when this subtle non-Euclidean geometry of sanitation is broken or ruptured—as when, for example, a hungry rat bursts into a café kitchen and so, from there, into what is known as the front of house. The patrons shriek! Now suddenly everything is contaminated! And now, wrenched unwillingly in one direction, we must wrench ourselves back. The economy of the *cordon sanitaire*, once exploded, can only be restored by collective forgetting. "Control" is revealed as not control at all, but rather its opposite, namely, a surrender performed through a willed act of amnesia.

These are familiar insights, and the rescue of garbage for aesthetic interest is, by itself, a minor achievement. If these works did only that they would not be terribly interesting. But a new line of thought opens up when *Beautiful Infections (urban)* and *Speeding* are juxtaposed with four other works, the three *Untitled* pieces from *Limited Activities*, and the other *Beautiful Infections* piece. This last work, a winsome installation of brilliant simplicity, presents a six-foot-high aluminum stepladder, apparently fresh from the hardware store, in the act of being colonized by a creeping invasion of readymade plastic blocks, uniform in shape but multicolored. Like *Speeding*, this piece seems to grow more complex, and more compelling, with every installation, such that the most recent version had the blocks not only infecting the ladder, but also running along the floor and even the wall, a sort of Lego trail of death. The stepladder, once a means of our ascent, is rendered still and nonfunctional. It appears powerless to fight off the encrustation of the blocks, a tool overgrown and so destroyed by this multitude of tiny construction units, whose bright colors twist together the benign appeal of toys with the bright menace of laboratory models of molecular viruses. A beautiful infection makes a beautiful confection.

One thinks here, perhaps, of Coupland's aesthetic play with scale and toys, as in his own Lego works, or the molded plastic soldiers rendered at half-human height. But also, more deeply, of An Te Liu's recent "sanitation architecture" installations, wherein whole miniature cities of buildings and streets are created on the white-cube gallery floor by arranging and stacking air filters and other technologies of purification in the standard matte white of the studio model or vitrine. Again, Blue Republic's related reflection is unstinting. Nearby stand the three *Limited Activities* installations, witty and unnerving commentaries on dirt and control: the demented quartet of industrial push brooms, forever thwarted in the act of sweeping; the push broom locked and limited in its wooden box; and especially the circled vectors of personal space literally carved out of a field of rubble, lumber, crushed concrete and Gyprock.

All three works suggest some deranged but fundamental

janitorial impulse that is constantly confronting its own limits, indeed its built-in defeat. Dirt forever encroaches, and every act of cleansing is another sign of dirt's domination! We may hold out against this power, and so define ourselves, but we can do so only negatively. That is, we understand ourselves as, for the moment, holding the line—*not giving in.*

iii. Measure

Incomplete projects of control and domination are thematized in a different way in the evocative works from the *Simulations* series. The best of these, *Measuring the Meter*, establishes the rich theme of measurement and mapping deconstructed as desperate attempts to find a priori regularity in a contingent, even arbitrary natural world. The standard unit of measurement, a length so sacred it is established by the speed of light and held in trust by the headquarters of French bureaucratization, is mapped off with bits and pieces of found elements, suggesting both the meter's vulnerability and its necessity. There must be a unit, if measurement is even to be possible; but any unit is no more than a sign of assumed consensus or, sometimes, applied force. The meter's authority is established in its policed uses, not in some transcendental fixity.

The work, here offered in homage to Jacobs, also recalls Michel Foucault's remark that there may be a category of the contingent a priori: not the self-contradiction it seems, rather an awareness that all practices require presuppositions that, from within the practice, can be neither defended nor questioned but must be always already assumed. The notion further echoes R. G. Collingwood's suggestion for a "descriptive metaphysics" that does not seek to justify, only to identify, the absolute presuppositions of a given practice.[3] Only on the basis of these are the relative presuppositions of the practice—the rules of the game—available for use; and only on the basis of those relatively assumed notions are propositions, or moves in the game, possible. Thus the proposition "The table is 1.5 meters long" rests, as it were, atop an unspoken relative presupposition, namely that my ruler is an accurate rendering of meters. That in turn sits upon the assumption, so deeply unspoken as to sound bizarre if phrased, that *measurement is possible* because there is a unit of measurement.

Collingwood is what we today would call a *quasi-realist*. He is content to describe this layering of truth claims, and approve its local functionalism, without feeling any need to justify the practice independently of itself; whereas Foucault reminds us—as Blue Republic likewise does—that these taken-for-granted elements of practical life are among the most contestable political sites we know. Or rather, we don't *know* that because our knowledge—both what counts as knowledge, and the individual elements thereof—is disciplined by a "regime of truth" that renders its deepest presumptions invisible. Measurement, so apparently innocuous, is one of these, arguably the dominant modern one. Here, Foucault's distinction between *conaissance* (generated surface knowledge) and *savoir* (assumed depth knowledge) offers a useful level. *Savoir*, he says, may also be understood as *episteme*: the assumed project of a disciplinary knowledge hygiene. In the modern, which is to say post-Cartesian, era that hygiene is one of rendering the world of lived experience into an abstract space that can be subjected to a grid-based logic. The ancient world harbored this dream as *mathesis*—a universal science of measurement and order—but only Descartes's modern triaxial geometry made it realizable in practice.[4]

Mathesis is the link between meters and maps, and so from *Measuring the Meter* to the map-based *Simulations*, especially the perforated and shredded city maps of *Untitled* and *NEWTOPKA*. Here, the mapping project is literally dismantled or punctured, taken apart. *Mathesis* disciplines knowledge but, by the same token, it also serves to discipline subjects: maps render individuals into locations, such that one's position can always be found on the relevant document, and one can, in principle, be addressed as a set of coordinates. On the map I am never without such coordinates, even if I am in constant motion. So powerful is this Cartesian desire that many cities, especially in the New World, will adopt its conceptual grid as their own physical reality, carving the natural site into hard right angles and regular rectangular lots, numbering rather than naming the streets and avenues. And so the map becomes the ultimate form of panopticon technology, making everyone and everything localizable and subject to spatial determination.

But, like hygiene more generally, the map's peculiar spatial hygiene fails just to the extent it succeeds. Considerations of scale, deployed here in the poster pieces *8,000 years* and *Check Your Vision* as well as in features of the large installations, make the point vibrant. The branching, map-like elements of the installations hint at it too, fractal mathematics being, in one sense, a recognition of the paradoxes of scale. A map must accept, as one of its relative presuppositions, a relevant scale; a map that depicts everything is a nonsense relic out of Lewis Carroll, the one to one-scale map that is so large it covers the entire county it seeks to represent. The relativity of the scale presupposition depends on, but also unsettles, the absolute presupposition that accurate mapping is possible. Once scale is chosen, things are left out and so not covered by the map. The map can only present its truth under the aegis of a larger falsehood, or suspension of disbelief. Its comprehensive provisionality is masked by the air of authority it offers; but that mask may be removed to uncover the desires in which *mathesis* is rooted.

iv. Cities of Desire

Desire itself is thematized through the artists' work, letting us know that this republic of blueness, of wry but melancholic reflection, may also be a site of therapeutic investigation. The cities and scales, the tools and trash, here put into play are all, in their different fashion, implements of desire. They carry our wishes, but at the same time show that those wishes—for direction, for control, for hygiene—are liable to be thwarted, or stalled, or turned back upon themselves. The future yawns before us because we fail, over and over, to possess the past of our longing.

But what, after all, is desire? It is as much an *avoiding* as it is a *seeking-after.* "The paradox of desire," says Slavoj Žižek, "is that it posits retroactively its own cause."[5] That is, we confront, and think we understand, our desires in terms of its immediate objects, which we then label as the origin of the desire: the woman I cannot have, the car I must have, the victory I long for. But these are not the origin of desire, merely its coagulation or fixity. We know this, in part, because desire is constantly failing to be satisfied *even in its satisfaction*, and so is always renewing itself. Indeed, the paradox is deeper than just this one of causality; desire's satisfaction is also its death, and so we enter into a dangerous game whenever we satisfy a desire. Desire met is desire killed, and so satisfaction is necessarily dissatisfaction. This is more than just a matter of being disappointed with what we get, or finding victory anticlimatic. The economy of desire makes for a constant reproduction of longing in the space we call fantasy. Desire itself is what we desire! Thus there is an endless circulation around what Žižek (after Jacques Lacan) calls the *objet petit a*: the trace of the Real of desire, which fantasy conceals. There is a hole, or gap, that resists complete symbolization, even in fantasy: we cannot confront directly that which we really desire. We can see it only through a skewed view, a *looking awry*, as Žižek's 1991 book has it.

Desire's own perversions offer such a view, as do these artworks that cast their sidelong glances, their peripheral vision, along the traces of nostalgia's longing. Consider boredom, that "paradoxical wish for a desire," as Adam Phillips calls it.[6] Boredom, so common in the very urban experience of selfhood and scene depicted in these works, is desire stalled within itself. At one level, boredom reveals the nature of desire as suspended within temporality and meaninglessness: I cannot start anything, because nothing seems worth doing—nothing worth the casting of my self into the future which is desire's project. And yet, time still passes. Thus, as Arthur Schopenhauer put it, "boredom is direct proof that existence is in itself valueless, for boredom is nothing other than the sensation of the emptiness of existence. For if life, in the desire for which our essence and existence consists, possessed in itself a positive value and real content, there would be no such thing as boredom: mere existence would fulfill and satisfy us."[7] As it is, desire is instead constant and mere existence is insufficient. Boredom thus marks both the withdrawal of meaning from the self, and the endlessness of desire.

Kierkegaard accepted boredom as nestled in the ever-renewing quality of desire, not least because of the baseline principle that "all men are boring." Here we may simply agree, and note among other things the classicist Cornford's assessment of *Boring* as a prime tactic, along with *Wasting Time*, of the accomplished academic politicians. Boring, says Cornford, may be technically defined as talking with authority and at length at some distance from the main point, preferably on a matter about which you are known to be incompetent.[8] More deeply, Kierkegaard's bleak assessment may sound an overture to the general claim offered by poet John Berryman a century later: "Life, friends, is boring. We must not say so."[9]

Indeed, though, we *do* say so—albeit usually in a desperate attempt to avoid the reasons why life might be (might be found) boring. Fleeing our boredom is a version of Hegel's "bad infinite," which runs heedlessly from one longing to another, often in ascending spirals of Neronic or Caligulan distinction: from porcelain plates to silver, from silver to gold, from gold to burning half of Rome to experience the conflagration of Troy. "Boredom is the root of all evil," the aesthete *A* says in Kierkegaard's *Either/Or*, outlining his "Attempt at a Theory of Social Prudence." That is, given the baseline fact that "all men are boring," it follows that one must cope with the fact of boredom in oneself and others. But *overcoming* boredom is not an effective coping strategy; it self-defeats for the very same reason that boredom arises in the first place, namely that we are indefinitely suspended in webs of desire whose only cessation is death. Boredom arises as an overwhelming middle term, or ground, between memory that has succumbed to nostalgia and hope that has allowed itself to reduce to expectation. Boredom is an awareness that our grasp of the temporal, even in thought, is vanishingly slight.

Instead of overcoming, then, which merely recapitulates that failure at greater degrees of complexity or desperation, A recommends a method which is a refinement of the cultivated idleness advocated by, among others, Samuel Johnson (before) and Bertrand Russell (after). A's idleness is not mere aestheticization of experience; it also has a social dimension, which lies in converting the boring person into someone interesting. "When sensitive people, who as such are extremely boring, become angry, they are often very diverting. Teasing in particular is an excellent means of exploration." This is not an exercise to be undertaken lightly, since "[t]he whole secret lies in arbitrariness" and "it requires deep study to succeed in being arbitrary without losing oneself in it, to derive satisfaction from it oneself." Thus *crop rotation*, the art of arbitrarily exciting one's interest in otherwise boring things.

Phillips is not so pessimistic, nor so ironic. For him, what Schopenhauer and Kierkegaard describe is not boredom itself but the "nihilistic waiting" that marks a stage of despair when boredom gives way, or gives up, surrendering to meaninglessness—and then responding with either articulate surrender or elegant ironies. But boredom itself, properly viewed, is not nihilistic in this sense; it is still a struggle, and hence not yet meaningless; it is experienced as frustration, and therefore as an active (if perverse or paradoxical) desire. Boredom is, in fact, what philosophers call a second-order desire, a desire about desires: I want to want something. In this sense, it is akin to other second-order desires and likewise related to various conditions where first- and second-order desires are in conflict, such as addiction, procrastination, weakness of the will and so on. Boredom still negotiates hope through expectation; it still wishes. But it is clutched in its wishing, an engine running without the gears engaged.

One common reason for this is not, as we often imagine, a lack of object, but rather a lack of obstacle. Desire cannot know its object until it is thwarted; then the object *I do not have* arises for me as the "cause" of the desire. Desire needs the obstacle more than it needs the object—one reason why virtually anything, sometimes the strangest things, can be an object of desire. Having an obstacle allows me to avoid the two terrors that attend all personal economies of desire, and explain why wanting is so important to the very idea of self. On the one hand, I fear the *merging* of my self with my desire, such that there is no distance at all left between me and the objects of my wanting. This is a species of self-dissolution, or disappearance. On the other hand, however, I likewise fear the *isolation* of my self and my desire, such that I set myself against desire and its objects. This is a species of self-abnegation, or suicide. Both outcomes are kinds of death, whether I am swallowed up by my desires or so far repudiate them as to, in a final exercise of self, kill off the self.

What is the optimal distance between merging and isolation? Well, that is just what the self must negotiate. Personal identity requires obstacles more than satisfactions, because the ego's projects must be both thwarted and satisfied; obstacles are a link to the world, to knowing "where we are" and "where we are going." They tell us who we are, and how we are faring. Without them, we are not just cut adrift, we are literally nothing at all. And so desire must forever renew its dissatisfaction, its being blocked and challenged. Boredom is a hint at this forever, an illuminating hiccup in desire's otherwise apparently smooth functioning—especially in social economies of desire, where consumption is urged on us at every moment, a fever of longing and its satisfaction. This social economy requires, beneath its bright surface, a structure of swift discard and built-in obsolescence. We must be constantly throwing things out—clothes, or tools, perhaps even trends and ideas—in order to consume new ones afresh each day. The city becomes a mechanism for this economy, a massive machine of desire circulation.

v. Hope

And yet, beneath the dust and chaos of the city, within the forever renewed excitations of longing, there runs a current of hope. The works offered here extend a critique of current economies of longing, but they may do something even more valuable: they exhibit the elements of play that are boredom's antithesis and rescue. Boredom is not vanquished, merely postponed, by exciting a new desire. Only play, with its roots in undirected and nonutilitarian desire, its utopian overtones of refusing to assimilate or end or be located, can free us from the stalls of self. We cannot escape the economy of desire, for that way lies death, but we can renegotiate our engagement with it in a self-fashioning, open-ended manner. This is where desire transforms itself into the specific kind of non-nihilistic yearning we call hope.

Derrida defines hope as "the affirmation foreign to all dialectics, the other side of nostalgia." He means that hope is the unresolved remainder, the forever leftover, in any process of rational assimilation. The dialectic project shows itself most clearly in its failure, not its success: there is always something more, some further antithetical gesture that forces it onward. And this *more* is that which constantly evades the project, just as the possible future reiterations of my speech or writing are mutually destabilizing. The past use of words and phrases makes available—avails—my present use, but also all other present and future uses, and these in turn render mine not so much finite (for this is obvious) as spectral and uncontrolled, unlimited.[10]

As with words, so with ideas: the principle of universal democratic inclusion, for example, is revealed most clearly—perhaps exclusively—in its limit-moves, at the very moment it goes beyond what was previously accepted. Just as the success of the map is given only in the moment of its twinned failures of *edge* (what lies beyond) and of *scale* (what is not shown), universality is never invoked as a stable achievement, only as a demand to expand the circle, to allow more in. Once more, the *more* is everything, for universality is an empty signifier except for it. Universality is visible only in its forward movement, which is to say in its previous failure.[11]

And so again: as words and ideas go, so go forms and materials. The nano-architectural experiments of these works, the sustained micro-reflection on the act of building and the fact of built forms, presses us towards a precipice of awareness about our macro-level acts of urban dwelling. We use materials according to the sum total of their previous uses, and so subject them to the same iterational (il)logic as words, making a given use unstable even (or especially) when apparently firm; but we also, sometimes, expand on their range of uses and so shift the limit, both of use and of experience thereof. Stuff becomes garbage and garbage becomes stuff. Consumption is produced even as products are consumed. And so, finally, the constraints of personal space, the inside and outside of individual consciousness, are further folded in, or suspended within these tangles, creating the rich, funny and disturbing layering of thought that marks this exhibition.

Derrida suggests that hope is the other side of nostalgia, and here we might follow his argument along lines like these: nostalgia is criticized as false hope, the longing for a never-was harbored by someone in a never-is. John Berger, in a sub-Benjaminian insight, associates nostalgia with *glamour*, the quality, he says, of reflected envy.[12] The glamorous do not possess an essence or intrinsic quality so much as they sit at the center of a reciprocal economy of desire, a node of envy. My wanting to be you (that is, what I imagine, via mediation, you to be) is what makes you into the glamorous person. Glamour is a positional good. Unlike other, more straightforward positional goods such as *taste*—i.e., my sophistication in art or sport enjoyed precisely in the act of being demonstrated as superior—glamour, like *cool*, has the peculiar feature that it can only be discerned by the entire desire economy. The glamorous, in other words, need the nonglamorous in a manner as tight and inevitable as Hegel's dialectic of lordship and bondage. You are not envied for some talent or skill or possession; you are envied simply for being enviable. And so, absent the enviers, there is nothing left to envy.

From this vantage, nostalgia is just a generalized envy for, and so glamorization of, an imagined time or condition. Nothing is revealed in it except the aimlessness, indeed emptiness, of our yearning. If the economy is reciprocal in this fashion, nostalgia, even under analysis, simply throws us back upon ourselves and our now revealed lack. Nostalgia is indeed a sickness, but not homesickness so much as sickness at heart. We want to believe—we want to want—but every moment of our wanting is forever turned in upon its own energy, negating and canceling it.

And so nostalgia for the present once more doubles and redoubles. Longing for a past moment is experienced in a present one, and so determines our constant, inevitable entry into the future. Engagement with things and their effects—with systems of measurement and design—is revealed as ontologically nostalgic. We can never recover the originary presence that orders those very systems. We can never, any more than we can return to the longed-for past, penetrate the systems themselves to find, or uncover, what lies beneath. The message of this exhibition's sustained reflection on sense making and scale is not merely that access to originary presence is blocked. It is, in addition, that there is no beneath or origin, any more than there is a truth to the recalled and cherished golden moment—a moment that is, by definition, golden only in the glow of memory. By the same token, presence is basic only in being the desire for solidity we experience as a result of the *lack* in instability's heart. Presence is always felt in being gone.

There is a more hopeful possibility, to be sure, and that is that nostalgia will precipitate its more robust, indeed robustly political, cognate of hope. Perhaps we can work through nostalgia, not to lay it to rest but to perform a sort of autopsy of our heartsick condition. Hope is the most activist of virtues—not because it always issues in action, still less because it is motivated or guided by a total dialectical understanding. No, rather because it remains by definition open-ended and incomplete. Hope is a variation of what Derrida means by hospitality: the waiting and welcoming that does not demand the answer or insist on the resolution, but makes a space of receptivity for whoever may come to visit.

Thus we shift our attention from the standard Heideggerian demand to *be at home*, to achieve dwelling and so thinking, into a more demanding project: *making our home available to the other*.

This is the extra-dialectical logic of the gift, offered without expectation of return, the stranger welcomed without question or
demand. Odysseus returns and we do not ask to see his scar; we
assume that he has scars, as we all do, and simply offer him a place.
As it has with a variety of past works, Blue Republic redeems the
idea of the present through an insistent play with its meanings,
thematizing the cultural and material force of Past and Future in
rich textures of humor and insight. The gift of this complex and
moving artwork is to make us feel at home in our worldly moment
even as it recalls just how homely and unwelcoming the wider
world remains.

Notes

1.   It is an odd twist of naming and necessity that "Blue Republic" is also,
     as of the moment of this writing, the name of a political weblog dedi-
     cated to progressive liberal causes in the United States, a nation whose
     present includes a struggle between "red" and "blue" states. A legacy of
     demographic mapping and (presumably) the American political
     palette, red states are conservative and Christian, blue states progressive
     and secular. The resulting map, with blue patches concentrated in the
     Northeast and California, and red dominating the Middle West and
     South, is just the sort of attempted sense-making visual document that
     Blue Republic—the artists—would find worthy of perforation. Indeed,
     it is a short step from this red/blue splitting of a nation's consciousness
     to the satirical remapping of North America, proposed by a Swiss car-
     toonist, into two psychographic nations: the United States of Canada
     and Jesusland.
           The rich layers of meaning that cling to blue—a separate investiga-
     tion—are examined brilliantly by William Gass in *On Being Blue: A
     Philosophical Inquiry* (Godine, 1976). Its long opening sentence (also
     repeated near the end) begins this way: "Blue pencils, blue noses, blue
     movies, laws, blue legs and stockings, the language of birds, bees, and
     flowers as sung by longshoremen, that lead-like look the skin has when
     affected by cold, contusion, sickness, fear . . ." Blue is the color of desire,
     but also of desire's renunciation.

2.   For an extended meditation on this project of control in the modern
     urban, see Dominique Laporte, *History of Shit*, Nadia Benabid and
     Rodolphe el-Khoury, trans. (MIT, 2000); orig. *Histoire de la merde*

(1978). Among other insights, Laporte notes how the underground sewage system is a kind of subconscious echo of the circulatory economies of the "legitimate" surface, the movement of bodies, goods, and money along the streets and shopfronts (nowadays, also phone lines and swipe systems) of the city.

3.   R. G. Collingwood, *An Essay on Metaphysics* (Oxford, 1998; orig. 1940). Collingwood's position, a direct challenge to the logical positivism of A. J. Ayer and others, successfully updates, without the transcendental commitments, the Kantian understanding of practices as *having to have* elements which are always already the case. Simon Blackburn's recent influential defence of quasi-realism, against the presumed challenges of postmodern relativism, works over similar ground; see, e.g., *Essays in Quasi-Realism* (Oxford, 1993).

4.   Michel Foucault, *The Order of Things*, Alan Sheridan, trans. (Random House, 1971); orig. *Les mots et les choses* (1969)—a bad English translation of the title, which forebears from endorsing (because it wishes to investigate) the regime of ordering. Foucault's historicism is often tendentious. Ian Hacking, while generally sympathetic with the archaeological project, takes issue with the conaissance/savoir distinction in "Michel Foucault's Immature Science," *Nôus* 13 (1979): 39–51 at 42. And in a recent conversation (June 2006) Hacking noted that the plausible-sounding assumption of a pre-modern universal science of order and measurement was unfounded, and Foucault's historical interpretation therefore flawed; also, in contrast to English dictionaries that list numerous historical citations of *mathesis* as a poetic usage (in Alexander Pope, e.g.), in French the word is labeled "rare" and the dictionary citations are all to Foucault!

5.   Slavoj Žižek, *Looking Awry* (MIT, 1991), p. 12.

6.   Adam Phillips, "On Being Bored," in *On Kissing, Tickling, and Being Bored* (Faber, 1993). Phillips's account of boredom is a mostly orthodox late Freudianism extended, via clinical reflection, into this key area of contemporary experience.

7.   Arthur Schopenhauer, "On the Vanity of Existence," in *On the Suffering of the World*, R. J. Hollingdale, trans. (Penguin, 2004; orig. 1850), p. 19. Boredom, for Schopenhauer, is characteristic of modernity because it marks the awareness that we no longer need to struggle with the bare facts of existence, and so lose the meaning, however primal, offered in that struggle. It is accurate to suggest that for him there was no such thing as boredom, though there may have been inaction and even

leisure, prior to the nineteenth century. It is a fortiori true that the contemporary city is a prime site for boredom, since it is a scene of constant desire-excitation combined with manifold stalls to desire. (*Stalls* must be distinguished from *frustrations*, for reasons suggested in the main text above.)

8.   Francis Cornford's enduringly relevant satire of academic life is *Microcosmographia Academica* (Bowes & Bowes, 1908; 1922). Among the many gems of Cornford's analysis are the *Principle of the Wedge* ("you should not act justly now for fear of raising expectations that you will act still more justly in future"), the *Principle of the Dangerous Precedent* ("nothing should ever be done for the first time"), and the definition of *Propaganda* as "that branch of the art of lying which consists in very nearly deceiving your friends without quite deceiving your enemies."

9.   The words form the opening line of John Berryman's "Dream Song 14," from *The Dream Songs* (Farrar Straus, 1969):

> Life, friends, is boring. We must not say so.
> After all, the sky flashes, the great sea yearns,
> we ourselves flash and yearn,
> and moreover my mother told me as a boy
> (repeatedly) "Ever to confess you're bored
> means you have no
>
> Inner Resources." I conclude now I have no
> inner resources, because I am heavy bored.
> Peoples bore me,
> literature bores me, especially great literature,
> Henry bores me, with his plights & gripes
> as bad as Achilles,
>
> who loves people and valiant art, which bores me.
> And the tranquil hills, & gin, look like a drag
> and somehow a dog
> has taken itself & its tail considerably away
> into the mountains or sea or sky, leaving
> behind: me, wag.

10.   See Derrida, *Limited Inc.* (Northwestern, 1988) for his notorious engagement with the hygienic speech-act theory of John Searle as defended in *Speech Acts* (Cambridge, 1969). Searle, claiming an inheritance of the project from J. L. Austin as set out in *How to do Things with Words*

(Harvard, 1962), engages in an extended exercise of containment, trying by the methods of analytical philosophy to eliminate the lacunae and slippages in Austin's original discussion of performative utterances. The attempt reveals its truth in its failure, and Austin's own ironic awareness is, as so often, lost in Anglo-American translation. A good overview of this triadic engagement is found in Simon Glendinning, "Inheriting 'Philosophy': The Case of Austin and Derrida Revisited," *Ratio* 13:4 (2000): 307–31. Christopher Ricks, meanwhile, alertly chronicles the untidy literary tropes and tics that run through Austin's prose in "Austin's Swink," *University of Toronto Quarterly* 61:3 (1992): 297–315.

11. A fine discussion of this point may be found in Judith Butler, *Excitable Speech* (Routledge, 1997), which attempts, with limited success, an amalgamation of Derrida's insights about reiterability with Louis Althusser's powerful concept of interpellation—the way I am established in identity by the literal call of the other, including the frightening limit case of being hailed on the street by a shout of "Hey, you there!" For Althusser and Butler, interpellation is always an act fraught with threat because I may be hailed as a miscreant or delinquent—that is to say, someone recognized at the moment of exceeding limits, in this case of the law. Althusser's extended autobiography/self-defence (including an attempted justification of murdering his wife) is, appositely for present purposes, *The Future Lasts a Long Time*, Richard Veasey, trans. (Chatto & Windus, 1993); orig. *L'avenir dure longtemps* (1992).

12. John Berger, *Ways of Seeing* (Penguin, 1972). Walter Benjamin's more nuanced, and far more extensive, engagement with nostalgia is featured throughout his works, both in lovely exercises in it (e.g., *A Berlin Childhood* [Harvard, 2006]) and in deconstructions of it (passim. in *The Arcades Project*, Howard Eiland and Kevin McLaughlin, trans. [Harvard, 1999]). Benjamin, who for better or worse gave the world of cultural theory the notion of aesthetic aura in "The Work of Art in An Age of Mechanical Reproduction" (orig. 1934; in *Illuminations*, Harry Zohn, trans. [Schocken, 1968])—a staple of analysis for Berger and many others—nowhere isolates the insight about positionality that is at the heart of Berger's too-brief discussion. Here there is useful joining of Benjamin's cultural awareness with the brilliantly but sometimes overbearing reductionism of Thorstein Veblen in *The Theory of the Leisure Class* (1899). For Veblen, aesthetic judgments always, and usually swiftly, reveal themselves as claims to status; but even without going so far we can accept the power of reading many qualities or essences as, in fact, claims of position. But even Veblen did not see what we can now

observe everywhere: positional goods don't even need to be goods, in the sense of material bearers of status; position can be established by reciprocal proxy, that is, by *being judged enviable* or *being thought cool.*

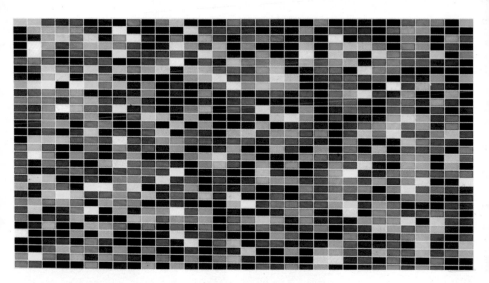

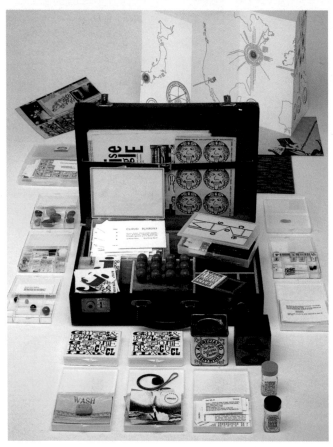

Above: Gerhard Richter's *1024 Colors* (1966). Left: Fluxus edition *Fluxkit* (1965–1966).

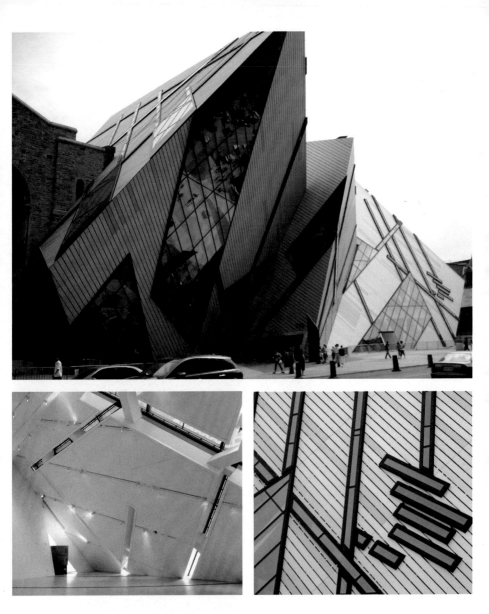

Monumental conceptual: (top left) Daniel Libeskind's Jewish Museum in Berlin (2001), and (above) Royal Ontario Museum, Michael Lee-Chin Crystal in Toronto (2007). Left: Frank Gehry's Guggenheim Museum in Bilbao (1997).

Works by James Lahey (from top):
Atlantic Ocean, Vero Beach, Florida, Dec 8 AM (2004); *Tulip, May 20 16:30.53.1* (2003); detail from *Cloud* (2001); detail from *Index Abstraction no. 17* (2006).

Works by David Bierk: (clockwise
from top) *Locked in Migration, River
Plain* (1990); detail from *Kawartha
Vista (Locked in Migration), Red
Cloud* (1993); *Eulogy for a Planet, to
Leonardo* (1992–94)

Works by Edward Burtynsky: (above) *Oxford Tire Pile No. 1* (1999); (right) *C.N. Track No. 8* (1985). Opposite page, top to bottom: *Manufacturing #4* (2005); *Shipbreaking No. 9a* (2000); *Manufacturing #17* (2005).

Unlearn: Ken Lum, *I wish I could start all over again* (2003) and Kelly Mark, *Broken Line #14* (2003).

Photographs of Michel de Broin's *Entrelacement* (2001). Below: *Help* and *Sorry* from Germaine Koh's *Signs* series (2002).

Images from Iris Häussler's *Legacy of Joseph Wagenbach* (2006).

Photographs from Blue Republic's *Nostalgia for the Present* (2006).

Gerhard Richter's *Woman Descending a Staircase* (1965).

PART TWO:

Philosophy After Art

10. Love and Philosophy

It is a notable irony that philosophy is both the only remaining academic discipline that has love in its name, and, as an academic discipline, probably the last place any of us would be likely to seek insight into the nature of love.

The reasons for this are obvious. According to a widely held view of the species, philosophers have not had much time for the emotions, nor been able to cultivate them very successfully, being (in the popular imagination, and sometimes also their own) dead from the neck down. If this widely held view is in fact inaccurate—philosophers are arguably more devoted servants of the emotions than poets, at least in terms of time spent writing about them and volume of pages produced—it does express an important partial truth. Philosophers have on the whole distrusted emotions, regarding anger and envy and passions of all kinds as distracting or even deleterious to thought, chaotic winds battering the walls of reason. Thus the main, eliminative form of their interest: philosophy has over the centuries devised many ingenious programs of emotional dissection and destruction, the better to facilitate the smooth application of cold logic. Call this the Vulcan school of philosophical aspiration: Spock-like contempt for and suppression of the emotions.

Ask a philosopher to speak of love and the result can only be deflationary and unintentionally hilarious, like watching an earnest child try to pick up Jell-O with a pair of tongs. It is not difficult to see why. Here is one contemporary philosopher, who shall go nameless, addressing himself to the topic of love in the jargon of our tribe. "An idea of the concepts analytically presupposed in our use of 'love,'" he writes, "can be gained by sketching a sequence of relations, the members of which we take as relevant in deciding whether or not some relationship between persons A and B is one of love." The relevant relations might include such things as "knowing about," "feeling affection for," "respecting" and "wanting the best for" the other person in question.

"These relations are relevant not in the sense of being evidence for some further relation 'love' but as being, in part at least, the material of which love consists," the same writer continues, still not kidding. "The connection between these relations which we will call 'love-comprising relations' or 'LCRS' is not, except for 'knowing about' and possibly 'feels affection for' as tight as strict entailment."

At this point, you can imagine poor old A and B—if those are their real names—turning to stare at each other, both mouthing the words "strict entailment?" with baffled amazement. But we need not accept this sort of "comically solemn ineptitude," as one critic has accurately called it. Nor need we allow the related pathology of indulging an emotional harshness that masquerades as clear-minded precision, as when the philosopher Russell, a notorious womanizer, one day mentioned to his wife, in tones better suited to detailing a grocery list, that he simply no longer loved her.

This apparently canonical attitude of disdain or insufficiency towards emotion in fact underestimates the extent to which even philosophers hostile to the emotions are respectful of both the power and the knowledge inherent in what they seek to stifle. The Stoics, in particular, are probably not best seen as Vulcans *avant la lettre*, despite what is often thought. Believing that emotions were irrational not in being unbidden and senseless (like hunger) but in being cognitive yet erroneous (like a belief in flat earth), the Stoics took seriously the personal and community challenges posed by passions. These two senses of "irrational," though often confused, imply a crucial distinction. For the Stoics, emotions are not infantile and incorrigible feelings, meant to be simply stifled; they are, rather, corrigible feelings based on mistaken judgments concerning the individual's place in the world, which can therefore be rationally addressed. It's not all a matter of iron control, in other words, battening down the mind against the threatening storms. Emotions are cognitive, and so reason has a foothold in understanding them.

Even if we are persuaded that emotions are forms of knowledge, however, the question is still whether this *eliminative* cognitive account is the right one. As Martha Nussbaum argues in her book *Upheavals of Thought*, the Stoics get the first part of the equation right: emotions are not mere gusts of feeling, but rather states that contain and express knowledge—of ourselves and our relations to things and forces outside us. Where the Stoics go wrong, and where Nussbaum seeks at some length to repair the damage, is in joining this cognitive understanding with a particular normative recommendation, namely to reform or get rid of emotions altogether: the resulting condition, known as Stoic *apatheia*, is the cool self-sufficiency aimed at by Epictetus or Marcus Aurelius. Nussbaum wants to keep the baby while losing the bathwater: intelligent emotions plus an ethical project, just like the Stoics, but now an ethical project of retention and respect rather than elimination, regarding emotions as key elements in the larger cognitive structures guiding ethics and politics.[1] In what follows I want to do the same, concentrating philosophical attention on the cognitive status of love, but I hope without descending into the self-parody that lurks within philosophical methods of attention.

Though their bewildered students may not know it, contemporary philosophers have for some time been trying to make greater room for emotion in the account of human personhood and agency. In addition to this larger rehabilitation, certain emotions, especially anger and vengefulness, but also sadness and grief, have lately arisen forcibly as political issues; and philosophers, in common with citizens everywhere, have been forced to confront some difficult questions. Is it appropriate to act out of anger when one has been injured very close to home? Why does the proximity of pain make mourning more acute? What are the limits of compassion when the objects of potential compassion look unlike us or live in ways quite foreign to our own? Is a strong feeling of attachment to one's national flag a virtue or a fetish?

To raise such questions in a useful way, rather than merely venting or declaiming, we must go beyond existing misperceptions of how emotion and reason stand in relation to each other. It is too simple to draw a line, as many do, between reason and emotion and leave it at that. That polarization leads to the Vulcan temptation on the one hand, but also to a peculiar form of (usually hawkish, right-wing and populist) anti-intellectualism on the other, according to which anyone seeking understanding or demanding nuance in a time of trial, or indeed during an intense emotional scene such as a lovers' quarrel, will be considered "too philosophical for decent company."

That is just calling your own suit trump when it benefits you. As long as we persist in seeing the emotions as simply ranged against reason, it will not matter which side we choose to support in the resulting endless battle; the situation will always resist resolution or even insight. Philosophy will be condemned for its bloodlessness and even borderline treason in times of crisis; and emotion, at least when business is more or less as usual, will be subjected to constant pathologization and medicalization, labeled an irrational disease in need of a cure. Such skirmishing is good sport for editorialists and polemicists, depending on the prevailing cultural winds, but it does not help us gain a better appreciation of our place in the world, or the limits of our ability to make sense of that world.

As a hard test case of that making sense, then, consider the prima facie most bewildering—or at least most fecund—of common emotional experiences, the one we call falling in love. Falling in love, as we most often regard it, seems quite mysterious. It comes upon us sometimes without warning, for unclear reasons, even occasionally against inclination or desire—we don't *want* to fall in love. It cannot be *entirely* mysterious, of course, as each of us perhaps has cause to know. There is—there must be— some element of intelligibility in the experiences, at a minimum the sheer fact of one's being present and able to have them, but presumably something more than that. What, exactly? It strikes me that this question, always a stumper, is lately more difficult than ever to answer.

Some people, not just philosophers, would have you believe that love is a cognitive condition, a state of knowledge. This view has both psychological and cultural sanction, from the common phrase "carnal knowledge" to the well-known condition, detailed in something like Jerome Kern's "They Can't Take That Away from Me," which itemizes the tiny details of love's knowledge: the way you tip your hat, the way you sip your tea. Anyone who has been in love can relate to that laser-guided attention to the insignificant, the sense that love is essentially *a way of looking*. This can be obsessive, even creepy (think of Holly Cole's version of "On the Street Where You Live," wherein Charlie Chaplin's song about devotion is transformed into a stalker's anthem); it may also, paradoxically, be the source of that most dangerous of romantic myths, that of falling in love at first sight. We might think love-as-knowledge would involve long experience of the other but, as devotees of the condition will tell you (usually over and over), some people *just know*, know *right away*, that the other person is the one for them.

This cognitive miracle often also involves another potentially dangerous myth, that of the *one true love*. A vision, let it be said, at least as old as Aristophanes' speech in Plato's *Symposium*, wherein the comic playwright suggests that love is a matter of some sundered roly-poly person finding his or her missing other half by a process of usually messy elimination. The basic narrative of romantic love, better called infatuation, is frankly utopian. Or, more accurately, originary-utopian. That is, there is the creation in mind of a perfect state, which, though perhaps validated by one or two features of experience, is then counterdemonstrated by future events and features such that one's energy is disproportionately directed towards recapturing the initial (and often delusional) condition of perfect happiness. Thus the routine violence of utopian longing is recalibrated as the attempts, repeated and increasingly desperate, to find again the open-window-fresh-air happiness of love's first moments—a project logically doomed to failure since there is never newness more than once (though there may be intimations or memories of newness for some time, one of the roots of nostalgia).

Many cherish this notion of sweeping romantic love, but it is hard to square with the more general experience of love once we agree to consider it at all objectively. Frankfurt has argued, in a no-nonsense manner, that the most cogent understanding of love is to construe it as "disinterested concern for the existence of what is loved," which might be a person or an ideal. This construal has an immediate, and uncomfortable, consequence. "It is important," he says, "to avoid confusing love—as circumscribed by the concept that I am defining—with infatuation, lust, obsession, possessiveness, and dependency in their various forms. In particular, relationships that are primarily romantic or sexual do not provide very authentic or illuminating paradigms of love as I am construing it." Such relationships may involve "vividly distracting elements" but these "do not belong to the essential nature of love" and "are so confusing that they make it nearly impossible for anyone to be clear about what is going on."[2]

The argument is not unprecedented. Here let us recall Sigmund Freud's gimlet-eyed analysis of the tension in *Civilization and Its*

Discontents—with what he labels sexual or genital love playing the role of what others usually euphemistically call romantic love. "[M]an's discovery that sexual (genital) love afforded him the strongest experiences of satisfaction, and in fact provided him with the prototype of happiness, must have suggested to him that he should continue to seek the satisfaction of happiness in his life along the path of sexual relations and that he should make genital erotism the central point of his life." But "in doing so he made himself dependent in a most dangerous way on a portion of his external world, namely, his chosen love-object, and exposed himself to extreme suffering if he should be rejected by that object or should lose it through unfaithfulness or death. For that reason the wise men of every age have warned us most emphatically against this way of life; but in spite of this it has not lost its attraction for a great number of people."[3]

Nor is that mulishness in the face of sage advice the only problem here. Clear thinkers among us might think to avoid the risk of suffering either by diversifying or by generalizing the love-object, such that we pursue happiness with a constantly changing variety of sexual partners; or direct our love, as Freud says, "not to single objects but to all men alike." The first option is dubious, since it closes off at least part of the satisfaction that motivated it, namely connection with a singular other who recognizes me as worthwhile and desirable over time. And the second option of unconditional or indiscriminate love is open to two apparently fatal objections that Freud himself notes: "A love that does not discriminate seems to me to forfeit a part of its own value, by doing an injustice to its object; and secondly, not all men are worthy of love."

Even were we then to apply a version of Frankfurt's love, which is discriminate though disinterested, we still miss something of the passional quality of love that linked it so closely to primitive satisfactions that remain central even to finely textured conceptions of happiness. That, surely, is one reason the appeal of romantic love is undiminished for the great number of people despite the centuries of wise warnings that Freud cites, often issued, indeed, by philosophers—and not just Stoic ones.

At this point, many people will be inclined to say, so much the worse for Frankfurt, Freud and philosophy. Many of us seem committed to the idea not only that romantic love is the paradigm case of love, perhaps of emotional experience *tout court*, but also that such love is a human birthright rather than, what might be the case, a stroke of luck or even, most often, an illusion. The Freud/Frankfurt move does not address this wish except negatively, and it does not address our current issue of whether such love is, or can be, cognitive. As a result, it misses an important nuance, namely that such love might be subject to relative aptitude, and hence unevenly distributed across a population—something that a different sort of sage sees immediately. "It's a funny thing," a wise Nancy Mitford character says in the 1932 novel *Christmas Pudding*, "that people are always quite ready to admit it if they've got no talent for drawing or music, whereas everyone imagines that they themselves are capable of true love, which is a talent like any other, only far more rare."

Observation of human activity tends to reinforce this view, but with results from which each of us likely holds ourselves exceptional: the paradox of unequal distribution, which holds that it applies to everyone except me. Hence the common retreat into subjectivism on the question of love, which guarantees that no standards of proof can ever be leveled against (my) claims of love. This move is of course irrational, and noncognitive to boot, hence self-contradicting: how can I have *knowledge* that is accessible only to me? But note that such a criticism is itself taken as friendly, since love on the subjectivist view is supposed always to be irrational. Such a move exactly parallels arguments for belief in the existence of God which turn on the fact that such belief is beyond argument: they are both species of fideist ideology, categorically immune to all rational challenge—and reinforced in that immunity by every gesture of challenge.

The subjectivist attitude to love is mistaken. However, we must not simply assert that but also ask, *in what way*?

Here is one sort of start to make on the issue. Whatever it really means and however often it really occurs, love clearly involves knowledge, but it is never, I think, as simple as the knowledge involved in distinguishing a sparrow from a starling, or even in deciding whether or not you like olives on your pizza. Or rather, it may be as simple in one sense, that is, acquisition; but not in another sense, namely consequences. Hence the common enough sense that one is in love unwillingly: cognition and will are not the same faculty, and indeed sometimes obscure one another.

The character Jim Dixon, in Kingsley Amis's first and most charming novel, *Lucky Jim*, makes this sort of point when he compares knowing whether you're in love to knowing whether you like greengages, alike in being equally simple. "People get themselves all steamed up about whether they're in love or not, and can't work it out, and their decisions go all to pot. It's happening every day. They ought to realize that the love part's perfectly easy; the hard part is the working out, not about love, but about what they're going to do. The difference is that they can get their brains going on that, instead of taking the sound of the word 'love' as a signal for switching them off. They can get somewhere, instead of indulging in a sort of orgy of emotional self-catechising about how you know you're in love, and what love is anyway, and all the rest of it. You don't ask yourself what greengages are, or how you know whether you like them or not, do you? Right?"

Well, let us say *partially right*. Here Dixon speaks effectively in the voice of the ordinary-language philosophy Amis would have imbibed at his contemporary 1950s Oxford, a point deftly made by the critic David Lodge about the comic appeal of Amis's fiction. The precise linguistic distinctions and wry mockery of mystification and sloppiness in usage that mark Amis's narrative voice are clearly reminiscent of the work of Austin. "Oh, don't say that; no, don't say that," Dixon yells quietly after the girl he's been talking to complains she doesn't care for the word "love" because she "doesn't know what it means." "It's a word you must often have come across in conversation and literature. Are you going to tell me it sends you flying to the dictionary each time?" The meaning of love is not opaque. Subjective, perhaps, but not incomprehensible—certainly not any more so than whether one likes greengages.

Unfortunately, this welcome insistence on clarity in language and hence in thought is often for Amis, as it never was for Austin, gender specific. Thus is revealed one deposit in the rich vein of misogyny that increasingly marks Amis's fiction: women don't mean what they say because they don't have to. The same author memorably shows his true misogynist colors in almost every single subsequent novel. "The root of all the trouble," says a typical male character in Amis's *Stanley and the Women*, "is we want to fuck them, the pretty ones, women I mean. Just try and imagine it happening to you, everyone wanting to fuck you wherever you go. And of course being ready to pay for you if your father's stopped doing that. You'd have to be pretty tough to stand up to it, wouldn't you? In fact women only want one thing, for men to want to fuck them. If they do, it means they can fuck you up. Am I drunk? What I was trying to say, if you want to fuck a woman she can fuck you up. And if you don't want to she fucks you up anyway for not wanting to." Not very helpful, even if widely held.

On the Dixon view, love's knowledge may be a condition simple to acquire—though that is surely open to further debate both personal and philosophical. It is certainly not a condition simple to understand or to act out—and confusing these two operations is unfortunately common, leading, among other things, to the self-inflicted brain death Dixon alludes to and perhaps even to the generalized gender-war hostility of the later character. Even when we do try to use our brains, we encounter difficulties, since love's knowledge appears to be complex, nuanced, layered, conflicted and, above all, demanding. In contrast to some forms of knowing, love is both volitional and activist—which is not to say that it is up

to us or within our control. Indeed, it is unlike other kinds of
knowledge precisely in not appearing primarily, or at all, cognitive
in the usual senses of consistent, predictive and reiterable. Thus it
is not subject to the usual controls on cognition, nor does it operate in the usual ways. Love more often confers value than, as we
often suppose, finds it; our love for our children or ourselves—
acknowledging that these are quite distinct, but related—does not
depend on discerning worthiness for love in the love object but,
instead, putting it there. That is how it is possible to love children
before they are born, after they turn out badly and at every point in
between. Likewise with selves, where self-love is indeed a condition
of having a fully human life, not least in the baseline sense of continuing it through time. Care is a state of being, not a proposition.

And that also is why romantic love poses a special problem
because it tangles even further the usual confusion of finding
worth and conferring it, the shifting sands between cognition and
volition. Do I love because she is lovely, or is she lovely because I
love? Mere logic will not—cannot—solve this kind of issue for us.
The problem is one that arises only at the margins, when falling
(as we put it) in or out of love. And yet, it is these margins that
mark our most intense and important human engagements. The
experiences of falling into and out of love are, as we know, among
the most wrenching and violent humans can undergo. One clear
reason they are so is that, as with all love, this species of love is
supposed to be action-guiding but without any clear or consistent
indication of what the right action might be. Love's knowledge is
normative, but it calls for a duty whose imperatives are ever shifting and opaque. We know that, here, tears or declarations are
not enough: love calls for accompanying actions, actions that, if not
performed, call the condition of being in love into doubt. *If you
really loved me, you'd* _____.

To compound that difficulty, sometimes it is not clear what
counts as the appropriate *range* of actions. No doubt this has
always been somewhat true, but perhaps the most obvious feature of contemporary love relations is their rampant cultural

indeterminacy. It is not merely that postindustrial gender relations are in constant flux, a minefield of unexploded potential miscues. It is also that love is a tangle of various and sometimes contradictory sources, allusions, role models and imperatives. Indeed, a good deal of those various and contradictory messages are coming from an immersion in the everyday mass of pop music, television and movies themselves, the conjoined contradictions typical of what Theodor Adorno and Max Horkheimer analyzed as "the Culture Industry." Because these cultural materials are at base profit driven, their action-guiding bona fides are comprehensively compromised and undermined. As the ever acute cultural critic Lisa Simpson put it in an episode *The Simpsons*: "Mom, romance is dead. It was acquired in a hostile takeover by Hallmark and Disney, homogenized, and then sold off piece by piece." And yet, where else are people to look for guidance in the actions that love seems to demand?

Take a familiar example. A friend of mine recently watched in horror as her best friend—let's call her *B*, what the hell—was proposed to by her boyfriend, *A*, during a big extended family gathering on New Year's Eve. *A* had not consulted the unsuspecting girl in advance, instead "romantically" springing a hulking diamond ring upon her between courses in the family dinner. You can imagine the stunned silence. *B* doesn't want to get married. Or she hasn't decided if she does. Or she doesn't want to marry *A*. Or she doesn't want to marry *A* yet. In any event, she can't possibly do so then and there. She runs away in tears. *A*'s face goes white. The gathered guests search their plates for hidden messages. *A* flees for California under cover of night, never to return.

What was poor old A thinking? That might seem baffling but it is actually pretty clear. Hearing this story recently a friend just nodded in a world-weary manner and offered a one-word interpretation: "Movies."

Too many movies. Too much Tom Hanks and Tom Cruise and Billy Crystal and even, bless him, Fred Astaire. Too many teary pop songs, Dionne Warwick singing Burt Bacharach or Jennifer Warnes covering Leonard Cohen. Poor *A* lost the plot—or rather, *got lost in* the plot, the so-called fairy tale mentioned over and over by everyone from Julia Roberts in *Pretty Woman* to every hapless contestant on *Joe Millionaire* or *Blind Date*, that triumph of the evil of banality. Like the hapless male protagonists of Nick Hornby's novels *High Fidelity* and *About a Boy*—both were made into successful films—*A* was a man who could not quite figure out the mixed-media messages of love, which comprise a disorder that is, as we say, *iatrogenic*, which is to say physician-caused. A television show such as *Sex and the City*, for example, is the very disease for which it poses as the cure, offering a glamorized and fantastic vision of dating with a deep core of despair beneath its pretty surfaces. So he sought redemption, typically, in an overdetermined notion of romantic devotion and monogamy. If space aliens were to observe us through the medium of nightly television—no bad anthropological method—they would surely come away convinced it is amazing we have managed to survive so long, given that we seem at once so stupid and so cynical about mating rituals.

That is only the beginning of the media dangers associated with love. The vast creative output on the subject can sometimes make us feel not so much inadequate—who can match the passion of an Abelard, the insane devotion of a Romeo?—as without a center. Bombarded with images and narratives, beset by tall tales and minor chords, who can be confident of being genuinely in love anymore? We wonder: is there anything *essential* left beneath the huge accretion of media product, both old and new, about love? No surprise, in the fact of this indeterminacy, that some people lurch over to the crude sociobiological accounts of human behavior, the sort of thing that reduces us all to so many posturing baboons or phenylethylamine speed freaks high on the neurochemical drugs of sexual attraction.

We want to say: going that far is surely a mistake. Such reductive accounts are a drastic and sad diminution of our human possibilities. Certainly they fail to acknowledge, let alone account for, why romantic love seems to matter to us *so much*, namely that it offers the promise of connection with a singular other. Which connection, we think, may be an expression of something profound in human life, a knowledge sacred and even transcendent. We want to say: even in the midst of all this media saturation, falling in love still happens—and it happens to us. We want to say: there is still something irreducibly meaningful about *my* love— something both delirious and delicious—even within an awareness of our insistent biology. We want to say: it is not the cultural images, it is what you make of them. It is not the urges, it is how you interpret them.

Fine. Nevertheless, a problem still remains. The move to the sacred or transcendent defense of love performs another endgame on love's cognitivity. What kind of knowledge is this, now? Can it be articulated? Or is it a mystical property that must be the province of love itself, never to be spoken? (And tough luck on those who have yet to experience it, or never will.)

Put the problem in more general terms as one of *discourse's limits*. No matter how detailed and nuanced the final prose rendering, the emotional states of even an ordinary consciousness, let alone a rich and tormented one, escape the boundaries of language. This does not stop novelists from writing, any more than perpetual disagreement has stopped philosophers from thinking; but even if a philosophical treatment of emotions were offered in the Proustian spirit—attempting a comprehensive account of a singular consciousness having the experience of love—there is a special difficulty that arises from the difference between fiction and nonfiction.

When it comes to emotion, a rational account in this sphere is not only necessarily partial (that is arguably true of any philosophical intervention) but also skewed. The Proustian novelist has the first problem too, but not the second (if he or she is any good). For a philosopher, no matter how sympathetic the approach, we are still functioning in the rehabilitative mode mentioned at the beginning of the present essay, trying to bring emotion back into the rational fold of discourse as a wiser alternative to dismissing or hating the emotions. This cannot help but domesticate feelings somehow, much more so than in even the most discursive kind of prose fiction. And so, despite the subtlety and apparent open-mindedness of recent philosophical treatments of emotion, a version of the old polarization and resulting relationship of priority is still up and running. Surprise, surprise: philosophers find emotions to be rational after all!

Is there any way out of this difficulty? Some philosophers speak here and there about the importance of the body to an understanding of emotion, in particular with reference to shame and disgust, opening up one possible avenue of escape. And yet, they still tend to view these bodily experiences through the lens of rationality: looking for the root causes of shame, condemning twisted male forms of disgust with the female body, and so on. They are never inclined *to put the body first*, to see rational thought as itself an outcome, a coping mechanism, generated by vulnerable, spongy creatures with an unpleasant awareness of their own weakness.

Where, for instance, is the force of David Hume's insight that reason is the slave of the passions, a faculty that forms ideas to justify and promote our feelings, not the other way around? What about the fact that changes in the body's chemistry, whether willed or involuntary, themselves create emotional surcharges? Low blood-sugar levels can make us irritable, coursing hormones can make us weepy, and ingested drugs can add all kinds of texture, welcome and unwelcome, to emotional life. This troubling but basic aspect of emotion is absent from the account, when it should really be a starting point. We get a hint—but only a hint—of the true stakes in, for example, Heidegger's analysis of "mood" in *Being and Time*, which so far from mere changeable feelings are indications of how one is faring, how one is situated within a world of existential concern.

The key here is the notion of "world." The critic Philip Fisher says this: "Each of the strong emotions or passions define for us an intelligible world, and does so by means of horizon lines that we can come to know only in experiences that begin with impassioned or vehement states within ourselves."[4]

Unlike Nussbaum and other crypto-Stoics, Fisher wisely stops short of draining the feeling from feeling. Fisher's particular concern are those experiences we call "vehement," when we are carried "out of our minds"—or, more precisely, out of the worlds our workaday rational minds allow us mostly to inhabit. We cannot know the limits of mind and world until we butt up against them in the passionate, unwilling form of conflict. Vehement passion is always rooted in affronts to the will, deep challenges to the integrity of the self. Aristotle, Spinoza and Hume are the main guides in this subtle phenomenology of contingency, revealing themselves not only as great systematic philosophers but as thinkers sensitive enough to see that my anger and grief tell me who counts and who doesn't, that my body with its quakings and blushings and hot flashes is not separable from my soul, and that there are "paths of passion": when grief gives way to anger, for example, and then to shame or bitterness; or when love, alas, gives way to hatred.

What can we conclude from these investigations? Emotions, including centrally the emotions of love, are cognitive *when and if* they light up our embeddedness in a web of existence we cannot completely control. If love and grief are the emotions usually associated with "higher" attachments between persons, compassion and fear are often associated with "lower" things such as physical deprivation and personal humiliation. But such emotions are not merely cognitive, nor are they reliably cognitive in expected ways, as we have seen. Instead, let us say that they are *revelatory*: they are all based in some deep sense on the fact that a human self is embodied consciousness, vulnerable and mortal. Emotions of all kinds are rooted in physicality, both as they are felt (the burning rise of anger, the sickly paleness of mourning, the flinty edges of jealousy) and as they are generated (responding to our place in a world of sharp objects and sharper personalities).

The essential problem of all philosophy is that *my* world—where I am afraid or riven with rage and resentment, where I am suffused with love for you and for the world, where I am always alone—is not, and cannot be, *the* world of the modern universalist imagination, that strange abstraction, at once useful and delusional. What I experience as my world is, rather, a fragile and risky shared life world where you constitute me as much as I you. Our patterns of thought, especially over the past three or four centuries, have attempted to play down this inconvenient phenomenological reality, but in vain—and often with bizarre or comical results, as I indicated at the beginning, when that thought's tools are put to the task of deep understanding. Indeed, we could take this insight a step further. The questions of philosophy—the questions of existence—are all, ultimately, insoluble puzzles in epistemology because they are versions of the old dilemma concerning the existence of other minds. What do I know about my place in the world? How do I make sense of what I am feeling? How can I possibly know what *you* are feeling? Maybe you love me, maybe you don't. I hope so and fear not. Can I ever know for sure? Thus does vehement passion take root . . .

Philosophizing about love teaches us this crucial lesson, namely, that love is about what we care about; it is an investment of meaning in an otherwise indifferent and confusing world, which makes that world ours. Such an investment, even more powerfully than other action-guiding emotions, is at the center of the life worth living. This love is not ultimately romantic love, at least as commonly understood, variable and culturally overdetermined, though it involves a special kind of romance. I mean the principled love of life and one's place in it, you might even say (with proper warning and explanation), the love of self; in short, the love of wisdom that in the Greek translates, precisely, as *philein sophia*. True love is not finding our missing other half so much as finding the reality of ourselves, there all along, in the encounter with an other.

And so the end brings us back to the beginning, perhaps wiser and better informed, but certainly no more than ever able to claim mastery over love—for mastery is not the game we should be playing. Upheavals of thought are still, primarily, upheavals; emotions, fleshy and wet, will not finally be colonized by intelligence, even their own, and philosophy has no consolation for that. It does have wisdom; however, not the same thing. To philosophize about love is not only possible, but also necessary—even, we might say, logically necessary. For philosophy is one of the few reliable routes to a form of genuine, disinterested love, capable of generating wisdom about limits and their acceptance. And yet, the thought of limits holds even, or especially, for philosophy too: the limits of thought. The antidotes with which philosophy has medicated the cup of life, to paraphrase Seneca, cannot give it salubrity or sweetness; they can at best allay its bitterness and temper its malignity. The balm that wisdom drops on the wounds of the heart may abate their pain, but cannot, finally, heal them.

Notes

1. Martha Nussbaum, *Upheavals of Thought: The Intelligence of Emotions* (Cambridge, 2003).

2. Harry G. Frankfurt, *The Reasons of Love* (Princeton, 2004).

3. Sigmund Freud, *Civilization and Its Discontents*, James Strachey, trans. (Norton, 1961), p. 56.

4. Philip Fisher, *The Vehement Passions* (Princeton, 2002).

11. Anguish as a Second Language

Like all languages, English inscribes within its phoneme patterns the possibility of puns, those minor collisions of meaning when words of disparate denotation sound alike enough to bring the routine traffic of sense-making to a temporary stop. They are the fender benders of wordplay. Often said to be the lowest form of wit, puns are nevertheless pleasing to a certain kind of listener, especially one willing to forego the need for more sophisticated jokes. Children adore puns, for instance; so do new users of a language.

The reason is clear: getting the pun means getting to a certain point of linguistic mastery, where we are capable of recognizing the juxtaposition of elements, the crash of homonyms, as both superficially inappropriate and subficially interesting, and the resulting entanglement therefore funny. Lots of humor relies on precisely this combination, of course. And so puns, even bad ones, can be quite funny. Admittedly, the pun deployed in the title, anguish/English, isn't a great one. The homonym pair is a little forced, the referent phrase is not really part of everyday language, and so the result lacks the immediacy of effect enjoyed by many other puns. But it has the advantage of being meaningful in present circumstances, though that may only become clear a little later. Again like all languages, English is a medium both linear and time-based, especially in its aural form but also in the act of reading. No matter how hard you try, you can't say everything at once—just one of the pleasant constrictions language places upon us.

What is anguish? It is, first of all, a euphonic English word, one of those typical combinations of Latinate Old French rendered into medieval English and thence into modern. It is defined by the *Oxford Concise Dictionary* as "severe bodily or mental pain," which pretty much says it all, but it comes more directly from the French word *anguisse*, which means choking. That, in turn, is rooted in the Latin term *angustia*, or tightness, which is itself related to the even simpler word *angustus*, meaning narrow. So anguish literally means constriction, though we have not in practice constricted ourselves to that literal rendering, using it to mean all manner and form of discomfort. Its English synonyms, if you are interested, include agony, angst, anxiety, desolation, distress, dole, dolor, grief, heartache, heartbreak, misery, pain, pang, rack, sorrow, suffering, torment, torture, tribulation, woe and wretchedness.

It is above all a useful word, resonant and powerful, and definitely not to be used lightly. Shakespeare wrote in *A Midsummer Night's Dream* of "the anguish of a torturing hour" which might be eased by imminent revels. John Keats, in "La Belle Dame sans Merci," describes his famous tormented lovesick knight, alone and palely loitering, as having "a lily on thy brow, / With anguish moist and fever dew; / And on thy cheek a fading rose / Fast withereth too." George Eliot, in *The Mill on the Floss*, describes Thomas à Kempis's *Imitation of Christ* as a work "written down by a hand that waited for the heart's prompting; it is the chronicle of a solitary hidden anguish, struggle, trust and triumph." The poet Christopher Fry, more jauntily, spoke of "a gay modulating anguish, rather like music" that one could hear in the celestial spheres above us. (In the same work, Fry defined the moon as "nothing but a circumambulating aphrodisiac divinely subsidized to provoke the world into a rising birth-rate.")

Thus the three main reference works of a language. But down to business: What is the peculiar anguish of English as a second language?

I was in Prague some years ago and had occasion to speak at length with a tall English hippie with wild hair and purple trousers. The two of us were attending a "Counter-Summit" organized by groups protesting the meetings of the World Bank and International Monetary Fund in the Czech capital. I was speaking at this event, and Ian, my new friend, had come from his home in Sussex to be part of the meetings and the protests against the effects of economic globalization. He was smart and troubled, well educated but charmingly weird. He was troubled mainly because he had just returned to England from a stint teaching English as a second language to children in Spain, and the idea that he was implicitly serving the very globalization process he wanted to resist made him uneasy. He had my sympathy, and the point is a good one. I had already decided that, when I stood up to address the crowd in English, I would have to acknowledge my own reliance on what is, despite everything, the de facto language of transnational markets.

Doing that was itself an unsettling experience, because I tried to pass it off as a minor joke, or anyway irony. Here we all are, fighting The Man using The Man's language. As I was making this feeble joke, the apology suddenly struck me as ridiculous, not least because of its pro forma character, unpleasantly reminiscent of those with-it male academics of the 1980s who used to pepper their abstract discourses with the pronoun "she": *If a person wants to make a valid moral choice, she must assess the maxim of her action against the Kantian principle of universalization.* Fine, but I always listened to those guys and thought, don't kid me; you say "she" but you *mean* "he." It seemed the worst, most superficial kind of fashionably political self-protection, getting extra credit at no extra cost.

My discomfiture was magnified by the fact that about half the audience, Czech and German and Spanish, were listening to my address on translation headphones. It is a well-worn truth that humor translates badly, if at all, and I suppose queasy minor-league irony, or attempts thereat, translates about the worst. It did not help that Praguers, in particular the black-clad anarchist youngsters who made up most of the audience, are notoriously humorless. Or not humorless, exactly; just uninterested in whimsy. They have a sense of humor the way Klingons have a sense of humor.

The real problem, though, as I realized standing there dying the slow roasting death of the unsuccessful joker, is that my immersion in the English language is blind and total. I can't help loving it. I love its sprawling disorderliness, its sinewy range. The massive, assimilationist vocabulary, so nobly and recklessly open to anything new. The freedom from syntactical rule, the verbs and nouns scattered not quite randomly, like Easter Sunday treats. Those startling, oddly welcome mood swings from Latinate formality to Anglo-Saxon crudeness, that bipolar vertigo. English offers a home in a way that no city or country ever could, and any love affair with it pushes all other friendships and romantic attachments into second place—a fact that is not always welcome to those it affects directly.

My profession is academic philosophy, which means that I am supposed to trade in the market of ideas. This I do to the best of my ability, trying, as Johnson prayed for all writers, to give a just account of whatever parcel of talent has been granted. No actual sentence I have ever written is a complete or perfect expression of what I thought I was trying to say, but in each case it is also true, perhaps paradoxically, that I did not know precisely what I was trying to say until a given sentence was written. This is one part of the odd surfing motion of being a writer, the source of so much joy and frustration as we try to give expression to what we think. But whatever the success or failure of that final expression, ideas come to me, always, in English. That is, they always assume a specific linguistic form. Some people deny this possibility, but reflection shows that linguisticality is basic to the experience of consciousness. I know students are lying, or confused, when they say, as they so often do: *I know what I think, I just can't express it.* But I say to them: no. Until you can express it, you haven't really had the idea. You may have had an inkling, or an intimation, or a glimmer, or a sense of possibility; but not a thought. To really have an idea, you must give it expression in language, whether you write it down or not; and only by writing it down will you know the precise contours of the idea, as opposed to its vague outline. As Wittgenstein put it in the *Tractatus Logico Philosophicus*: "Everything that can be thought at all can be thought clearly. Everything that can be put into words can be put clearly." (He also said, in that work's famous final line, "Whereof we cannot speak, we must remain silent.")

What your language allows therefore determines, in larger part than we would sometimes care to accept, what you can think, what ideas you can have. Heidegger argued that ancient Greek and modern German were the only truly philosophical languages, the only ones whose verb tenses and middle-voice capacity truly expressed the Meaning of Being. English, for Heidegger, was chatty and sometimes stringent, but it was not deep. (To be fair to us English speakers, who like to think we can think, Heidegger's use of German, especially in the early work *Being and Time*, is so bizarrely agrammatical and neologistic that, by some measures, he was not using German at all. Some people call it Heideggerese.)

The intimate, even isomorphic, relationship between thought and language is the real reason we need to worry about the increasing dominance of English in the globalized world. Despite some warnings, like the one recently issued by Barbara Wallraff in *The Atlantic Monthly*, that English is not going to be the lingua franca of Mono-Global-Culture-Corp, it does seem to be the case, as both investment bankers and philosophers have been known to assert, if you don't speak English, you simply don't exist. This is an issue for everyone who has to learn English in order to survive, but it is also an issue for those of us who are first-language English speakers.

Because a language does not go global without suffering severe consequences, not all of them salutary. As Heidegger further said, *language speaks us* more than we speak language. We are its servants, not its masters, and it delineates for us, whether we like it or not, the limits of who we can be. In Canada, of course, we have ample reason to know that language is politics, that whether you put "*arrêt*" or "stop" on the sign—even though "stop" is perfectly good French—is the sort of thing over which people come to blows. But language is more than politics, it is existence. We are prisoners of language like we are prisoners of gravity, or of mortality: these inescapable facts of the human project limit the possibilities of meaning, make meaning itself meaningful.

We are forever in danger of diminishing the range of meaning's possibility, even as, paradoxically, the new global English gets ever more expansive in vocabulary. A global English, like a global anything, can't help but be reductive in its effects: like the metalanguage of evolutionary biology, or the metanarrative of Christian salvation, it becomes a dominant story that makes all idiosyncratic locutions not so much odd as meaningless. Shakespeare's *Sonnets*, which many people regard as the best sequence of poems ever rendered in English, are already a vulnerable commodity in a world where university graduates, most of them native English speakers, cannot parse complex sentences, let alone detect internal irony or the compressions of meaning characteristic of the sonnet. What would it be like to inhabit a world in which those poems were understood by nobody, were mere scratches of black ink upon a dusty page?

We are not there yet, but there are certain danger signs—or anyway what lovers of English may choose to see as danger signs. The following quotation is from an interview that the novelist Kazuo Ishiguro gave a number of years ago, published in *January* magazine (October 2000). The problem of writing with a global audience in mind, Ishiguro said, "is like everything else to do with globalization. The downside is that a kind of grayness might sweep over literature too. That we'll all start writing in the same kind of way. I'm aware of this happening to me, too. There are a lot of things I don't write now. I stop myself writing certain things because I think, for instance, that it wouldn't work once it's translated out of English. You can think of a line that's brilliant in English—with a pun or two, you know—but of course it becomes nonsense once translated into a different language, so I don't use it."

These, then, are some of the deeper concerns we all must have when we consider what the globalization of English is doing to us, and to English. To see the full force of those concerns—the full force of anguish as the constant condition of those trapped in the honey of language—let us focus for a moment on the specifically political implications of language. My suggestion is that this focus will bring us back in a sharper way to the existential implications of linguistic globalization: the way anguish is not just the lot of those who acquire a new language, but also the inevitable consequence of being linguistic creatures at all.

Salman Rushdie, himself a brilliant product of linguistic globalization, said that a writer should re-read George Orwell's 1946 essay "Politics and the English Language" at least once a year. In general, this is good advice. There is no more brilliant, and brief, dissection than Orwell's of flabby euphemism and rhetorical wheeziness in the writing of English. But there are dangers. A minor one at any time is that the brisk vigilance counseled by Orwell will render a lot of what you commonly write unconscionable. You will find your hands tied, unable to write a word that does not offend. This is the linguistic equivalent of being a shortstop who thinks too much. The condition probably won't last long, but there is an even greater danger. Put baldly: if you take Orwell's counsel to heart as you listen to the campaign speeches written for the candidates, *you will go mad.*

The reason is that Orwell is too right. His view of the dodges and shortcomings of political language is just too clear-eyed, too exacting. While listening to political speech making and "analysis," it is all too possible that the awful truth of Orwell's demythologizing will expose you to the cold chill of metaphysical loneliness. I do not mean to imply that we would prefer it otherwise. Most people who force themselves to listen to that speech making will realize, in some far reach of their souls, that it is all nonsense, self-serving sham. They will. They just won't want to face up to the implications of the realization.

And who can blame them? The truth is a cold, hard thing. It's unsettling. "When one watches some tired hack on the platform mechanically repeating the familiar phrases—*bestial atrocities, iron heel, bloodstained tyranny, free peoples of the world, stand shoulder to shoulder*," Orwell says, "one often has a curious feeling that one is not watching a live human being but some kind of dummy: a feeling which suddenly becomes stronger when the light catches the speaker's spectacles and turns them into blank discs which seem to have no eyes behind them."

The hook line for an old magazine article was a simple question: *Can George Bush Think?* The answer was unsurprising. "Can he think in an organized, linear way about problems?" a former presidential staffer asked. "Can he pose the thesis and antithesis, and draw a synthesis? No. He's the least contemplative man I've ever met." (This was Bush Sr., not Jr.; readers are invited to reflect on heritability.) Now, is Bush an execrable speaker because he can't think, or does it work the other way around? Or does it matter? Orwell said it does. English "becomes ugly and inaccurate because our thoughts are foolish, but the slovenliness of our language makes it easier for us to have foolish thoughts." We all get into bad habits, the laziness and vagueness Orwell minutely examines. The point is that "[i]f one gets rid of these habits one can think more clearly, and to think clearly is a necessary first step towards political regeneration." So don't blame Bush for his laughable mangling of sense and syntax, but don't look to him for

Orwell's revolution either. Oh no. Logic demands that only a person who can think can think *more clearly*. Leave Bush out of it.

Orwell detailed many bad habits of writing and speaking that are still with us today, but his greatest scorn is reserved for euphemism. Pretentious diction, dying metaphors, passive-voice constructions and other carbuncles on the body of the language—the habits of the bureaucratic mind—obscure meaning with great efficiency; but only euphemism actively subverts it. Only euphemism substitutes false for real meaning. "The great enemy of clear language is insincerity," Orwell therefore concluded. "When there is a gap between one's real and one's declared aims, one turns as it were instinctively to long words and exhausted idioms, like a cuttlefish squirting out ink." The simple reason is that, in politics, most of one's real aims are too cruel, nasty or self-serving to be publicly aired.

What this means, ultimately, is that nobody can appeal to sincerity and make any headway; sincerity is debased coinage. When sincerity has lost the ability to speak in anything other than clichés like these, we know that one important battle against anguish is lost. Worse, contrary to Orwell's hope, thinking doesn't necessarily help. In an essay called "A New Refutation of the Very Possibility of Al Gore," published during the 2000 American election campaign, the philosopher Crispin Sartwell writes as follows: "The question before us is this: Does Al Gore exist? Let us approach this question from a phenomenological perspective, taking as our provisional starting point the following sentence by Heidegger, who wrote, in *Being and Time*, that: 'The nothing nothings' (or 'nothingness nihilates'). Consider, as a thought experiment, a speech by Al Gore. He is not really there, and he is not saying anything; he is nothing and he is saying nothing. Al Gore is a kind of hole or vacuum that expresses the essence of nothingness. Nothingness nihilates."

So the election, Sartwell goes on, "poses itself as a question: Will we trip over Al Gore's abysmal foot into the infinite void, falling eternally into dimensionless nonbeing?... Consequently, a vote for Al Gore is a vote not only against the universe in which we happen to find ourselves; it is a vote against the very possibility of any universe, of even a single merely possible lepton." We need not go so far, even in satire; and this was, to be sure, written before Gore's successful resurrection as an activist on the subject of climate change. Neither his success there, nor the scandalous stolen elections, can eliminate the inconvenient truth that, as a politician, Gore's form of thoughtfulness did not communicate well.

Orwell's warning about the way language inscribes ideology is timeless. So timeless, in fact, that one could grow weary of reporting examples of newspeak tendencies in the languages of bureaucracy and power: from Winnipeg's old "Public Safety Building," say, actually a jail, which those of us who visited it used to call "the Ministry of Love"; through corporate "right-sizing" and "outplacement," otherwise known as cutbacks and getting the axe; to former premier Mike Harris's "Common Sense Revolution" in Ontario, a thinly veiled right-wing crusade to undo the good of five decades of citizen-based social programs.

We are all aware of this capacity of language to hide domination, to erase all signs of the exercise of influence, such that influence itself becomes invisible and hence unquestionable. War theorists from Sun Tzu onward know that ideology, like all forms of true domination, functions by means of strategic envelopment, cutting off all normal routes of escape and creating various crippling dilemmas for those on the wrong side of the power balance. The weak face a series of Hobson's choices in which all options are self-defeating. They are caught in what Gregory Bateson, the influential communications theorist, called a double bind.

The idea of double binds was actually first advanced as a way of understanding schizophrenia. In Bateson's analysis, schizophrenia is only incidentally a disease of the brain; it is, first and foremost, a distorted pattern of communication, in which first-order claims are contradicted by second-order ones, all of it wrapped in a third-order contradiction created by the situation itself. As an example, consider this case, given to me by the psychologist James

Geiwitz, who helped work out some of the early implications of double binds with Bateson: "A young man who had fairly well recovered from an acute schizophrenic episode was visited in the hospital by his mother. He was glad to see her and impulsively put his arm around her shoulders, whereupon she stiffened. He withdrew his arm and she asked, 'Don't you love me any more?' He then blushed, and she said, 'Dear, you must not be so easily embarrassed and afraid of your feelings.' The patient was able to stay with her only a few minutes more, and following her departure he assaulted an aide and was put in the tubs."

Talk about anguish as a second language! A sophisticated reading of language and ideology brings to our attention this kind of all-powerful, no-exit style of communications pattern. This is not always a matter of obvious structures of domination, either, which makes the anguish all the more acute. As the critic Stuart Hall says, "Ideology pervades everyday life in the form of common sense." In a smoothly functioning culture like our own, the ideological forces can be disguised, even invisible, as the unquestioned, indeed unquestionable, taken-for-granted structures of daily existence: the things we do not pause to criticize because it never occurs to us to do so. Language, like all shared patterns of human interaction, can become a site of this commonsense domination. So can universities or bureaucracies, as Orwell knew: not so much in what they teach or do, but in their very structure, their presuppositions.

The question is always *what to do about it*. And this is far from obvious. To challenge these taken-for-granted structures is to court more anguish, of course, and it is, furthermore, to risk being thought mad. It cannot be done head-on, since it is in the nature of strategic envelopment to render open challenge not so much ineffective as incoherent. The person who bucks common sense too openly, who refuses to take the taken-for-granted for granted, is called insane. And if, lacking any other strategies of resistance, we fall into frustrated inaction, not only does everything stay the way it is, but also we feel that we have failed ourselves, that our anguish is bent back on our own desires and integrity. In a vivid

English phrase whose overuse has rubbed off its sharp edges of tragic, self-inflicted violence, we *eat our hearts out.*

Thus the need for oblique strategies of resistance, guerrilla actions that take on the dominant power structure in sidelong fashion, creating alien bodies within the landscape of normal, routine exchanges. Here, style itself—in clothes, music, writing, self-presentation—may be the only way to resist. But the constant danger, especially in our day, is that style will be assimilated by the very structures it seeks to criticize. Style becomes mere fashion, its tokens of resistance decontextualized and emptied, neutered and declawed, now to be bought and sold in further smooth exchanges of the all-enveloping market—the market of money, to be sure, but the market of discourse as well, where language lives. (For more on this issue, see chapter 14.)

The protesters gathered that long-ago week in Prague were there to oppose the actions of the World Bank and International Monetary Fund. They grappled with the double binds of protest that date from time immemorial. Should they engage in violent protests? If they did, they would be dismissed as thugs and anarchists; but if they did not, their protest movement would be dismissed as insignificant and minor. Should they accept an invitation to come and talk to the leaders of the World Bank and IMF? If they did, they would be tacitly granting those bodies a legitimacy they actually wish to deny; but if they did not, they would be accused of not wanting to negotiate, not being serious. Should they agree to proposals to reform those tools of economic globalization? If they did, they would undermine their own claim that the Bank and the Fund are tainted all through and should be abolished; if they didn't, they would be dismissed once more, now as unreasonable extremists.

It is one thing to think about these issues in a detached, academic fashion, and quite another to be a twenty-two-year-old in a foreign city, camped out in the cold, trying to figure out how to engage in meaningful political action. Language itself is part of the enveloping power, the hegemonic forces (as another kind of writer might put it). For, while language can be bent to revolutionary and subversive purposes, and at its best often is—this, after all, is the sense in which Percy Bysshe Shelley's line about poets being the unacknowledged legislators of the world makes sense—it is equally, at least equally, the case that language is the subtle instrument of power. If newspeak is the spectral form of language's ideological tendencies, more common and proximate forms exist, as Orwell knew, in euphemism, blandness, vagueness and other techniques of charlatanry. And the smooth phatic forms of language, the routine exchanges characteristic of television debate or newspaper editorializing that masquerade as public discourse, are more dangerous still.

I once wrote a book with the title *A Civil Tongue*. It attempts a defense of the virtue of civility in political life, the relation of discursive willingness to the pursuit of justice. Both the thesis and the title were criticized, especially by my friends on the left. Wasn't civility just another tool of oppression, and wasn't the phrase "a civil tongue" most often used in the discourse-ending imperative that we keep one in our heads? The broadcaster Edwin Newman, who has also written a book called *A Civil Tongue*, as it happens, says that he learned the phrase during early experiences as a reluctant office boy, when its clear interpretation was "Be respectful to your elders," or, less gently, "Shut up."

Newman goes on, in his book of this popular title, to defend what he calls "plain speaking" against the mutations and distortions of everyday English: the way our lovely tongue gets mangled by flight attendants and shopkeepers ("Have a nice day in Cincinnati or wherever your final destination may be taking you"); the way inverted commas are witlessly used for emphasis when they really signal doubt, as in so-called scare quotes, such that a shop sign enthusiastically offering "FREE" T-shirts with every purchase causes the literate passerby to wonder what the catch is. This kind of criticism is all well and good, and it mines a rich vein of (usually elderly and male) complaint against what the young folks are doing to the language. Amis and, less fogeyishly,

William Safire are Newman's proximate colleagues in this project. It is a mood that falls upon men of a certain class and education when they reach late middle age, and cannot digest the enormity of ubiquitous bad grammar and clunky usage, especially among the young.

If the war between plainness and euphemism were left to that, however, we would miss the point. It is not simply that languages are constantly evolving, sometimes in ways uncongenial to its most accomplished users—and Amis, whatever his other virtues or vices, was a precise and witty master of English prose. Rearguard actions have their pleasures, but the historical record is pretty clear that they rarely, if ever, succeed where popularity must of necessity rule. Nor is it even that the act of acquiring a second (or third, or fourth) language involves a process of infantilization that is capable of reducing grown men to stammering, gesticulating primates begging for food or directions to the bathroom— though, of course, this is the source of lots of routine anguish. What are now most often called teachers of English as a second language are, in some other contexts, called teachers of English as a foreign language, and so the resulting acronymic description is not TESL but TOEFL. (The distinction between "second" language and "foreign" language is not precise, but it has to do with the degree of mastery implied, and the size and complexity the vocabulary learned.) *Tessel* is an English word, as it happens. It most often occurs in the past participle form "tessellated," and it is most often used to describe pavement or reptilian skin. It means "in a regular checkered pattern." *Teufel* is more resonant, if less obvious: it is not an English word at all, but, perhaps fittingly, a German one: it means *devil*.

The deeper point—the point that moves the political argument into the existential realm—is always that being-in-language entails a constant feeling of anguish *for everybody*. This is what we need to remember. Language is the site of our interactions, the shared field on which our individuality matches itself against the assumptions and expectations of others. Here we acquire or discard scripts of identity. We try on accents and voices, finding the peculiar ventriloquy that will answer our needs. We speak of native speakers, as if they possessed a natural comfort unavailable to the new arrival, the immigrant to the land of language. But this is misleading, for we are all forever beginners in the classroom of words. As English makes its way around the world, as more and more humans take on the specific challenges and rewards of this pliable, sometimes civil tongue, that anguish can only continue.

Can we do anything about that? Only what we have always done, speaking and writing the language of our thoughts with the fullest generosity of which we are capable. And listening with a similar grace and openness to those doing likewise. Using language entails the responsibility of probing its political commitments, examining its existential freight. That, finally, is what civility really means: not the face-saving dodges or obscurantist locutions of the powerful, seeking to protect their power from challenge; but rather the constant vigilance of the good citizen, sometimes subversive and sometimes constructive, struggling with other speakers to realize here, on the uneven ground of shared language, a society—a world—that we can call, in that robust English word derived (of course) from the Latin, *just*.

Welcome to anguish.

12. Crayon in the Brain:
Machining Happiness in the Time of Homer

"Happiness is for idiots."
—Charles de Gaulle

i.   Homer and Lisa

A story of two people, one happy and one sad.[1]

In an episode from the 2001 season of *The Simpsons*, Homer discovers that he has a crayon lodged in his brain, the result of a childhood incident in which he was dared to insert a whole box up his nose, and hence his brain. A sneeze brought all but one flying out, but in the interval Homer lost count of the crayons, and one remained.

Now that it has been surgically removed, Homer discovers he is actually a man of towering intellect. His wardrobe, vocabulary and demeanor all change instantly. So does his relationship with daughter Lisa, to this point the sole intellectual in the Simpson family, maybe in all of Springfield. Formerly distant, father and daughter now find they are close friends, together living the life of the mind.

There is a cloud, however. Homer's restored intellect allows him to realize that the nuclear power plant where he works is a maze of safety violations. He blows the whistle, much of the town's population is laid off, and Homer is vilified as a conscientious troublemaker. He is burned in effigy in the local bar, Moe's. As he is saying "I notice a distinct strain of anti-intellectualism in this tavern," one of the patrons hits him in the head with a plank and the rest throw him out of the bar. He goes to a popular movie starring Julia Roberts and Richard Gere, *Love Is Nice*, and watches with growing irritation and boredom as the clichéd plot lurches towards its banal conclusion, perhaps reflecting on Adorno's complaint in *Minima Moralia* that "every visit to the cinema leaves me feeling stupider and worse."

People notice that he is not enjoying the film. "Don't blame me," Homer says. "This movie is tired and predictable." He complains that of course they all know the two main characters will end up together, and the audience, shocked by this thoughtless revelation, attack him, hit him with a plank, and eject him from the theater. "Point out your plot holes elsewhere," the pimply usher shouts. Despondent Homer wanders the streets in a forties-style cinematic montage of despair, neon signs of a dumbed down culture floating past: Smart People Not Welcome, Dum-Dum Club, Lunkheadz, Disney Store.

Homer goes to Lisa and asks her why she never said that being intelligent was so painful. Why is he unhappy if he is smart? She acknowledges that it is true, and in fact shows him a graph she's plotted demonstrating the inverse relationship between intelligence and happiness. "I make a lot of graphs," she says sadly. How does she cope? "Tai chi," Lisa says dreamily. "Chai tea."

At this point, Homer decides that he no longer wants to be smart. The scientists who removed the crayon will not help him, so he goes to Moe, the local bartender who doubles as an amateur surgeon, to have the crayon reinserted in his brain: a procedure Moe calls "the old Crayola oblongata." Moe positions it in his nose and begins hitting it with a ball-peen hammer; the further it enters

Homer's cranial cavity, the dumber he becomes. When he says "Extended warranty? How can I lose!" Moe knows he has gone far enough and Homer has been restored to his former state of happy stupidity, retaining no memory of his crayon-free condition.

Only Lisa is devastated at the return of the familiar Homer. Her father hands her a letter he has discovered in his back pocket, apparently written before he underwent the backroom operation. In it he explains that he "took the coward's way out" in returning to his status of blissful stupidity. He could not endure the sense of isolation and discontent, not to mention the plank blows to the head, entailed by being a smart man in a dumb culture.

ii. The Happiness Delinquent

This story may be read as a cautionary tale, or fable, for intellectuals, and hence of Lisa's isolated plight—that is, happiness is indeed for idiots, as de Gaulle said, and the necessary corollary is that nonidiots are debarred from happiness. Being smart means being sad, because if you have a brain it is impossible to be happy *in the terms the culture typically offers.*

But the story has other resonances. Perhaps most poignantly of all, it is a miniature operatic tragedy. Homer is briefly transformed, by a complicated and implausible accident, into another version of himself. We are made to understand that this, indeed, is his *true* self: he has not so much altered as returned, *becoming who he is,* to use the Aristotelian argot. The crayon was a barrier, a foreign object, a xenocyst lodging in the soul of an otherwise brilliant man. But having experienced the other side of existence, that is, the form of life we might simply call, after the cliché, blissful ignorance—a state, notably, to which Lisa has no access barring the insertion of her own crayon—Homer cannot take it. He cannot bear to remain in the realm of intellect because there he is manifestly unhappy. He submerges his true self in order to return to a condition of consonance with his culture, and therefore a cheerful consumer of all the things that culture has to offer, not least its idea of what it means to be happy. Not even the awareness that he is, in effect, stranding Lisa

in her role as the family's, if not the town's, single *happiness delinquent*, is enough to sway Homer (the intelligent, "genuine" Homer,
we must remember) from this course.[2]

As in the phrase "juvenile delinquent," or "J.D."—a term now
almost archaic—the happiness delinquent is a lawbreaker, here
not the youthful violation of the actual (say criminal) law, but
rather violation, by anyone, of the norms of expected behavior.
(Delinquent, from Latin *delictum, delinquens, delinquere*—to
transgress or violate.) The happiness delinquent refuses to play the
happiness game by the culture's consensual rules; he or she opts
out in favor of some other vision. The alternative need not be self-
consciously "intellectual," as it is in *The Simpsons* example, but it
often will have that coloring simply because sophisticated criticism of the dominant culture and a refusal to "play along" are so
often intertwined. (Leave aside for now the corollary question of
whether the critic can ever be happy in the culture's own terms—
engaging what Žižek calls "the idiotic enjoyment of popular culture.") But this opting-out, however personal in motivation—not
every intellectual wants to change the world—is necessarily taken
as a challenge to those still playing within the rules. Hence the hostility to the smart Homer, the constant marginalization of the
squeaky-voiced, conscience-driven Lisa.

Even knowing this it is hard to accept Homer's defection from
the newfound but, again, *fundamental* position as his own happiness delinquent. Indeed, the return to happiness enacted here
poses questions similar to those familiar from thought experiments in utilitarianism, in particular what is sometimes called the
happiness machine. If it were possible to put yourself into a
machine capable of generating consistent and comprehensive
happiness, with no opportunity or exit costs to speak of, would
you do so? Or rather, since most people have strongly negative
intuitions about this choice when it is actually posed to them, why
wouldn't you do it? After all, the principle of utility, at least in
some of its cruder forms, enjoins a maximization of happiness
to which this machine, and your entry into it, would contribute

significantly: you may even have a positive duty to enter the happiness machine! How can you not? Might we, as society, even be in a position to *force* you inside, or forcibly *prevent* you from leaving?

A number of responses are typically offered for a refusal to enter the machine. One trades on the recurrent conflation in utilitarian theories of happiness and pleasure. If the happiness machine is a kind of "Orgasmatron" (as fancifully depicted in the Woody Allen film *Sleeper*), the choice becomes clearer—if also, for adolescent males especially, momentarily more tempting, not less. For most people, though, a life of pure pleasure is not substantially attractive, not least because they understand that pleasure is a function, in part, of limits and contrasts. We savor things because they stand out from other things: a fine meal after a week of ordinary ones, a glass of wine after a hard day, a vacation to relieve months of drudgery. If we had these "pleasures" all the time, their piquancy would fade, the enjoyment dull. A treat like ice cream is not a treat in a steady diet of ice cream. Too much pleasure makes the palate, and the soul, grow weary and jaded. Despite the film's comic scenes, even an Orgasmatron eventually becomes boring.

Or so we prefer to believe. Nothing in this argument ought to prevent one from entering the happiness machine, however, for two reasons: one, the machine promises manufactured happiness, not pleasure, and so in principle to avoid what we might call the jaded-palate objection; and two, even if the machine were only capable of generating pleasure, and if pleasure contributed to the maximization of utility, our duty to enter the machine would be unchanged. Nevertheless, people still resist. Often, at this stage, they enter a version of John Stuart Mill's own utility argument, really the substantive rejoinder to Jeremy Bentham, that even pleasures need to be nuanced by an analysis of quality over quantity. The happiness generated by playing pushpin is not equivalent to the happiness unleashed by reading poetry, and so cannot be measured on the same scale; moreover, the person who has experienced both is in a position to judge between the two, whereas the person who has experienced only one—especially the presumptively "lower" one—is debarred from that judgment. The consequence is that sometimes local, lower-level unhappiness will be consistent with, perhaps even entailed by, the duty to a larger, higher-quality kind of happiness. The calculations of utility need to be vectored and rank-ordered to make room for high and low, and the resulting duties change likewise. Famously, therefore, it is better to be Socrates unsatisfied than a pig satisfied.

With respect to the happiness machine, this judgment of quality is shifted in an interesting direction, concerning reality. Now the judgment addresses less the alleged "height" of the pleasure and more the *artificiality* of the alleged comprehensive machine happiness. In other words, the person who has experienced real happiness, or at least who inhabits a real world, is capable of judging that happiness—or, to be precise, its possibility—as superior to anything that can be generated from within the machine.

Again we observe confusion, though. The person standing outside and refusing to enter the machine has not, in fact, experienced both kinds of happiness. He is a happiness delinquent, in fact, who does not want to fulfill a duty to happiness that is otherwise reckoned valid. Why? Because the machine's happiness is artificial. But what if that information could be factored out of the equation? That is, what if we could tweak the happiness machine so that any memory of existence prior to entry is erased? This is exactly what is modeled in Homer's "Crayola oblongata" self-mutilation, after all. He doesn't want simply to return to a state of easy cultural enjoyment; he wants to do so with no lingering awareness of his time as a cultural critic. Indeed, it is impossible to imagine doing one without the other: if he retained memories of his intellectual period, blissful ignorance would not be facilitated. The essential ignorance involves not just a lack of awareness of the (alleged) emptiness of the culture's pleasures, but also of any residence in the conceptual region—here figured as an outlaw territory—where that emptiness is noticed, analyzed and debated.

iii. Cypher and "I"

In this sense, Homer's crayon maneuver parallels the return to a comprehensive and oppressive virtual reality effected by Cypher, the disaffected rebel in the epistemo-action thriller, *The Matrix*. Joe Pantoliano's Cypher—a man whose name notably means both code or secret and nothingness, nonentity; the magic zero, in short—is the film's essential antihero, directly paralleling the messianic self-awareness that clings to Keanu Reeves's developing kung-fu Christ, Neo. Cypher betrays his fellow resistance fighters in exchange for reinsertion into the blissful—though artificial and exploitative (the computer running the virtual reality uses human subjects for energy)—program. Here is a world where steaks taste delicious, even if they are not real, whatever "real" could possibly mean! Cypher is no fool—indeed, he is philosopher enough to have seen the main issue at stake in the betrayal: not the hapless colleagues he reluctantly leaves behind, but the prior self he profoundly wishes to abandon. Though we see him discussing the deal as himself with Mr. Smith and the other Matrix-minders, he reminds them that a complete memory wash is a condition of the deal. Only by obliterating awareness of the boundary can crossing the boundary be made plausible.

This is one of the many Cartesian moments of the film, which, despite visual nods toward Baudrillard and Carroll is essentially conservative and foundational, almost Platonic, in its epistemology. Like Descartes's dreamer, Cypher realizes that shifts in perceived reality are only available to perception if memory is retained of *both sides* of the boundary. The dreamer knows he is— that is to say, *was*—dreaming only by virtue of waking up. From within the dream there are no tests that can establish the independent reality of the world experienced. The threshold and its crossing underwrite the metaphysical judgment, just as they do in Plato's cave, with its laborious upward ascent. For Descartes, however, in contrast to Plato's transcendental solution, the reality of a world can never self-justify: there is no standpoint that vouches its own reality without condition. That is precisely why Descartes's doubter, the fictional *I* of the *Meditations*, must cross an *inner* boundary and try to secure the clear and distinct ideas that are, as it were, lying within the core of everyday experience and may, under analysis, support the rest.

Though Descartes seems scarcely aware of it, the meditation form is essential to this undertaking. It is more than a matter of establishing intimacy and first-person immediacy—however important these remain. The meditation narrative is a personal-identity narrative. The *I* of the *Meditations* goes to bed each night of his six-day thought experiment and then wakes the next morning *as himself once more*. He is not a giant beetle, nor has he lost his memory (two conditions we will examine in a moment). This continuity of personal identity, even more than the searching doubts so celebrated in the text, are what make Descartes's foundational epistemology possible. Absent it, in particular absent the memory of self from day to day, from stage to stage of perception, and the argument would not run. Memory, and the narrative that both depends on and creates it, is more essential to perception than traditional epistemologists, Descartes included, ever acknowledge.

They likewise underestimate structures of intersubjectivity and what we sometimes call multiple subject positions, concentrating instead on an isolated *I* that is no mere rhetorical device of representation but rather a misleading philosophical fiction. Note that personal narrative, while it necessarily arises as egocentric to each subject, is impossible without others likewise occupied; and moreover, that it is no more than a useful fiction to presume a single, unified or essential person at the heart of such a narrative. There is no *I*, and a fortiori no happy *I*, absent you; and there may be more than one *I* in even the most coherent narrative. (The present text is obviously a demonstration, in minor key, of those two points.) Moreover, memory is often false, and perhaps just as often—though, again, how would we know?—a species of shared cultural experience. That is, some of our memories may turn out to be not false but shared: not so much implanted via some Philip K. Dick conspiracy scenario—see, for example, the vivid tangles of action and identity deployed in

Blade Runner ("Do Androids Dream of Electric Sheep?") or *Total Recall* ("We Can Remember It for You Wholesale") as ingested or absorbed osmotically from the general memosphere of our being in the world. This evidently complicates the idea of memory as the key to identity, and hence happiness.

Nevertheless, this issue of memory is, finally, why the happiness machine thought experiment consistently generates so many negative responses. We cannot accept putting ourselves inside it from the position of being, remembering that we are *our selves*. We see, even if we do not always articulate it clearly, that to be in the machine would have to mean abandoning the person we are at the moment of entry. Anything else would fail to allay the persistent objections concerning the artificiality and hence illicitness of the happiness so experienced. We want happiness, but we want it to be real; and we want it, even more to the point, to be ours. The happiness machine test is really one of identity, not happiness. Happiness is not happiness if it is not for me. The supposed utilitarian duty is rejected not because the calculus fails to make sense, but because it fails to place a burden on me. Any fulfillment of the duty, after all, would include elimination of me, and so how can I feel such a fulfillment as my duty? The happiness machine is a theoretical option, but it is not, cannot be, an option *for me*— whatever that is taken to mean.

This is the point at which the happiness machine discussion is usually concluded. Note two things, however. First, there may indeed be duties, such as self-sacrifice in times of war or threat, that enjoin precisely the elimination of individual selves in favor of larger goods. It is hard to imagine the happiness machine as such a case, perhaps, but nothing in principle forbids it. (This is the sort of entailment that is often used to give utilitarianism a bad name, as "not respecting the difference between persons," to use John Rawls's terms. Still, if one grants the principle of utility, it is difficult to avoid the conclusion. Second, the eventual focus on identity is significant in the real-world cases of happiness as much as in the thought experiment. What does that mean?

Think again of Homer. If we expand the idea of machine from the rather literal "device of representation" in the utilitarian thought experiment to a larger, Deleuzoguattarian conception of "machine" as a system of control and normativity, including possible lines of flight and ruptures as well as connections, the issue becomes clearer. This is the machine against which, if we were so inclined, we might rage. The culture at large is a happiness machine in two senses. First, a space where happiness is sold in machine form (in technology, pharmaceuticals, goods, services, reproducible effects, even, crucially, social position—commodities, in short, whether material or otherwise); and second, as a system, promising to cast the die of happiness on each of us, to machine satisfaction in one product after another. Positional goods are the *ne plus ultra* of this two-sided machining, since they demand one's attention and capital, engaging desires and aspirations, without any need for real production, or even real qualities, to underwrite them. That is why "cool" is the ultimate in happiness machining: everywhere and nowhere, it structures large chunks of human life in the developed world, without being anything in particular. The happiness machine is to a large extent organized around it. Who among us can hope to avoid, in some form or other, the lure of being cool? We might even begin to fear, legitimately, that our personal narrative and sense of identity is organized around consumer preferences; an identity not just contingent, in other words, but contaminated and stolen.

When we regard matters in this light, we see that the happiness machine is really just a small-scale version of the comprehensive truth that Homer's happiness dilemma indicates. He asks himself—or we ask on his behalf, since he seems in little doubt once the plank blows begin raining down on his head—whether he can justifiably leave his "genuine" self behind in order to achieve the sort of satisfaction, or lack of dissatisfaction, offered by the dominant culture. But in what sense is the crayon-free Homer his genuine self? He has spent more time, and formed more of his personal story, in another condition. Does it even make sense to speak of a genuine self in this context? It seems like a rather more basic choice: crayon or no crayon, that is the question . . .

At first Homer's defection back into cultural idiocy looks hard to justify, again not least because he is aware, in his "cowardice," of leaving poor Lisa behind. We have trouble with this because his decision is presumably rational, made from within the "smart" Homer universe. But smart Homer is indeed smart, and not merely cowardly. He knows the crayon will eliminate memory of his intelligent interlude. He also knows, more crucially still, of his own previous existence as a happy moron! That is, unlike most of us, who regard the happiness machine with distaste even though we have not actually experienced it, Homer has fulfilled the Millian injunction not to judge two qualities of happiness without intimate knowledge of both.

Homer is thus the anti-Mill: he has first-hand experience of both poetry and pushpin and, giving the lie to Mill's smug confidence, chooses the latter over the former! "Higher" pleasures are rejected in favor of lower ones. It is too much work (and too painful) to be Socrates dissatisfied. Smart Homer calls this "cowardice" in his letter to Lisa, but since he chooses it anyway, we may be forgiven for wondering if *he does not really believe that*, perhaps says it merely as a sop to Lisa's likely feelings of betrayal. Reading the letter, she will be able to reinforce her feelings of intellectual superiority as a result of these events. Briefly joined, then abandoned, by her father, her position as the happiness delinquent is invigorated. The episode, like the series more generally, implicitly defends a position of intellectual refusal with respect to the culture of which it is a part.

iv. Me and Myself

That irony is structural. Though we have been considering the story, and the happiness machine, as if there is a clear boundary between forms of existence, this is of course a handy fiction. Smart Homer and Dumb Homer may have no future knowledge of each other, just as (if I personally were to take the plunge posed by the utilitarian thought experiment) Happiness-Machine Mark will not remember Philosophy-Professor Mark, but this depiction does not accurately model the choices we actually face. The status of *The Simpsons* as a cultural critique, a kind of refusal, which is nevertheless embedded in the machine of the culture—on network television, indeed, than which there is no greater cultural envelopment—is not necessarily a strike against it. On the contrary, this embeddedness and its implications are really where the happiness question is best investigated. The show opens up a crease in cultural experience that is central to our concerns, namely the status of personal identity at once independent of and servile to general economies of desire.

The issue of memory, or its loss as demanded by the notional passage from without to within the machine, is crucial. One obvious reason for this is that memory is, along with bodily continuity, one of the twin pillars supporting personal identity. This becomes fully clear in the century following Descartes, when the limitations of his solution to the appearance/reality problematic began to confess its limits. In a crude philosophical shorthand, the former criterion is insisted on by Hume, the latter by Locke; but all convincing accounts of personal identity must argue for both. Consider literary examples that illustrate each kind of concern.

When Gregor Samsa wakes one morning in Franz Kafka's "The Metamorphosis" to find himself a giant beetle, he feels himself the same "on the inside," but others do not find him the same because, necessarily, they interact with him via his "outside." Here, bodily continuity has been ruptured, in this case irremediably. (We could imagine other, less severe cases where there was a breach in bodily continuity that might be bridged or healed over: a disfiguring accident, for example, or even a science-fictional exchange of bodies. If my beloved suddenly took on another [humanoid] form, it would be extremely difficult for me to maintain the attachment, but arguably not impossible. A beetle is too much to ask.)

If, on the other hand, memory is ruptured, as in the tragic central character of the film *Memento*, identity is likewise threatened—perhaps even more devastatingly, since felt from the inside out, rather than the outside in. The character has no short-term memory, and "blacks out" of his experiences without warning. He uses Polaroids and tattoos in a desperate attempt to hold himself together—images and words being, though demonstrably unreliable, his only lifelines of coherence. No matter what he does, however, no matter how elaborate his system of tattoos and stacked snapshots, there is no possibility of linking experiences together in even a loose narrative of aspiration and achievement—the sort of narrative each one of us has, even if banal or predigested. And so the character organizes his identity around the one solid memory he retains, of the murder of his wife, and makes himself a weapon of revenge. To complicate matters, and give an experience of dislocation, the film's narrative runs backwards and so we learn that this revenge plot is meaningless only at the end—a bleak and rather horrible denouement.

Personal identity, requiring these two criteria, also requires what they allow, namely, the telling of a personal story. This also avoids any looming essentialism in our accounts of identity, the sort of view that gets tangled in thickets of seeking "authentic" or "true" self that is somehow lying somewhere (where?) waiting to be discovered (whatever that might mean). Such views are confused, if tempting. There is no such thing as this true self, because any self that I am must necessarily be an achievement rather than a discovery: we become who we are over time. We do this, crucially, via story construction—to ourselves and to others. Daniel Dennett puts it well when he says the self must be considered a "centre of narrative gravity."

We can now appreciate the full challenge of the happiness machine dilemma. How can we enter the machine's promised oblivion without abandoning ourselves? How can we abandon ourselves without losing the subjective position (or cluster of them) that constitutes our very idea of ourselves? The answer is that the machine must be supplemented by something else— something that will render it temporal and, therefore, compatible with narrative. The machine's apparently static apparatus must be made dynamic: it must be joined to the very structures of aspiration and achievement that are typical of human identity formation. The machine must become a dream, a dream of a very particular kind, the one most often called, simply and somewhat misleadingly, American.

The American dream is many things, and has many features, often a list of material goods or relationships drawn from an idealized depiction of postwar American life: large automobile, house with picket fence, loving family.[3] The particular items aside, certain basic structures of the dream logic can be articulated.

Perhaps the most basic (and familiar) feature of the dream is the constantly renewed desire, frankly paradoxical, that suggests satisfaction is forever *just around the corner.* This is the dream initially and openly declared in the Declaration of Independence, founding a republic on the protection of life, liberty and the pursuit of happiness. "Pursuit" is naturally the key term here. Unlike the Cartesian dreamer, the American dreamer is based on forgetting, not remembering. This paradox of memory and desire is captured by the mocking sign seen in many bars: "Free drinks tomorrow." Since from today, tomorrow is always not-yet, and what was tomorrow yesterday becomes today with the passage of time—casting forward the promise into another tomorrow—this rather silly sign captures the profound influence of desire satisfaction when combined with structures of temporality. Desire is here understood as a lack, as an "aspirational" fact of life—an adjective that magazines and advertisers now brazenly appropriate; but this lack is both painful (hence up for elimination) and endlessly renewable (hence impossible to eliminate). Indeed, it is no exaggeration to say that this conception of desire, immersed in an impossible temporality, is the very thing that so worried Plato and Aristotle and drove the latter, anyway, toward the eudaimonism he wished to replace *pleonexia* and appetitive madness. A genuine narrative of happiness—a narrative of virtuous commitment—was offered as a corrective to the unlimited longings and psychic conflicts of the unreflective soul.[4]

There are at least two important limits on this kind of critical account, however. One is the very problem of critical position that has arisen already in the discussion of Homer and Lisa. This illuminates a feature of current critique that was arguably absent in earlier generations—though they had their own challenges. Consider this passage from John Kenneth Galbraith's *The Affluent Society*, one of the key texts in postwar criticism of the dominant culture associated with the American dream. "Any direct onslaught on the identification of goods with happiness would have had another drawback," Galbraith notes of those inclined to Aristotelian critiques of the dream.

> Scholarly discourse, like bullfighting and the classical ballet, has its rules and they must be respected. In this arena nothing counts so heavily against a man as to be found attacking the values of the public at large and seeking to substitute his own. Technically his crime is arrogance. Actually it is ignorance of the rules. In any case he is automatically removed from the game. In the past this has been the common error of those who have speculated on the sanctity of present economic goals—those who have sought to score against materialism and Philistinism. They have advanced their own view of what adds to human happiness. For this they could easily be accused of substituting for the crude economic goals of the people at large the more sensitive and refined but irrelevant goals of their own. The accusation is fatal.

Galbraith is correct but out of date. This was indeed true of those "moralistic" critics of material goods, and even today an old-fashioned economist may reject one's value-based arguments by asserting that goods are simply what people want, freedom merely the concrete expression of preferences.

But critics today face a barrage of other difficulties, centrally the instability of their position. Rejection by "the people at large," after all, is for many critics a sign of virtue, an emblem of success; nowadays the happiness delinquent is as likely to be welcomed by the people at large, a sort of cultural sideshow to provide the illusion of dialectic! How does one maintain a stance of critique vis-à-vis a dominant culture of which one is, inevitably, a part? Despite the suggestion of a logic of inside and outside, and despite Homer's cowardly resort to the crayon, the reality is far more slippery. Lisa displays a greater degree of complexity and tragedy when she sighs about her pathetic coping mechanisms—tai chi, chai tea. For her, as for most of us, there is nowhere to go: one cannot escape the cultural conditions of life, especially if one wishes to assess them critically; and yet the critic is forever in a position of being either marginalized or—worse—smoothly assimilated by those very conditions. One of the most glaring cultural contradictions of late capitalism is that critics of late capitalism are so susceptible to the mechanisms of exchange and (de)valuation typical of the entire system.[5]

An even more alarming difficulty, or anyway a specific alarming instance of the larger problem, is that narrative and even apparently eudaimonistic conceptions can be colonized by the larger machine of happiness. That is, the existing forms of aspirational desire can be cast in stories of commitment and virtue that look Aristotelian but are really just implicit reinforcements of the current arrangement. The American dream offers an influential example of this appropriation. Perhaps it is better to say that this narrative structure allows the greatest degree of unexamined desire to remain in play while still suggesting the telos of a well-ordered life. In that sense, the American dream is the vehicle of the culture's consistent, and consistently renewed, dominance. Happiness is a matter not just of machines but of dreams, a matter of machining dreams—renewing the narrative in slightly altered forms, over and over—and machining dreamers, subjects of the narrative who believe the story is truly theirs, personally and validly. As the ads say, we all have to live the dream!

v. Specters and Realities

We cannot hope to resolve these contradictions here—or maybe anywhere. Some would regard this analysis as unduly alarmist, or pointless, or both—people are dreamers, and they dream of happiness (even while failing to interrogate happiness). It was ever thus, and critics are powerless to change it. But there are larger stakes here than merely the plight of critics, and I want to conclude with at least a suggestion concerning the political implications of Homer's abandonment of Lisa. For the American dream does not exist in a vacuum, despite its ostensible first-person status. That is, the Americanness of the dream is essential. Consider for a moment two related ironies of the current happiness logic, which gives every indication of being both spectral and contradictory: a dream gone bad.

The first irony is, like so much recent political experience, at once amusing and bleak. Speaking to *New York Times* reporter Ron Suskind on the eve of the 2004 United States federal election, a Bush administration aide explained the new postmodern condition to the liberal intellectuals of the Eastern Seaboard (and whoever else may be presumed to read the *New York Times*). Such people belong to "what we call the reality-based community," the aide said, where people "believe that solutions emerge from your judicious study of discernible reality." This was a view of things for which he clearly felt some pity, so deluded did they remain. "That's not the way the world really works anymore. We're an empire now, and when we act, we create our own reality. And while you're studying that reality—judiciously, as you will—we'll act again, creating our new realities, which you can study too, and that's how things will sort out. We're history's actors ... and you, all of you, will be left to just study what we do."

This rhetoric is startling for many reasons, including its disdainful aggression, but its most unsettling feature is the out-of-hand rejection of the so-called reality-based community, that hapless coterie of disconnected intellectuals and other assorted *naifs* who still believe there should be some matching of action to reason. In this postmodernism of absolute power—we might give it the appropriately paradoxical name of postmodern political realism—there are no standards of right and wrong. Nor are there even standards of true and false. No values; but also no facts. Only the pure exercise of power, understood now as the creation of reality; with the attendant denigration, typical of American anti-intellectualism, of anyone who has the temerity to suggest reality might be a master, not a servant, of power. This conjunction of ideas far surpasses the might-makes-right realism of a Thrasymachus or even a Niccolò Machiavelli. Here, might makes not *right*, but *light*: power is the only source of illumination, the only allowed standard of judgment. Empire is reality, reality empire. And those of us still struggling to forge understanding, to judge and measure, are left in history's dust. Nothing that Jean-François Lyotard or Derrida or Foucault said about the variability of truth could have hoped to achieve so comprehensive a dismantling of the idea of reason and the norm of truth. The appearance/reality problem is finally solved—by banishing reality.

The second irony is less philosophical and more practical. The American empire is not only postmodern, it is also *allegedly liberal*. That is, in contrast to previous empires, which were more straightforward in their designs on domination, or found quasi-moral justifications thereof, as in the case of Britain assuming "the white man's burden," the current example clings to a position of exceptionalism and even isolation. It employs a rhetoric of liberation and human dignity, and remains unwilling to offer clear admissions of aggression. Its violence is real and undeniable but rendered always inexplicit, hidden behind claims of national security or distant oppression. It will not acknowledge any moral authority outside of itself, yet appears untroubled by internal contradictions in its own moral position, the recourse to lies and false justifications for exercising power.

This is no mere lack of honesty, however; it is a fundamental incoherence in the idea of liberal empire. As the political scientist Greg Grandin has argued, this "easy acceptance of brutality in pursuit of an elusive liberal empire bears more than a passing resemblance to an earlier willingness of Soviet apparatchiks to justify repression in the name of a distant utopia."[6] This contradiction is not news, because it is a matter of conflicting values. Arendt, in *The Origins of Totalitarianism*, made the very same point of an earlier generation of imperialists. British politicians who believed they could maintain a liberal imperial regime without recourse to racist violence were, she said, "quixotic fools of imperialism." Empire means violence, the imposition of will. It is not, and cannot be, a program of liberation, no matter what a given inauguration speech might say.

American conservatives, meanwhile, who might have been thought sympathetic to the Christian moralism underlying this project of liberation, reacted with a mixture of concern and bitterness, making strange bedfellows with American leftists of the old American-dream school. The imperial policies of the first years of the twenty-first century seemed to violate the central promise of American politics, namely that they would put Americans first, making the homeland not just secure but a land of opportunity. One commentator, writing in *The American Conservative*, summed up the linked ironies this way: "The launching of an invasion against a country that posed no threat to the U.S., the doling out of war profits and concessions to politically favored corporations, the financing of the war by ballooning the deficit to be passed on to the nation's children, the ceaseless drive to cut taxes for those outside the middle class and working poor: it is as if [the Bush administration] sought to resurrect every false 1960s-era left-wing cliché about predatory imperialism and turn it into administration policy." Which is, of course, just what the left wing itself was thinking all along, though perhaps less wryly.

Nor is it even clear that the vaunted democratization and market liberalization, promised as the goods of the spreading American empire, are in fact coming. Experience in Latin America, for example, shows that economic liberalization, achieved there without recourse to invasion, has led not to prosperity but rather to a form of "dismal growth," where disparities between rich and poor are exacerbated and the national debts mount because of unfair trade practices. If one were cynical, one might be forgiven for thinking that liberal empire really means making the world safe for more American prosperity, "liberated" nations held in a soft-noose system of vassalage whereby they can trade with the Mother Nation, with its big hungry market of consumers, but only unevenly, so that debts accumulate faster than wealth to service them: the nation-state equivalent of the wage slave earning just enough to buy more than he can afford at the company store.

Paul Virilio calls the resulting condition endocolonization, that state wherein an imperial power begins to consume itself, eating up its own resources and citizens in a war set in motion theoretically to protect those very commodities. The machine of war is such that only total mobilization, which is to say eventual total self-consumption, is sufficient to the logic at hand. The powerful emblem of endocolonization might be the literal machine of the massive sports utility vehicle, growing larger by the season, which hurtles along American highways at seventy miles an hour—and, example after example, sports a yellow ribbon or red, white and blue decal enjoining support for the troops, fervent desires to bring the soldiers home from Iraq. These are material paradoxes, automotive contradictions! But perhaps even more effective, and necessary, to the process of endocolonization is the ongoing maintenance of a dream logic that continues to allow desire to flow in the concrete form of consumption. Happiness is itself colonized as part of the larger movement of colonization, made into a machine so complex—so spectral and multifarious—that it becomes almost impossible to decode its rebuses and condensations.

As analysts—which is to say, as members of the reality-based community—we must of course, with full awareness of our tricky position and various troubling susceptibilities, continue to try. That is our own narrative of happiness, our own form of personal identity. We wish to side with Lisa, perhaps, but we must also remember that we are, like it or not, the sons and daughters of Homer.

Notes

1. I used this story before, in the Introduction to *Practical Judgments* (University of Toronto, 2001). There it illustrated some dilemmas of intellectualism. I reprise it here to make the salient related point about the relationship between being "intellectual" and being "happy." In public talks I like to illustrate the story with the appearance of Pez dispensers featuring the heads of Homer and Lisa, respectively. Pez dispensers are small toys that produce a candy when the head is pressed back, one after the other, as in a cartridge. The promise of the Pez dispenser is the promise of the happiness-machine: that there is *always one more candy*.

2. The term happiness delinquent was first used, to my knowledge, by Aernoud Witteveen, and I borrow it here with his permission.

3. I pursued line of thought further in an essay on the American Dream called "The American Gigantic," *The Walrus* (June 2006), pp. 64–72; also, with respect to technology and ambition, in *Nearest Thing to Heaven: The Empire State Building and American Dreams* (Yale, 2006).

4. *Eudaimonia* is the word Aristotle employs in the *Nicomachean Ethics* (and elsewhere) to describe the flourishing life that is proper to humankind. *Eudaimonia* may be translated as happiness but, in so doing, we lose the connotation of a full and well-lived life—one of social commitment as well as personal satisfaction—that is our proper task. Eudaimonistic conceptions of happiness therefore contrast with any kind of merely hedonistic (i.e., pleasure-based) or psychological (i.e., desire-based) notion of happiness.

    Pleonexia, meanwhile, is the specific vice associated with the general economy of desire: the wish for more, the more one has. There is no adequate English translation, but the phenomenon is clear enough in everyday consumer culture. Satisfaction of desire is not satisfaction, because it leads to further desires, not a laying to rest of desire. Plato distinguishes between appetites, which are first-order desires, and reasons, which can be considered second-order desires: desires concerning desires. Example: I want the ice cream, but do not want to want it. If my will is strong enough, it combines with second-order desire to control appetite; this will-and-reasoned control of appetite is one essential structure of Plato's tripartite soul as seen, for example in the *Republic's* goal of psychic harmony.

    I attempted to defend a version of this eudaimonistic conception of happiness in *Better Living* (Viking, 1998), using the contemporary culture of "machined" happiness as the consistent counter-example. The limits of this virtue-ethics critique of culture are acknowledge in a later work, *The World We Want* (Viking, 2000). The present essay is a sort of meta-commentary on both earlier discussions.

5. These critical paradoxes are discussed at greater length in "Representations of the Intellectual in Everyday Life," in *Practical Judgments*.

6. Greg Grandin, "The Right Quagmire: Searching History for an Imperial Alibi," *Harper's Magazine* (December 2004), pp. 89–93.

13. Let's Ask Again: Is Law Like Literature?

i. The Problem

Many recent debates about interpretation of the law, familiar to students of legal theory, are determined by a rather simple question—the one I take as my title here—which has, surprisingly, received little *explicit* attention. These debates are vexed and complex, and have been exacerbated by the personalities of some participants and the professional jealousy aroused by real or imagined transgressions of disciplinary boundaries. More seriously, the recent entry—or, as some would have it, the infiltration—of contemporary literary and interpretive theory into the realm of law has vastly complicated the issues. Those issues include: divining the precise role of intention in legal documents, especially the United States Constitution; considering the relevance or redeemability of claims to truth and objectivity in legal interpretation; deciding the law's epistemological and moral status; and, ultimately, assessing the relevance of legal theory itself to the practice of law.

These questions were not absent from the minds of lawyers and legal scholars before this groundswell of theoretical interest.

The study of legal hermeneutics, including much abstract and subtle theorizing about textual indeterminacy, has a long and honorable history—one longer, arguably, than that enjoyed by the study of literary interpretation.[1] The "infiltration" problem is rather that the many controversies, innovations and philosophical questioning of one realm of study—contemporary literary theory—have translated, and even proliferated, when similar concerns were raised in the realm of law. The so-called law-and-literature movement and its attendant debates are the legacy of this proliferation. But reading the current debates shows that most can be organized around divergences and confusion concerning the analogy between law and literature. We still need to decide how similar, finally, are the concerns of legal and literary theory. Do they speak to subjects that are relevantly the same? In what way or ways is law really like literature?

That is the central question, and though it is indeed a rather simple one, we cannot pretend on the same score that it has a simple answer. Nor can we expect, for related reasons, a *definitive* answer. All available answers to the analogy question, including the one offered in this paper, are complicated by various dimensions of indeterminacy, disagreement and simple cognitive failure. That is, it may prove no easier to say—in a dispute-ending way— whether law is like literature than it is to say what art is, or what constitutes the good life, or whether a person is trustworthy. Indeed, one of the salutary things about asking the analogy question explicitly is that it shows us the limitations of our desire for a simple and definitive answer to the question. Having thus hinted at paradox, let me confirm the hint and offer a blunt version of a good answer to the analogy question: law is utterly like literature; it is utterly unlike literature; and, in the end, the question of analogy hardly matters.

The question hardly matters, yet it remains significant. Why? Because, ranging from those (like Ronald Dworkin) who think law very much like literature to those (like Richard Posner) who think it very much unlike, it is the question that drives a widely shared concern: to find a plausible general theory of legal interpretation. The motive to find such a theory derives from an even more general desire, namely the desire to distill *clear meaning* from legal texts. Such meaning can take many forms and there is a bewildering variety of opinions on what status it has; but in general people concerned with the question wish there to be *something like* the "valid" or "correct" or "true" or even "objective" meaning of the legal text.

Just what that something is, and how much like "valid" or "correct" or "true" it needs to be, are questions that take us into the heart of recent law-and-literature controversies. What we will find, in exploring those controversies, is that a general theory of interpretation is indeed available, a theory that is both interesting and useful in understanding the law's status. But whether, in addition, such a theory secures "true" meaning, or is practically useful in guiding the practices of legal interpretation, are distinct questions, and I will take them up only in the final section.

To get to that point, I will proceed as follows. The next section assesses several controversies that have become familiar in recent debates over legal interpretation, in particular the set of allegedly all-or-nothing choices that seem to define the theoretical discussions of law. These debates clarify the stakes in the analogy question. Next I examine, in sharper focus, various versions, pro and con, of the analogy argument: the claim that there is (or is not) a relevant similarity between law and literature. My claim here will be the fact that the question has, for the most part, remained inexplicit; and in the rare instances in which it has been asked explicitly, the answer has been clouded by what the writer imagines "the other side" to be saying. In the third section I attempt to sketch the outlines of a superior general theory of interpretation, but also to suggest its limitations. These limitations lead us back to the fundamental questions, broached in the fourth section, that are ever in the background of this discussion: Can truth ever be secured in interpretation? Does interpretive theory represent the only way to secure it?

ii. The Forks of Legal Interpretation

Students of interpretation theory in law are familiar with the experience of being asked to make a series of *choices* as they consider the question of what a legal text means. Each of the choices comes with a related label, and writers in the field invite readers, in effect, to pledge their allegiance: positivist or nonpositivist; interpretivist or noninterpretivist; intentionalist or formalist; originalist or contextualist; determinist or indeterminist; objectivist or perspectivist; foundationalist or pragmatist. To add to the confusion, and the reader's sense of being put-upon, these choices frequently overlap and seep into one another. Is being a positivist the same as being an intrepretivist? Can a pragmatist be an originalist? Disputes over entailment are also endemic: when is an originalist also an intentionalist? Always? Never? Sometimes?

Supporters of the various parties, who very much want the reader to choose, may elevate the stakes to make the choices starker. If you are not an objectivist or a foundationalist, they might say, chaos will be loosed upon the law. Nietzschean nihilism (or skepticism, or indeterminacy, or quietism) will reign.[2] Society will crumble. If, on the other hand, you are not (say) a contextualist, you risk supporting the tyranny of reason, the chilly determinacy of the dominant worldview, the devastation of empire and capital, or simply fascism. The tropes of writing about legal interpretation often reduce to two: the fork and the specter. The fork demands that one choose this path or the other; the specter is the vision of disastrous consequence, fear of which is supposed to ensure we make the right choice.

The stakes are rarely as serious as the specters would suggest, and it is tempting to agree with Stanley Fish that the choices, and the labels, are of mainly rhetorical and political import.[3] But we should resist taking Fish's next step, which he does not bother to distinguish from the first, namely that the theoretical consideration of these questions *has no bearing* on the practices of legal interpretation. How we pledge ourselves—what we understand ourselves to be doing when we engage in textual interpretation—

will affect both the kinds of interpretation we produce and (a distinct but closely related issue) what status we take those interpretations to have. Indeed, Fish's kind of reductionism, which sees most of these fraught debates as really nonexistent, has the unfortunate effect of leaving everything as it is and reducing theoretical reflection to no more than a pleasant parlor game.

That he would not regard that effect as unfortunate, indeed that he would not regard it as an effect, is consistent with Fish's urge—one he holds in common with many other sophisticated thinkers, usually (though not always) influenced by Wittgenstein— to cure us of certain theoretical desires. These include the desire to draw distinctions and to force choices in an effort to say how things really are in the world. That this set of desires, which can go by the shorthand name of "philosophy," has exerted this hold on us is undeniable; that Fish's practice-based account of legal interpretation has much to recommend it is also true to say.[4] Yet ultimately his efforts at intellectual therapy, the attempt to get us, as Wittgenstein put it, to stop scratching where it does not itch, in effect simply leads to one more fork in the legal theory road: theorist or therapist.

Before assessing *that* fork, and giving a suggestion for how we can detour around it, I will briefly examine the most influential of the other forks. Though there are many complexities in the debate surrounding these choices, I hope to provide enough detail to clarify the stakes in the central question of analogy between law and literature. I hope also to avoid exposure to another argumentative trope common in the literature. That is the one played out in reply to someone who attempts to "overcome" certain canonical distinctions. Here the common charge is that by refusing to take the fork seriously one has shown oneself to be someone who wants to have his cake and eat it too. The fork is reinstated as a choice between "thinking clearly"—that is, thinking dichotomously— and not. Yet the charge fails to hit the mark; although there are indeed choices to be made in interpretive theory, they rarely involve the all-or-nothing propositions suggested by the forks.

The two most influential forks posed for the practice of interpretation—as opposed to forks concerning the status of interpretations, or the status of the law itself—arise out of different scholarly
contexts. The interpretivism/noninterpretivism debate is a legacy of
legal debate, while the intentionalism/formalist debate is a direct
inheritance from literary criticism, especially the American criticism that was influential during the middle part of the last century.
(That is, the so-called New Criticism, which held sway when literature was still thought to be a subject of criticism, and the discipline
called "literary theory" did not yet exist on this continent.) Cynical
observers, reflecting on the origin of these debates, have found it
amusing that lawyers found themselves able to advance a theory of
interpretation that denies the value of interpretation as most of us
understand it—and to call that theory, perversely, interpretivism.

In general terms, interpretivism is the view that adjudication
is a matter of reading a legal text (a statute, a founding document
like the U.S. Constitution, or even a body of precedent) and rendering a decision that tries to express simply "what the law says."
According to this view, judges "should confine themselves to
enforcing norms that are stated or clearly implicit in the written
Constitution."[5] In the judgment of Mark Tushnet, interpretivism
is one of "[t]he two leading constitutional theories" in contemporary legal circles.[6] And indeed it has a straightforward appeal:
what else could adjudication do but say what the law says? But the
real thrust of interpretivism is that "statements" or "clear implications" in legal texts are in practice limited to a very small number
of noncontroversial (and for that read "nonpolitical") clauses and
features of legal writing. Thus, in practice, as Owen Fiss remarks,
interpretivism is really a kind of legal determinism: it draws a (usually undefended) distinction between the controversial and the
noncontroversial, and purports to speak only of the latter, and to
do so moreover "in plain terms." Fiss is correct to say that this distinction is itself a controversial interpretive property, and that
interpretivism of this sort is necessarily committed to a pre-reflective
view of what the law is, hence is deterministic.[7]

Some commentators, attacking the determinism of interpretivist stances, have gone so far as to argue that even apparently uncontroversial clauses—such as the Constitution's Article II enjoinder that the president should be at least thirty-five years of age—are themselves open to interpretation. That he or she should "have the maturity and station in life of an average thirty-five-year-old" is, for example, one possible interpretation suggested by this clause. Posner is the most vocal of interpretivist-style critics of this interpretation. The interpretation is implausible, he says, because Article II is meant to be merely an arbitrary cutoff. But this "merely" is charged: Posner will not be bothered to ask both what the clause says and what it means—that is, he won't interpret it as well as read it.[8] We can agree that the limit is simply an arbitrary and fixed cutoff (we're not asking for exemptions for some exceptionally mature thirty-year-olds) *and* argue that its meaning is discerned only in some account of maturity and resources. But strict interpretivism shuts down *ex ante* this effort to secure meaning, leaving us, in this case, with a clause whose very arbitrariness, unless unpacked in interpretation, can appear simply authoritarian and prejudicial. Could it even be, in the jargon of our own day, "ageist"?

Interpretivism can also be considered a species of legal positivism, for it claims to treat the law as if it were an object of quasi-scientific study, something that will cough up its relevant truths when subject to the proper methods of impartial judicial investigation.[9] Two familiar slogans from legal theory clarify the specter that is thought to motivate the choice in favor of interpretivism. Interpretivists want a law that is found, not made; and they want a government of laws, not men. Noninterpretivists for their part have worries concerning the validity of interpretivist judicial decision-making, namely that interpretivists may misconstrue the law in their efforts to treat it as what Richard Rorty has called "a lump"—that is, as a preexisting, unconditioned something that lies, without any prior determination by human concerns, waiting to be examined.[10] In addition, by refusing to grapple with parts of the body of legal texts that are controversial, interpretivists in effect obviate the role of adjudication. We do not have judges just to provide interpretations of the apparently plain—even recognizing that plainness can be deceiving. Interpretivism is therefore an inaccurate picture both of the law and of judicial decision-making. Taken as a *normative* picture, it will skew judicial reading of the Constitution or other statutes and/or render the law irrelevant to changing social conditions.

The choice posed between interpretivism and noninterpretivism is really no choice at all. Lawyers will sometimes speak as if there were a genuine decision to be made about whether judicial decision-making could be interpretive, but in fact judges—like all readers—are interpreting all the time, whether they like it or not. From this point of view interpretivism is really just a rather strict and somewhat old-fashioned school of interpretation, which has the added deficiency of insufficient self-awareness. The notion of uncontroversial clauses and "plain speaking" are red herrings that, at best, obscure the contextual features of a practice that make some elements of a text less problematic than others, and, at worst, conceal a political agenda that is conservative in nature.[11] Moreover, as developments in philosophy of science make more and more investigative practices appear less positivistic, the appeal to standards of scientific "lump" examination will make less and less sense.[12] Owen Fiss, commenting on these matters in his influential paper "Objectivity and Interpretation," claims that interpretivism is no longer a serious choice for students of legal interpretation; yet he nevertheless organizes his opening comments around the issue of whether adjudication is indeed interpretation, suggesting the question (if not the choice) is still a live one.

This fork has a strong bearing on the analogy question because it may suggest, as Fiss puts it, the possibility of an "essential unity between law and the humanities."[13] The clue here is a proliferation of the notion of *text*, which Fiss says, correctly, is now applied to almost every aspect of life. Hermeneutics has long insisted on the essential similarity between texts in the usual sense, which is to say books and other written documents, and what are called text analogues. Text analogues may be spoken words, rituals, practices, nonverbal artworks or even a definable set of political or moral values. Indeed, the thrust of *philosophical* hermeneutics, especially as associated with Heidegger and Gadamer, is that all aspects of human life—what we may simply call "the meaningful"—are relevantly addressed as texts by a general interpretive theory. Overcoming the nonchoice concerning interpretivism and noninterpretivism, which has confused the issue with its narrow commitments concerning the noncontroversial, can free us to the possibility that all adjudication is indeed interpretation.[14] The relevant texts will be the statutes, defining documents and precedents of the legal practice to which we belong. The relevant question to ask of ourselves as interpreters will be not whether we are or are not interpreting, but rather what commitments we bring to the task of interpretation, and how defensible they are.

Fiss is right that adjudication is always interpretation. Whether this general statement actually confirms an essential unity between law and the humanities is, however, a separate question. Fiss moves too easily from one to the other, and he does so because like many legal theorists he has not paused to examine the analogy issue in detail. Because law and literature both involve generally accessible written texts, it is perhaps too easy to assume an analogy on the level of interpretive principle that is more difficult to establish than is generally assumed. The proliferation of texts and text analogues makes the question an easy one to elide, but we cannot allow it to remain so.

The intentionalism/formalism fork makes it clear why. Put crudely, this fork poses a choice between those who are willing to take authorial intention into account and those who claim not to be so willing. In legal theory it is closely related to the earlier fork because many, if not most, so-called interpretivists are strong proponents of intentionalism: they argue that the clearness of clear Constitutional statements (or clearly implicit messages) can be recovered only by examining the historical record and accounts of the Constitution's writing to discern, or anyway imagine, Framers' intent.[15] The nonintentionalist side of the choice, associated with certain well-worn positions in literary criticism (W. K. Wimsatt, Monroe Beardsley, Cleanth Brooks et al.), is called formalism because it suggests that the only relevant criteria of interpretation are those that inhere in the work itself: the work considered, in the language of these authors, as a kind of artifact, a "verbal icon" or indeed a "well wrought urn."[16]

Authorial intention is irrelevant to formalist critics because it cannot tell us anything about the success or failure of the work in terms of its formal perfection, its achievement of aesthetic goals concerning, say, coherence and uniformity of effect. Indeed, the notion of "recoverable intention" is thought by some to be a chimera—inaccessible, even imaginary, and only claimed when one has achieved a satisfactory interpretation on other grounds.[17] Literary critics committed to some form of intentionalism (like, say, E. D. Hirsch, Jr.) argue, by contrast, that no text can be fully understood without assessing the important issue of what its author intended it to mean.[18] For them the text is a kind of message, something that we could in principle ask the author to repeat or expand upon in line with what he meant to say. Reading the text, as a result, involves placing a written text in a context of those (usually counterfactually presumed or historically reconstructed) authorial intentions.[19] Formalists often reply, at this stage, that if authorial intentions have any bearing at all, they will be realized in the text itself and will not have to be sought in biographical or historical or otherwise extraneous information.

The remarkable persistence of this debate has overshadowed numerous commonalities between the two positions, positions that ultimately collapse into each other. As before, this is not so much a genuine choice as it is another fork in the rhetorical road. And once again, this fact has important consequences for the question of whether law is like literature.

A clue to the commonalities is provided by the unsatisfactory nature of extreme versions of the fork. There have recently been critics who felt no compunction in declaring the author—conceived as a locus of intention—dead, his or her texts no more (but, of course, no less) than nodes of textuality in a great linked chain of writing and reading. On the other side, certain interpreters of some texts—law texts perhaps among them—claim that formal or aesthetic criteria are entirely irrelevant to the meaningfulness of a message. The first position appears to destroy the really interesting fact about texts, namely that in them someone is trying to say something to someone else. And the second position appears to ignore that no text can be meaningful unless it follows *some* formal criteria, shared between author and reader, that combine to render the text readable.

The specters conjured up by the respective parties also differ, but they are united on another common theme, namely that the other side's interpretations are going to be subject to error and distortion, and hence loss of validity. Formalists think that opening the door to the evidence of intention will lead to impressionism, subjectivism and even relativism. At the same time, intentionalists, many of whom find their bogeymen in more contemporary literary criticism, think that taking close account of intention is the only way to halt a different form of impressionism and relativism, the kind threatened in "reader-response" criticism or (a favorite bugbear of the late 1980s) deconstruction.[20]

As with most of the specters, the danger posed by this "relativism" is overstated—a subject we will return to in the final section of this chapter.[21] For now, notice a third commonality that bears directly on our central question. Both formalists and intentionalists in literary criticism can find good reason to reject the law/literature analogy: formalists because the formal properties of law are not, allegedly, of the kind that bear on its interpretation; and intentionalists because the law poses far-reaching problems concerning the accurate reconstruction of the intentions held by numerous people in a complex process of negotiation and argument that makes for creation of legal documents. The debates concerning the intentions held by the Framers of the Constitution are from this second point of view central. Even if we prize intention in literary evaluation, can we ever say what those varied and dis-agreeing people intended, especially when combined with the usual problems of distance in time and culture and the profound difficulties in divining what vision of the future they held?

Since no single person could hold both these views, a more common version of rejecting the law/literature analogy is by using the intentionalist/formalist fork as a fulcrum. This is the course defended by Posner, who declares himself a formalist in matters lit-erary and an intentionalist in legal interpretation—incidentally adopting in each arena the more "conservative" of available choices. I will explore his position in more detail in a moment. We should notice first, though, that recent moves in the intentionalist/ formalist debate have actually sought to collapse the distinction— and from both sides. Fish no longer holds (if he ever did) a straightforward reader-response view, and has argued that we have no choice about taking intentions into account when we read texts, for they would make no sense considered from any point of view other than one that regards them as meaningful attempts to say something—in this sense we are all, like it or not, intentionalists.[22] And the strict intentionalist Hirsch, clarifying his position, has recently said that we have no choice but to assess interpretations in terms of our own responses, and *not* against an always deeply prob-lematic attempt fully to reconstruct what the author intended.[23]

These thinkers might see themselves as forcing the choice rather than collapsing it, but that is inaccurate. Fish and Hirsch doubtless disagree about much, but in these recent clarifications of their views they both appear to agree that interpretation is something we do with texts, and that intentions of the author are relevant in some sense to this enterprise. Once we admit intentions, of course, the question is no longer "formalist or intentionalist?" but instead "which intentions, and why?" The notion of *relevant intention* thus acquires increasing importance, though perhaps with no attendant increase in clarity. (Why relevant? To whose ends? By what reckoning?) Nevertheless, this convergence suggests a more convincing general account of interpretation than any of those mooted by the confirmed intentionalists or formalists, an account that attempts to define and take account of context, including a context of intention. The precise boundaries of these contexts may prove difficult or even impossible to place, of course, and such a theory may provide no more than some rules of thumb. But it would bypass the limitations of the posed forks.

This theory will be sketched in section iii. A more immediate concern is what such a theory can say about the analogy argument. Can we have a theory that specifies relevant intentions for law and different ones for literature? Or will the similarities that remain in such a theory be so trivial—the shared words "text" and "interpretation," for example, but little more—that the many differences will obviate it? To appreciate the depth of these issues, and with the theoretical ground now cleared, we must now examine in more detail some influential versions of the analogy argument as it arises in legal theory.

iii. Analogies and Disanalogies

In his influential work "How Law Is Like Literature," Dworkin made one of the broadest possible appeals to the pro-analogy argument in the recent literature, an appeal that continues in his more systematic studies of judicial interpretation in *Law's Empire*.[24] The law, he said, was like a chain novel: successive interpreters of the law were like the composers of a novel whose discrete chapters are written, through time, by different authors.[25]

This image captured a sense shared by many legal theorists that the interpretation of law, which unlike literary criticism produces binding results that can alter the relevant canon, is a shared authorial enterprise and not a relationship of critics to (original) author. The novel is put in motion by a first author, and the first chapter may determine many aspects of the resulting novel by introducing characters or themes, but he or she has little control over what exactly happens thereafter. Subsequent authors feel themselves bound to honor the intentions of the previous author—but only up to a point, the point at which they decide how the novel can best go forward as a whole. New chapters have to be written in a manner that both preserves continuity with what already exists and advances the story in a positive way.[26]

On the basis of this analogy, Dworkin identified two *constraints* that operate on the efforts of subsequent authors in the chain novel, and, by extension, on the efforts of legal interpreters. First there is a notion of "fit," a constraint that preserves the coherence and consistency of the whole text. Fit works, in other words, as an anticipation of completeness—a sense, shared by all contributors, that the end product will be a complete whole and not an incoherent patchwork of unconnected stories. But since fit is not enough to guarantee that the text will be the best it can be, Dworkin adds a second constraint called "best light" or, sometimes, "the aesthetic hypothesis": the requirement that a given text be interpreted (and added to) so that it is *the best example possible* of the "form or genre to which it is taken to belong."[27]

The aesthetic hypothesis, the importance of genre, is clearly essential in literary criticism. We do not ordinarily assess a novel by Proust in terms of its ability to sustain nail-biting suspense to the last page, nor ask of a Shakespearean sonnet that it contain a rousing patriotic message. To do so is to make an elementary category mistake concerning genre that would lead our interpretations astray. I say "ordinarily" because in literary criticism—unlike in law—we may indeed sometimes assess a work this way, for the sheer interest of it, or for the possible new light it will throw on an old and much-interpreted text. (We might also do it in jest or for satirical purposes, thus using the gap between ordinary and extraordinary for other purposes.) We may want to call genre-bending interpretations mistaken, but in literary criticism the most we can typically say is that they fail to take account of the whole text or, more damning, that they are uninteresting.

Such counter-genre interpretations are anyway not common. Usually the aesthetic hypothesis operates (and it may even operate in a negative way in these unusual interpretations, as that which we are flouting). So in addition to asking whether a work is complete or coherent, we *will* also want to know whether it is good of its kind. Indeed, according to Dworkin this necessary interplay between fit and best light in effect constitutes a third constraint on the interpreter, namely that the balance between them be honored— a balance governed, in Dworkin's example, by W. V. O. Quine's[28] claim about a mutually adjusting "web of beliefs"; or, according to Georgia Warnke, by something like reflective equilibrium.[29] When the three constraints are put in play in interpretation, they have the ability to render a reading "constrained and valid, even if it cannot be considered uniquely correct."

But does the aesthetic hypothesis guide us in legal interpretation? Dworkin's claim is that it gives us something other kinds of legal theory do not, namely what he calls *integrity*. When we ask not only whether an interpretation fits, but also whether it makes the law the best it can be, we add a necessary dimension to adjudication: we make it accord with basic moral principles that, providing a fundamental normative structure, hold the law up. Without that structure the law has no legitimacy; and without integrity in adjudication, the law has no access to principle in its decisions. Law as integrity allows us to explain, then, why so-called checkerboard decisions should be ruled out, for they fail to take account of the moral status of persons and our convictions that that status is important. For example, a law that allowed abortions for women born in even years but prevented it for those born in odd years could be considered fair; it might even, more doubtfully, be politically satisfying to some affected groups. But it would lack integrity in Dworkin's sense because it would fail to join the law up to some shared moral principles that underlie the project of community, namely that rules concerning life and death should not be arbitrary the way lotteries or rote selections are.[30]

Warnke, for one, finds Dworkin's interpretive commitment initially encouraging. It suggests, she says, a new hermeneutic awareness among theorists of law. Yet Dworkin, the thinker widely held responsible for "the interpretive turn" in legal theory, lets the side down when it comes to discussing actual cases. As Warnke demonstrates, his discussions of *McLoughlin v. O'Brian* and *Brown v. Board of Education* both indicate that the hermeneutic commitment here is, in practice, quite small.[31]

In the first case, Mrs. McLoughlin sued Mr. O'Brian for emotional injuries suffered as a result of his car striking Mr. McLoughlin's car, killing one of their children and injuring three others and Mr. McLoughlin. Mrs. McLoughlin was informed of the accident two hours after it happened, and her emotional shock began when she visited the hospital and saw the condition of her family.[32] Hercules, the super-judge of Dworkin's thought experiment (who has no time constraints and ample intelligence), decides the case by choosing from a readymade list of interpretive options—i.e., competing thumbnail statements of what we think people have a right to in recovering for injuries. We choose one of these options, according to Dworkin, when we add in consideration of what public morality will bear. But selecting from this shopping list of choices is not interpretive adjudication, which is perforce unable to set choices into such neat categories. Law-as-integrity might indeed demand reference to public morality, but that would involve sensitive and contextual appreciation of conflicting demands. A successful interpretation is one that resolves these conflicts in a plausible, if not final, manner. We do not, in other words, successfully interpret *Moby-Dick* by choosing from among a range of competing (and reductive) options.

The appeal to public morality is not firm, either, in Dworkin's theory. In *Brown*, the well-known segregation case argued under the Constitution's equal protection clause, Hercules couldn't let public morality hold sway. Why? Because the Constitution deals with matters of fundamental importance, and public morality may be divided or confused on such an issue. The decision therefore turns on an even more problematic appeal to "basic political values," values that are presumed to be more apparent to judges than to ordinary citizens. But what is the source of such values, assuming they exist? Dworkin cannot retreat to an impoverished Framers' intent position to secure them, so he must refer—rather hopefully, it seems to me—to the glue of society and the importance of law's legitimacy. But this is to enter the realm of political theory.

Let me be clear: these may be valid interpretations of the cases. But there is nothing hermeneutic about deciding them in these ways, and the chain novel criteria of fit and best light seem no longer much in evidence. Warnke concludes, correctly, that Dworkin has here sacrificed the most valuable aspect of an interpretive theory, namely its ability to educate both interpreter and his or her community, not merely recapitulate the existing community norms. Perhaps even more obviously, there is no explicit attention to an analogy argument here. The aesthetic hypothesis, when applied to law, is no longer aesthetic in any meaningful sense: the sense of "best" we appeal to in making the law the "best it can be" concerns standards of public morality or political value, and it is at the least unclear how these standards are related to the kind of aesthetic criteria that would govern a literary judgment. Since the point of asking the analogy question is that law is not usefully thought of, even trivially, as just another genre beside the romance or the epic, the pro-analogy position has not been sufficiently defended by the thinker many consider its foremost proponent.[33]

These drawbacks may not be the most obvious. For critics who simply see too much making and not enough finding in Dworkin's theory, the image of the chain novel is vastly overstated, and Dworkin's interpretive constraints dangerously misleading. Consider: a chain novel has what Jessica Lane calls "a thrust toward closure," something the law by definition has not.[34] There is also some measure of agreement in literary criticism about the formal values associated with a given genre. Although this agreement is often overstated by outsiders, it is clear that the prospects of agreement on the formal values governing legal interpretation—the values of public morality—are much worse. It is not even certain that there exists genuine commensurability between text and reader in this kind of interpretation (hence the interminable disputes about Framers' intent). In short, Lane argues, Dworkin's version of the analogy argument must fail: law

and literature have different needs, impulses, associated practices and communities.

Perhaps the most important of these differences concerns the
relative power of literary and legal interpretations. Because of the
social practices and structures of the law, its interpretations are
demonstrably binding in a way barred to a literary critic. As Fiss
says: "There can be many schools of literary interpretation, but ...
in legal interpretation there is only one school and attendance is
mandatory. All judges define themselves as members of this school
and must do so in order to exercise the prerogatives of their
office." More bluntly, "even if the rule of law fails to persuade, it
can coerce."[35] And this recourse to coercion, though it says nothing in itself about the correctness of an interpretation, does ensure
the binding quality of it. Fish, emphasizing the presence of interpretive communities, attempts to argue that there are appeals to
finality and authority in literary interpretation, too, and he is
right. It is also the case that defenders of the disanalogy tend to
overstate both the uniformity of consensus in law and the lack of
consensus in literary interpretation. Yet despite all this shading,
there remains a clear difference. In law, an interpretation can be
backed by state power—and so, if there is not a single right
answer, there is at least a single answer.[36]

It is because those two things are distinct, however, that objections of the kind that worry Fiss are able to get a foothold in legal
theory. If an interpretation could be binding but not correct, is the
door not open to "political realist" theories of law that see it as the
mere expression of political power? Fiss himself drives a wedge
between the binding character of certain judicial decisions and
their correctness. *Plessy v. Ferguson* and *Brown v. Board of
Education* are both, in his view, "objective" in that they were
arrived at under the practice-sanctioned constraints—or "disciplining rules"—of legal interpretation. Nevertheless only *Brown* is
correct and it, in effect, overturned *Plessy*. According to Fiss, *Plessy*
could be incorrect for a variety of interpretive, or internal, reasons: the judges may have failed to understand the authoritative

rules correctly, or misapplied them. But the decision may also be incorrect, Fiss says, in terms of external reasons, i.e. moral, religious or political reasons not strictly related to law. But Fiss never satisfactorily clarifies the relation between these realms, or the issue of how the second kind of reason can be built into the "objective" disciplining rules of legal interpretation.

What does it mean, after all, to both follow a rule and misapply it? Or to follow it even while misunderstanding it? Fish's main objection to the Fiss account is that this notion of disciplining rules, supposed by Fiss to secure objectivity (and therefore ward off the specter of nihilism), is itself incoherent, and the language of objectivity is simply unhelpful.[37] Fish's notion of "doing what comes naturally," Wittgensteinian in inspiration, is that there simply exist practices of various kinds, including the one we call legal interpretation, and that these practices carry on perfectly well in terms (at some level) of our various needs and interests. An exhaustive set of rules for a practice is a logical impossibility, and any set of formal rules—which would really be guidelines or rules of thumb—can only ever be articulated by abstracting out of a practice that already works and with which we are already familiar: that is, a practice about which we have a high degree of "tacit knowledge."

Game analogies are popular in making this kind of point, in the manner of Wittgenstein's *Philosophical Investigations*.[38] The rules of chess are not the game of chess, and memorizing the rules will not make me a good player—indeed may not make me a player at all, unless we understand as well some of the "unspoken" aims and guidelines of chess. Or consider the game of baseball: as coaches we might give a rookie pitcher the excellent advice to "throw strikes."[39] But as a rule to constrain his conduct on the mound, this will prove worse than useless. The simplest strike is a fastball through the zone, and the rookie pitcher, following our rule, serves up a succession of heaters that get rocked by quick-swinging hitters. Following the rule, he is nevertheless not playing the game, or anyway not "really" playing it. The issue here is not only that he had to know already what a strike is, and how it fits into the game. He must also know some of the subtle and deceptive ways to get strikes—often the only way to get a strike is to throw the ball outside the strike zone. He must further understand crucial exceptions and the situations that call for them: the pitchout, the intentional walk, the retaliatory beanball. The rule does not constrain anything; it is useless as a rule—too general, uninformative and misleading.

Fish's argument, then, is valuable not as a statement in favor of political interpretation, or as a manifesto of legal nihilism (or realism), but as a reminder that *specifying* rules of interpretation is a mug's game. By calling attention to the degree of practice-specific knowledge operative in interpretation, he also manages to challenge the disanalogy Fiss was keen to maintain. The difference in law and literature is not that there are objective interpretations in one and not the other; or that there is an available notion of correctness in one and not the other. Fish even challenges the widespread notion that literary interpretation is not binding or authoritative, and does so consistently by drawing attention to institutional features of the practice that govern such interpretations: publication record, personal reputation, explicit hierarchies of universities and journals and presses. That there is one answer in law does not mean that it is the right answer; and that there is no right answer in literary criticism does not mean that there is no answer. In short, it is not nihilistic to claim that all meaning is practice-based. The theoretical task is to show how that meaning is generated, and which features among the many possible ones practitioners consider relevant.

This sort of claim is anathema to Posner's strict division of law and literature, and his related worries about a creeping contagion of skepticism in law. Indeed, it appears—in Fiss and Posner anyway—that motivation to advance a disanalogy argument is provided by the largest specter of them all, the destruction of "objective" meaning. Hence Posner's two-step theoretical commitment, to be what he calls a New Critic (or formalist) in literature and what he calls an intentionalist (which may in fact be a kind of originalism) in law. The division is predicated on a sense that the criteria of meaning or success diverge in literature and law, and Posner is distinguished as one of the few thinkers who devote explicit attention to the question of analogy.

Literature, he says, is governed by values of aesthetic pleasure, while law is governed by values of truth. A legal text is like a message, something that in principle we can ask to have repeated. Like a command or a communication, it is not suggestive, ironic, ambiguous, multifaceted or multileveled—all things we might want, or even demand, of a literary text. It has a single meaning, and we can only discern that meaning by attending to the intentions of its authors. Legal interpretation is akin to asking of an indistinct or distant interlocutor, "How do you mean?" Hence Posner's reductive position: "At the level of message most works of literature are clear," he says, inaccurately; "what makes them unclear is that we are not interested in staying at that level. But the message level is the only interesting level of a statutory or constitutional text. That is why the Peller-Tushnet interpretation of the age-35 provision in the Constitution seems obtuse rather than ingenious."[40]

This view has an attractive commonsense feel, but it is misleading. As mentioned, the difference between straightforward and ambiguous texts does not lie in features of the texts themselves, but rather in features of the contexts in which the texts are advanced and understood. The crucial difference between law and literature may lie precisely in this: not that their relevant central texts are metaphysically different, but rather that their contextual practices are constrained in different ways. It is precisely because *we* desire stability and finality in legal interpretation that we insist on single answers to questions of interpretation; by the same token, desiring novelty and innovation in literary criticism, we prize new and plural answers to the question of what a given text means. Feeling the stability of legal interpretation threatened, a Posnerian might balk at the very presence of interpretation theory in the realm of law. These interventions from literary theory seem to represent, after all, a challenge to the law's status as binding. But that status resides not in the texts of law, but rather in the practices of using those texts, and no general theory of interpretation has the power to put that entire practice into question.[41] Yet this, after all, is what worries Posner and Fiss about the rise of deconstruction in literary theory and the related—if it is related—rise of critical legal studies in law. The danger is overstated. Such "academic" disputes do not overturn practices of themselves. Deconstruction no more undermined the simple act of reading a book on the beach than Critical Legal Studies has undermined the myriad acts of judges and lawyers.

Still, there is a challenge here, and to be too sanguine about the ineffectiveness of theory is to collapse into Fish-like reductionism. Legal theorists worry about the challenge of skeptical theories of interpretation because it matters a good deal whether their practice is stable and in good working order. Nobody's life would be lost if the practice of literary criticism were suddenly to collapse; but a collapse of the system of legal interpretation, including especially Constitutional interpretation, could easily wreak social havoc. Defection from the republic of letters does not compare in seriousness with possible defections from the republic if the law were shown to lack legitimacy. So it is crucial that a theory of legal interpretation take account of these practice-specific demands of law: its need for a final adjudicator, for a final answer, for stability and commonality, and so on. Literary interpretation has different needs, and theory must be equally sensitive to them. It follows that if practices diverge, then their products do too. What is denied here is a third claim—a claim usually assumed, and not defended, by writers on these issues—that divergent practice and divergent product are equal to divergent texts. If true, that claim might indeed defeat the prospect of a general theory of interpretation. But it is not true.

To get a clearer sense of this, consider the following tables of elements. The first expresses some relevant features of the practices of legal and literary interpretation, while the second expresses

some features of typical interpretations offered within those practices. In the practice table the terms are divergent answers to the
same implied questions; the second table is merely an attempt to
articulate some relevant features of each kind of interpretation.

	LAW	LITERATURE
Practice	hierarchy of courts	parallel, multiple authorities
	binding precedent	novelty
	commonality	individuation
	stability	upheaval
	regulation	proliferation of possibilities
	coercion	persuasion
	truth?	pleasure?
	one (right?) answer	no (right?) answer
Interp.	utterance	art
	information	pleasure
	governance	complexity
	consistency	unity
	publicity	coherence
	authority	instruction
	legitimacy	thematic commitment
	constraint	subtlety

Notice that most of these features appear to support a disanalogy position. How could two such different practices, with
such different end products, be relevantly linked? "At a sufficiently high level of abstraction," says Posner, articulating a view shared
by many, "the interpretive tasks in the two fields may seem to
merge. But as soon as we get down to cases the commonality of

the legal and the literary inquiries disintegrates."[42] Apart from an implicit disregard of abstraction, a lawyer's forgivable preoccupation with cases, the failure of this statement is that the general theory of interpretation employed by Posner is too unsophisticated to give the commonality between law and literature its due. I suggested at the beginning that law would prove to be utterly unlike literature, and yet utterly like it. Here we see the first part of that apparently paradoxical position.

The trouble is that this is indeed only part of the story. By taking as his targets overstated pro-analogy arguments, like Sanford Levinson's crude statement about the multiplicity of Constitutions being comparable to the multiplicity of *Hamlet*s, Posner does the debate a disservice.[43] We are forced to an extreme where we must choose between saying that reading law is just like reading literature or nothing like reading it. Operating with an implicit but undefended standard of "aesthetic judgment"—a standard even less nuanced than Dworkin's pro-analogy version—Posner naturally rules law out of interpretive court. So committed before the fact to the disanalogy, it is impossible for him to canvass a theory of interpretation that would usefully include both legal and literary texts. I will now attempt to bolster the analogy argument with a more sympathetic version of such a theory.

iv. Talking Texts

A general interpretive theory allows us to assess, precisely and explicitly, the limits of the analogy between law and literature. Such a theory is best understood as a descriptive account of the presuppositions of interpretation—not rules in the prescriptive sense, impossible for reasons already mentioned, but a reconstruction of what goes on in attempts to say what a text means.[44] In the realm of law, this hermeneutic emphasis on practice-based presuppositions has the effect of moving us beyond what Alan Wolfe has called, in a felicitous phrase, "algorithmic justice."[45] But whether the raising of a practice to theoretical clarity has any normative significance, and thus recovers a prescription after all, is another question. I will address it in the final section of this chapter.

The model of interpretation most helpful in settling the analogy question is Gadamerian in origin. Its most obvious and immediate benefit is an ability to overcome some of the traditional disputes associated with the forks discussed in section i. The conversational features of Gadamer's model, the associated notions of horizon, horizon-fusion, and the third language, are the keys here. Instead of accepting a choice of emphasizing one side or other of the interpretive process, this model attempts to bring both into play, and thus to transcend the extremism of the debate between New Critics and reader-response theorists. It also has a more sophisticated account of the interpretive weight owing to authorial intent, suggesting that the text-in-context must be considered as itself the object of interpretation—an act with its own contextual limitations.[46] Finally, it makes room for reason and truth in interpretation without endorsing a strict or absolutist conception of transcendental justification.

The process of interpretation is represented here as contact between two spheres or horizons—mine as interpreter, and the text's (or text analogue's) as something separated from us in time or cultural distance. Interpretation involves, then, an attempt to "fuse" these two horizons by rendering the claims or import of the text into terms we can understand. But this model of horizon fusion is indeed only a *representation*, something that is often forgotten. In interpretation we do not perform the impossible feat of leaping beyond our own horizon; instead we find the text within it as something that needs to be understood—and so extend our horizon's boundaries in the act of understanding.[47] Understanding involves finding a place for this alien lump in our already existing sphere of meaning. Coming to understand an alien or distant text is not a static process. It calls for transformative effort, and so the reader-in-context does not remain unchanged by an encounter with the text-in-context. Gadamer's suggestion is that interpretation, like true translation, *creates a third language* and this notion captures the ability of the interpretive process to alter both reader and reading. The conversational nature of the process is demonstrated in interpretation's imperatives to honor what Dworkin called "fit"—the anticipation of completeness. A valid interpretation is one in which we, as sensitive interpreters, attempt to take account of as many elements of the text as possible. We do so by, among other things, playing parts off against whole, matching elements of the reading to other elements in a way that strives for some kind of unity.

But is this all that validity in interpretation consists in? Gadamer emphasizes, in well-known passages of his work, the role that prejudices or "forejudgments" play in interpretation and understanding. Indeed, the conversation between the text and us is impossible without them, according to Gadamer. We "talk to" the text in the sense of implicitly asking for support of a given reading, a reading that puts our forejudgments into play—meaning that we implicitly offer them up for critical assessment. The text "talks back" to us in the sense of providing internal evidence that a proposed reading is, in both senses, too partial—too limited, not complete enough and/or too overdetermined by our prejudices. But no act of interpretation can get off the ground without the presence of forejudgments, for they provide the background of assumptions and presumptions of meaningfulness that make understanding possible.

We could not even begin talking to the text, or take any of its evidence as replies to our interpretive enquiries, unless the forejudgments defining our horizon of concern were present. Hence Gadamer's celebrated dismantling of the Enlightenment "prejudice against prejudice," and hence, too, his taking on of Heidegger's notion of the hermeneutic circle.[48] Putting our prejudices into explicit contact with the text does not necessarily mean overdetermining the text, because this contact is itself transformative. We can only begin to understand on the basis of what we now believe; but coming to understand inevitably alters what we believe; and this in turn will affect our acts of understanding themselves.

The value of the process is expressed in the Heideggerian slogan, equally applicable to Gadamer, that the important thing is not to get out of the hermeneutic circle, but to get into it *in the right way*.

A third element, or feature, of Gadamer's descriptive account of interpretation is the central role played by *Wirkungsgeschichte*, or the history of effects, accumulated through time around a text. This history, sometimes misleadingly called tradition, is crucial both in an obvious sense (previous interpretations of a given text are relevant to my own attempts at understanding), but also in the sense that *Wirkungsgeschichte* is another way of expressing the context that determines my horizon of concern when approaching the text. It includes prejudices we might think of as specific to us but that are in fact legacies of a long history of community interaction and agreement. (This is one obvious sense in which we are determined by where we happen to stand.) It also includes interpretive legacies— theoretical or disciplinary commitments, practice- or community-specific norms and interests—that will guide our acts of understanding, and indeed prevent them from "going off the rails."

In this sense, the precise limits and contours of the reader-in-context are set by a history, or tradition, in which we find ourselves. Likewise for the text-in-context, which is determined both by a history of interpretive efforts and by the kinds of things we are able to see the text saying. I said that the Gadamerian picture overturned the intentionalist/formalist debate because it took account of authorial intention without sacrificing the authority of the text as object. The reason is that no text is separable from its context— but the precise limits of that context, the line separating relevant intention from irrelevant, cannot be placed in advance, theoretically. These limits only become obvious within the process of interpretation itself, and they are affected in large measure by the kinds of things we, as readers, are already prepared to see as meaningful.

What is the right way to get into the hermeneutic circle, then? It may be disappointing to find that there is no precise—no methodological—answer to this question. Gadamer mentions the need to cultivate sensitivity to the text, to approach it with "the right touch"—to abandon the imperatives of method and cultivate the imperatives of understanding and truth. Yet this is something one can only judge by entering, and becoming adept at, the practice of interpretation itself. There are no rules to guide us here; or, if there are rules, they are like the rules of a game that is much more complex than, and inexplicable solely in reference to, its rules. This inability to play the game except by entering the game, together with Gadamer's emphasis on *Wirkungsgeschichte*, have led some critics to view his interpretive model as excessively conservative. In a variation of the same charge, it has also been suggested that the theory is relativistic: it allows too many interpretive flowers to bloom, providing no definite standard of judgment. Because the circle described by Gadamer allows for no "transcendent" assessment of text or prejudice, this account of interpretation may indeed appear to leave everything as it is. The debate between Gadamer and Jürgen Habermas turns on numerous points focused around this central concern, that Gadamer's model does not provide any room for genuine critique and is therefore conservative in orientation.[49] Without critique, the charge goes, we are caught in an endlessly spinning round of interpretation that finds only what it set out to find, a quickly turning rotor that fails to engage a critical engine.

There are two options here. We may, as Gadamer did in work subsequent to *Truth and Method* (especially in replies to Habermas), emphasize the possibilities of "immanent critique" in this model. Because understanding is a transformative process, from which we never emerge unchanged, the very act of interpretation is itself critical: in the search for a shared language of understanding, it alters both text and reader. Immanent critique assesses acts of interpretation by playing them off against provisionally fixed elements of our horizon. We continue the critical process by assessing new aspects of our horizon against other elements, now themselves taken to be provisionally fixed. In this way we are able to be critical without performing the allegedly impossible feat of getting out of our horizon of concern—an act akin to jumping over our own shadows.

But that may seem insufficient. We may instead begin looking for a transcendent pivot by means of which genuinely critical assessments can be put into play. Habermas's work can be fairly described as an elaborate and detailed attempt to find a transcendental fulcrum not plagued by the difficulties made obvious in critiques of earlier attempts, especially those associated with thinkers in the Cartesian-Kantian tradition.[50] His answer is, like theirs, a characterization of what it means to be rational; unlike theirs, it is a characterization reconstructed from basic competencies, especially those of communication, and which therefore avoids the problems of ideality and formalism associated with, for example, the Kantian account.

According to Habermas, this reconstruction demonstrates that rational beings share a "transcendental-pragmatic" anticipation of agreement in communication. That is, when we make a claim, we are implicitly asking for (and expecting) all rational persons to agree with it. This implication, obvious for Habermas in normative as well as descriptive claims, points towards a shared commitment to what is sometimes called the unforced force of the better argument. The presuppositions of communication—that we all are making arguments, and are committed to be being moved by superior ones—are modeled by Habermas in the so-called ideal speech situation. Though our actual communication often fails to be rational, in that it does not issue in agreement, Habermas's claim is that the very act of communication commits us to the rational possibility that all disputes could be resolved by common reference to a superior argument. This possibility then acts as a "regulative ideal" that can guide and assess the rationality of our actual debates and the legitimacy of the norms secured in those debates.

What do Habermas's criticisms tell us about the Gadamerian model's relevance to legal interpretation and the analogy question?[51] Is immanent critique enough to deal with a conflict of interpretations? If it is not, is the model any use for legal interpretation, where conflict must be resolved? In other words, even though we might be inclined to agree that the general account is a useful description of interpretive acts *tout court*, if it fails to provide a decision procedure when competing and incompatible interpretations arise, disanalogy will ultimately outweigh analogy. The differences between Gadamer and Habermas are what move David Hoy to call the former an interpretivist and the latter a noninterpretivist, and make Warnke seek release from interpretive conflict in a Habermasian "rational" pivot.[52] Since legal interpretation cannot tolerate a plurality of interpretive options in the way literary criticism can, Habermas's criticisms and reforms may show the Gadamerian general theory to be just what Posner and Fiss suspected—a true but trivial account, emphasizing similarity on a highly abstract level, but one that breaks down similarity when it comes to cases. How fair is this point?

Conflict among interpretations has always been a source of worry for legal theorists because it seems to threaten the possibility of a unique result, a strong practice-based desideratum. Yet that is not the real problem. The real problem is that conflict threatens the justifiability of any actually generated unique result. We can easily imagine, and use, mechanisms that achieve unique results but that nevertheless fail to justify their answers as the single right one. So it is not simply that law cannot tolerate plurality in result; it cannot tolerate plurality in interpretation either, if that plurality casts aspersions on the legitimacy of results, however unique and enforceable they are. Hence the conflict that concerns us here is not so much conflict concerning rival judicial decisions, since that is in practice ruled out by, among other things, a determinate (if imperfect) decision procedure that includes the hierarchy of courts. The conflict in view really boils down to differing (descriptive) views of what judges are doing when they decide cases, and therefore what status those decisions have. Confusion enters when these descriptive conflicts are run together with normative theories concerning what the law should be, and what judges should be doing.

Dworkin's recent work provides an example of this. The background struggle in *Law's Empire* is between a form of legal positivism, characterized (or recast) as the interpretive theory of conventionalism, and Dworkin's own constructivist theory, law as integrity. Though his presentation of the positivist case may indeed be weak and skewed, as some commentators have suggested, this conflict provides a way to see an important distinction.[53] Dworkin argues that when judges disagree about law, the issue is not always one where shared rules have been differently applied to the same matter, or where shared tests have (or have not) been met in particular cases. The issue may be one concerning what law is. The disagreement may be, in other words, theoretical and not empirical. The positivist claim that all judicial arguments are empirical in nature, attempts simply to articulate the facts of law or previous decisions of legislatures and courts, fails to account for such nonfactual controversy concerning law. The possibility of nonfactual controversy—the idea that judges may disagree not over facts but over philosophical commitment—undermines traditional theories of law based on the idea that law could be described semantically, in terms of its truth conditions. It also provides the first point in favor of law as integrity, which allows for a plurality of interpretations as long as they are governed by the criteria, or constraints, discussed earlier.[54]

Yet, even if we accept Dworkin's motivation for the interpretive turn, even if we were to accept his view that interpretation is "constructive" rather than "conversational" (this choice is a false one—genuine interpretation is both),[55] we must still be disconcerted by the thought that disagreement remains a possibility. There is no reason to expect that two interpreters, each approaching the same material and each employing the constraints of law-as-integrity (or indeed of some other sensitive model), will always arrive at the same answer. And if they do not, how do we decide between the rival answers? It was at just this point, noticing that Gadamer's interpretive model could validate rival and incompatible interpretations, that Habermas was moved (as Rorty has put it) to "go transcendental and offer principles."[56] It is only because Habermas claims to find those principles in the structures of communication themselves that he is saved from an accusation of merely descending into positivism.

But it is also possible that Habermas makes his move too soon. Interpretations are never, after all, offered in an assessment vacuum, and we are rarely, if ever, faced with a choice between two (or more) interpretations that seem just as good as each other. (This was Warnke's point in challenging Dworkin's version of *O'Brian*.) Even in literary criticism, where plurality is arguably more desirable, there are strong personal and institutional pressures to find an interpretive "band" in which the acceptably interesting is separated off from the unacceptably uninteresting. This part of the interpretive process is not governed only by factors peculiar to the act of interpretation itself, but also by practice-based constraints that have to do, as always, with knowing how to play the game. The mistake often made in thinking about rival interpretations is to forget their embeddedness in such practices, which over time have developed ways not only of guiding interpretation but also of deciding between different interpretations.

In short, we give up on Gadamer's model too soon. Being in constructive conversation with the text is not something we do in isolation; it is something we do as members of a given community, whose shared goals and limitations govern our acts of interpretation as much as any goals or limitations we consider individual to us. Perhaps we give up on Dworkin's model too quickly as well: when we try to make the law the best it can be, we can only do that with reference to the moral and political values we think important to the community governed by the law. Since our sense of those values is an element of our interpretations, that sense too is available for assessment when members of the community try to decide whether our interpretations are any good. Awareness of contextual and institutional features of interpretation does not entail the absence of reason in our assessments. Any choice—as posed, for example, by *both* left-wing political realists like Roberto Unger *and* some extreme objectivists—between a miraculous harmony of reason and law and a cacophony of competing power claims is a false fork. We need not accept this account of the choices, or of the demand to choose.[57] The truth of an interpretation concerns both its "plain message" and its embeddedness within practices and institutions with determinate features (including ones of political and personal interest), for neither makes sense alone and we cannot recover one without the other.[58]

Of course, this practice-based view of interpretation does not provide us any definitive way to validate a given interpretation as objective or true, if those adjectives are taken to extend beyond the practice in question. Within the practice, however, many theoretical debates will concern precisely this question; the legacy of scholarship on law and literature is evidence of that. We have a practice called legal interpretation. What does it mean, and what status do its products enjoy? These questions exercise us because we want the practice to have a theoretical or rational sanction— we want it to be a legitimate practice, and not simply one with enormous but unjustified decision-making power. Yet, because there is another practice called scholarly debate, with its own set of ends and purposes (continuation high among them), there can be no *final* answer to these questions. As we will see in the next section, even those who claim not to be offering an answer cannot escape the round of statement and reply that marks the theoretical practice of philosophical debate.

It may be that the strongest benefit of seeing the limitations of any general interpretive account is a highlighting of the limitations of theory in general. There are those, like Hoy and arguably Gadamer himself, who want to save the account from false assessment. It provides "heuristic recommendations," in Hoy's phrase, but not rules.[59] Since it was never intended to be systematic, rule-governed, precise or normative, they argue, the account cannot satisfy demands that associate those features with a valid theory, either as necessary or as sufficient conditions. Thus it may succeed as an account, if not as a theory, once we surrender certain unrealistic aspirations presumably inherited from philosophy. But if the account is not a theory in this sense, how are we to explain (a) why it nevertheless appears to make cognitive claims, apparently redeemable via evidence or reflection, that interpretation has a certain and definite character; and (b) its associated normative weight, that a reading that fails to exhibit that character is in some sense invalid or incomplete?

These issues take us back to where we started, namely to the related questions of validity and status in interpretation. These questions were raised by asking the analogy question explicitly. Can they be solved by answering it equally explicitly?

v.   Theory v. Therapy

In an essay called "Rhetorical Hermeneutics," Steven Mailloux tells an affecting story of conflicting interpretations in a classroom situation. Noting the absurdity of a defense department interpretation of the 1958 *Space Act* ("We interpret the right to use space for peaceful purposes to include military uses of space to promote peace in the world"), he is dumbfounded to find a student disagreeing. As their conflict escalates, he finds to his chagrin that he possesses no knockdown way of defeating what he regards as a false interpretation. "It was at this point," he says, "that I felt the 'theoretical urge': the overwhelming desire for a hermeneutic account to which I could appeal to prove my student wrong. What I wanted was a general theory of interpretation that could supply rules outlawing my student's misreading."[60] It is probably obvious from the title of this essay that Mailloux thinks the theoretical urge is one that cannot be satisfied. His scheme for "rhetorical hermeneutics" is a nonfoundational pragmatist account that emphasizes persuasive ability within a given institutional setting, or context.

By acknowledging his desire Mailloux is, in common with other thinkers of recent vintage, in the business of trying to cure us of it. We must surrender the wish for a knockdown theory of interpretation, complete with explicit rules, that stops disagreement with finality. The posed choice, between theory and therapy, represents only the latest fork in contemporary interpretation theory. The attendant specters are easy to characterize. If we choose theory, we will skew our practices (and our understanding of those practices) as we worship before a false god; we will be blinded to the rhetorical, institutional and political elements of interpretation and so fail to see the most important influences on what we are doing. If we choose therapy, on the other hand, we will surrender any claim to interpretations that can be called valid, true, correct or objective; disagreement will never be overcome, and we will descend into a bottomless squabble of institutional forces. If we are very worried, we could go further and raise up the specters of nihilism and relativism, perhaps not bothering to define them, and just suggest that mere anarchy will be loosed upon the world. Everything will be as good as everything else, and so (what does not actually follow) nothing will mean anything anymore.

As before, the choices—and the consequences—are rarely so stark. The theory of interpretation discussed in section iii does not, apparently, have the knockdown status associated with the "theoretical urge." It has, moreover, no strict rules that attempt to guarantee validity and rule out misreading. On the contrary, it is a theory that emphasizes precisely the institutional, contextual and historical elements of interpretation, while insisting at the same time on the importance of the intentions and context of the work interpreted. It is a theory not in its generation of precise rules, but in its attempt to say what goes on in the practices of interpretation. Even Fiss, when he defends "disciplining rules" or "professional grammar" in interpretation, does not attempt to articulate them in detail. That is a matter for the practice itself. (To that extent, there is no conflict between Fiss and Fish: Fish does not deny that you can have rules of basketball; he just denies that you can have them, complete and before the fact, as defining the practice.) And from the other side, Fish's emphasis on institutional elements in interpretation—the fact of interpretive communities— is exactly *not* intended to make interpretation a bottomless pit of disagreement: some interpretations will be ruled out, as uninteresting or simply not sufficiently accomplished.

Both theorist and therapist, in other words, are attempting to say *what goes on* in interpretation. Both are making claims about the status of certain interpretive practices. If one were inclined to be reductive, one could say that the therapist is just another theorist: he or she intends claims about interpretation, including the claim that we cannot have a theory of interpretation to be cognitive. If they can be redeemed at all—that is, if the therapist can be right or wrong, accurate or inaccurate—then therapy is indeed theory in some basic sense.[61] Or, like Barbara Herrnstein Smith, one could distinguish theory from the narrower desires of "axiology": the precise rules and discussion-ending fixed points of human rationality that were, and are, supposed to be the only reliable guides of judgment.[62] The real conflict here, it seems, is a disagreement about what the law is, and whether legal theory has any bearing on the law. Therapists incline to the view that the law is "a surface play of forces," a social practice that has no grounding in metaphysical truth or objective essences. Theorists allegedly cling to the view that the law is in the business of securing objectively true answers to questions of contract, liability, rights and the like, answers that bind a society together in a strong way.

The choice is a false one because the positions are not so different from each other. But it is also false because it is possible for people to hold both positions, though perhaps not at exactly the same time. What posing the choice misses is the irony, in Rorty's sense, that we might be capable of exercising in this realm.[63] It also misses the ability to distinguish (again following Rorty) *causal explanation* of a practice from *justification* of it. As lawyers or judges, we will certainly argue for an interpretation's truth and will regard the decision reached by an appeal court as binding, even if we think it wrong. At the level of practice, in other words, we can all behave as realists about the law—just as, at the level of practice, we want our surgeons to treat us merely as bodies. In addition, at the level of a practice-specific theory—a theory called legal interpretation—we will attempt to say as clearly as possible what goes on in the acts of interpretation themselves. Only at the level of philosophy, which is to say the level of nonspecific and justificatory theorizing, will we attempt to say what is "really" going on in interpretation.

And it is this last level that creates the problems, for here it is possible to entertain alternative claims about status, including pragmatist or skeptical ones that appear to undermine the authority of the law. Posner, responding to Fish, says, "skepticism is an interesting and perhaps irrefutable philosophical stance, but, when pushed as far as Fish pushes it, one incapable of guiding action or interpretation."[64] Even if this is so, it misses the point. Fish's skepticism is not about guiding action or interpretation, and he is not worried (as Posner seems to think he should be) about "reconciling" his skepticism with the existing consensus in some interpretive communities. His skepticism concerns the *justification* of such consensus, not the fact of it, which he does not—and cannot—deny. Posner, by contrast, seems to think, like Fiss, that demonstrating the fact of legal consensus is tantamount to justifying it philosophically. Fish may be wrong about his skepticism, but he is thinking more clearly than the lawyers here.

When philosophizing, we have traditionally tried to join our accounts onto something called "the nature of reality" or "the world" or "the truth." When theorizing in the specific sense, we merely try to say as clearly as possible what is going on in a practice: we try to state the rules of the game, knowing that without the game there are no rules. And when practicing, we sometimes do our best only by, among other things, forgetting the kinds of doubt and uncertainty possible in the philosophical realm. Strong theorists—those who confuse specific theorizing with nonspecific theorizing—think that practices flow from theories, and therefore that they need to bolster the law's objective security philosophically. Strong therapists think by contrast that theories flow from practices, and therefore that they need to construct theories of indeterminacy, institutional forces and social pragmatism.

Once we break the strong connection between these realms,

however—once we see the obscuring force of philosophy—the fork disappears. We should be able to stop scratching where it does not itch. Of course, what we find is that even the best therapists, the ones who counsel leaving philosophy behind, cannot in fact leave it because their counsels are themselves philosophical. Self-contradiction may threaten; or else they are left remarking (like Rorty) that their general theoretical speaking is just another practice or (like Fish) that it is just something some lucky few of us get to do for a living—"nice work if you can get it." But the issue is not as pressing as it appears. Philosophy has always also been meta-philosophy: reflection on the nature of reality is perforce reflection on the possibility of such reflection. Pragmatists like Rorty and Fish, like other "end of philosophy" or "against theory" thinkers, are merely continuing a long and honorable tradition.

Does this mean, as Fish is keen to maintain, that theory simply doesn't matter? Fish's views on the issue have certainly contributed to a small but vocal antitheoretical pragmatism in some recent legal and literary theory.[65] And in the sense that no philosophical theory, however knockdown, will of itself alter a practice as complex as law, he is right. But in the sense that our philosophical commitments *will* alter how we view practices, and what status we grant the products of those practices, he is wrong. Pledging philosophical allegiance is not merely, as he suggests, of rhetorical importance. Among other questions, finding no sanction for thinking a legal interpretation objective in the strong sense will certainly alter how we view our imprisonment in the county jail, say, though it will not change the fact that we are prisoners. More than this, future acts of interpretation and lawmaking will certainly be shaped by philosophical views concerning what status is owing to the acts of interpreters and lawmakers. In short, philosophy, theory and practice are on discrete levels, and there is no straightforward or precise—no axiological—relation between them. But there is a relation, and discerning it is one of the things philosophy is for.

Where does this leave us with regard to the analogy question? As always, literature seems more tolerant of diversity and ambiguity here. Competing theories of literature do not seem to cause the same outrage among literary theorists as the same situation does among legal theorists. This may be a question of training, since many legal theorists are lawyers and not philosophers and so less inclined, possibly, to facing vertiginous epistemological possibilities. If we were to introduce nonprofessorial readers of literature into the theoretical debates, we would quickly see similar confusion, reaction and objection to antirealist or indeterminist theories. (Indeed, such a reaction was evident when a fad for theoretical innovation caused some elements of literary theory to trickle down into general reader consciousness.) And, in both realms, we can no more vouchsafe validity in advance than we can specify the rules of a complex game. To say that literary interpretation is more given to diversity than the legal kind is to say something about a difference in goal, but it does not get us very far because it does not say what counts as acceptable diversity in either realm. We are left wondering if it is a difference in degree or in kind, or indeed whether those are the only choices. We are left, in other words, with all the interesting questions still unanswered.

I suggested at the beginning that the answer to the analogy question would be that law is utterly like literature, utterly unlike it, and that it hardly matters. Law is utterly like literature because it consists of written texts that are subject to interpretation. To the extent that a general theory of interpretation is valid—a limited but very important extent—law and literature are two instances of the same human activity: divining meaning from written artifacts. But law is utterly unlike literature in that the practices governed by its texts have quite different goals. This may mean that the texts themselves have a different character, but that claim is often misstated. There is no metaphysical or essential difference at work here: law and literature are not different in any "deep" (which is to say, practice-independent) manner. Attempts to identify such a difference, and answers to the analogy question based on such a difference, just foster confusion. The issue hardly matters, finally, in that the general theory of interpretation—and theory generally—does not have a locked-in relationship with practices of interpretation. Theory can affect practice, and vice versa, but why and how much are questions that cannot be answered in advance and in general—that is, philosophically.

So we do not need to stifle the theoretical urge. By the same token, the therapeutic urge should be seen accurately, as itself an attempt to "get it right" with respect to practices. We are still philosophizing, like it or not, when we advance strong practice-based accounts of interpretation. The more self-aware our efforts become, however, the more disappointing they may appear. In this, we cannot except the present effort. It too leaves all the hard questions unanswered, postponed to the practices themselves, where they belong, and so leaves the strong theoretical urge unsatisfied. We cannot say what a valid literary interpretation will be. We cannot say what a valid legal one will be. And though we can say that their respective answers will be different, we cannot, beyond articulating some features of the practices, say just what that difference consists in. For there is no essence of the difference there to be discerned.

I also suggested at the beginning that this disappointment concerning the law-and-literature analogy would be itself instructive. Seeing our limits is a crucial aspect of seeing ourselves, and our practices, clearly. I can now say, in true philosophical fashion, that I told you so.

Notes

1.   Together with Biblical and philological scholarship, legal study provided the controversial texts that prompted the first study of general interpretive theory by German scholars in the early nineteenth century. See the Introduction and early selections in Kurt Mueller-Vollmer, ed., *The Hermeneutics Reader* (Continuum, 1990). James Farr demonstrates in his "The Americanization of Hermeneutics: Francis Leiber's Legal and Political Hermeneutics," (in Gregory Leyh, ed., *Legal Hermeneutics: History, Theory, and Practice* [California, 1992]), that the German style of theorizing about texts was alive early on this continent. Leiber, a Prussian immigrant to the United States, published the first edition of his work in 1837.

2. It is fascinating to note how often Nietzsche gets the blame for loosing nihilism upon the world, and ushering in the era of textual indeterminacy. See, for example, Sanford Levinson, "Law as Literature," in Sanford Levinson and Steven Mailloux, eds., *Interpreting Law and Literature: A Hermeneutic Reader* (Northwestern, 1988), pp. 155–73. An effective reply is made in the same volume by Richard Weisberg ("On the Use and Abuse of Nietzsche for Modern Constitutional Theory," pp. 181–92), who demonstrates the well-balanced character of Nietzsche's views on interpretation. Richard Posner, in *Law and Literature* (Harvard, 1988), makes a similar point—after an egregiously oversimplified reading of Nietzsche in ch. 3—when he notes (p. 219) that Nietzsche's views on textual coherence underwrite the conservative New Critical position in literary criticism. Randall Havas, in a forthcoming volume, makes a convincing case that for Nietzsche nihilism means *not* that there is no meaning in the world, but rather that all the meaning we have is *of human origin*.

3. Stanley Fish, "Play of Surfaces: Theory and the Law," in *Legal Hermeneutics*, pp. 297–316.

4. The extended defence of the practice-based account, including our practice-relative notions of truth and correctness, is contained in Fish, *Is There a Text in This Class?* (Harvard, 1980).

5. John Ely, *Democracy and Distrust* (Harvard, 1980), p. 1.

6. The other is the "neutral principles" view, which Tushnet suggests is equally misleading. See Mark Tushnet, "Following the Rules Laid Down: A Critique of Interpretivism and Neutral Principles," in Levinson and Mailloux, eds. *Interpreting Law and Literature*, p. 193. Tushnet's critique of these "programmatic" or "rule-driven" theories constitutes a negative argument in favor of a hermeneutical alternative. See pp. 199–203.

7. Owen Fiss, "Objectivity and Interpretation," *Stanford Law Review* 34 (1982); also, as reprinted in Levinson and Mailloux, eds. *Interpreting Law and Literature*, at p. 232.

8. See Mark Tushnet, "A Note on the Revival of Textualism in Constitutional Theory," *Southern California Law Review* 58 (1985) and Gary Peller, "The Metaphysics of American Law," *California Law Review* 73 (1985). Posner criticizes these two "critical legal studies" thinkers for their attempt to bring the "skepticism" of literary interpretation, especially deconstructionism, to statutory interpretation. See Posner, *Law and Literature*, pp. 219–220, 242.

9. It is not, for that reason, a legal *realist* position, since it remains committed

to interpreting the text of the law as what Fiss calls, misleadingly, "objective." Realist objections to this enterprise come in old and new forms: the political realism of the early twentieth century, and what Fiss calls the "nihilist" realism of the late twentieth century, both of which claim that judicial adjudication is about power, not objective legitimacy. (See "Objectivity and Interpretation," p. 230.) But, as I attempt to show in the final section of this paper, the issue poses another false choice. We can both recognize the role of politics in adjudication and preserve all the claims to legitimacy necessary to uphold the legal practices associated with it.

10. Richard Rorty, "Texts and Lumps," in *Objectivity, Relativism, and Truth* (Cambridge, 1991), pp. 78–92. The other essays in that volume continue the defence of Rorty's views on "anti-representationalism"—an account "which does not view knowledge as a matter of getting reality right, but rather as a matter of acquiring habits of action for coping with reality"— begun in Rorty, *Philosophy and the Mirror of Nature* (Princeton, 1979).

11. The issue is similar to the one conjured up when people claim that "politicization" of the law (or some other social practice, e.g., the academy) is illicit. Being honest about the political stakes of a practice is not tantamount to reducing it to plays of power—the usual specter in view here. On the contrary, refusing to acknowledge political elements of a practice capitulates to whatever politics are then dominant, and that in itself is a political act. "If someone agrees with us on the aims and uses of culture, we think him objective," the critic Robert Hughes notes; "if not, we accuse him of politicizing the debate." See his bracing essay, *Culture of Complaint: The Fraying of America* (Oxford, 1993), p. 60.

12. This point has become a commonplace with the expanding influence of Kuhnian philosophy of science, which emphasizes the practice-based elements of scientific investigation and lays to rest many of the axiological excesses of the Enlightenment view. See Thomas Kuhn's *The Structure of Scientific Revolutions* (Chicago, 1962). Despite important divergences, Kuhn's work has affinities, interesting for the present point, with the work of W. V. O. Quine and Donald Davidson. See especially Davidson's influential essay "On the Very Idea of a Conceptual Scheme," in John Rajchman and Cornel West, eds., *Post-Analytic Philosophy* (Columbia, 1985), pp. 129–44.

13. Fiss, "Objectivity and Interpretation," p. 230. Fiss's point seems to be that this unity, if real, would allow the application of humanistic techniques in the realm of law, and clarify the study of law as itself a kind of humanistic discipline.

14. But for a contrary view, from a perspective that is sympathetic to the critical legal studies movement, see Robin West, "Adjudication Is Not Interpretation: Some Reservations about the Law-as-Literature Movement," *Tennessee Law Review* 54 (1987).

15. Tushnet argues that the link between intention and interpretation can only be maintained by a commitment to "flawed historiographical methods," especially in viewing authorial intention as divorced from "social and conceptual context." See Tushnet, "Following the Rules Laid Down," p. 198 ff. We might be interested in distinguishing here between intentionalism *tout court* and originalism, the doctrine that interpretation is validated by reconstruction of (in this case) the Framers' original intentions. Some literary intentionalists, like E. D. Hirsch, are not originalists: in their view, this reconstruction is impossible and attempts at it lead to antiquarian fallacies. For a good discussion of the various options in legal interpretation, see Paul Brest, "The Misconceived Quest for the Original Understanding," in *Interpreting Law and Literature*, especially part 1. Terence Ball offers some novel anti-intentionalist arguments, showing that conceptual change makes genuine reconstruction impossible, in "Constitutional Interpretation and Conceptual Change," in *Legal Hermeneutics*, pp. 129–46.

16. Two essays by W. K. Wimsatt and Monroe C. Beardsley are considered the ground zero of formalist literary criticism. They are "The Intentional Fallacy" (1946) and "The Affective Fallacy" (1949), both included in Wimsatt's book *The Verbal Icon: Studies in the Meaning of Poetry* (Kentucky, 1954). They argue that authorial intentions and states of mind, as well as affective responses excited in the reader, are irrelevant to the objective judgment of aesthetic objects. Less uncompromising, but committed to the same goal, is Cleanth Brooks's close formalist reading of a collection of well-known poems in *The Well Wrought Urn: Studies in the Structure of Poetry* (Harcourt, 1947).

17. I thank Matthew Parfitt for sharpening this point. Formalists are not the only critics who reject intention as a criterion of assessment in interpretation, of course. (This is one reason the fork does not represent a genuine choice.)

18. E. D. Hirsch, Jr., *Validity in Interpretation* (Yale, 1967) and *The Aims of Interpretation* (Chicago, 1976) constitute the most sustained recent defence of an "intentionalist" position in literary interpretation. Hirsch makes a convincing case for the role of counterfactuals in usefully recovering intentions in "Counterfactuals in Interpretation," in

Interpreting Law and Literature, pp. 55–68. He suggests that "[i]nter-preters sometimes need to imagine what a text *would* mean if it were authored in the present." Without this awareness, the text is reduced to its present meaning in what he labels an *irresponsible* reading. But tak-ing this counterfactual awareness too seriously can lead to what Paul Brest calls "the misconceived quest for the original understanding," or the fallacies of antiquarianism or strict originalism (see Brest's essay of this name in the same volume). The problems of accurate historical reconstruction of intention have been much remarked; Hirsch's counter-factual account is free of most of them, and indeed closer to the model of interpretation I defend in part three of the present paper.

19. The "death of the author" claim, now much abused, is associated most closely with the French structuralist critic and philosopher Roland Barthes. See, e.g., Barthes, *Writing Degree Zero* (Hill & Wang, 1967), *Elements of Semiology* (Beacon, 1968), *New Critical Essays* (Hill & Wang, 1980), and *The Semiotic Challenge* (Farrar Straus, 1988). Barthes's cen-tral argument is that a text must be interpreted in terms only of its tex-tual functions, that is, wholly apart from truth values and from any con-cern with the irrelevant figure of the author. Echoes of this position are audible in deconstruction's emphasis on indeterminacy in textual meaning and intertextuality (i.e., the claim that "there is nothing out-side the text"). See infra. note 20, and, for a helpful discussion of decon-struction's relevance to legal interpretation, Michel Rosenfeld, "Deconstruction and Legal Interpretation: Conflict, Indeterminacy and the Temptation of the New Formalism," in Drucilla Cornel, Michel Rosenfeld and David Gray Carlson, eds., *Deconstruction and the Possibility of Justice* (Routledge, 1992), pp. 152–210.

20. The most influential of the new, more sophisticated literary theories in literary criticism were developed by Paul de Man in his *Blindness and Insight* (Minnesota, 1983), *Allegories of Reading* (Yale, 1979), *The Resistance to Theory* (Minnesota, 1986), and numerous accompanying articles. Deconstructionism was itself "begun" by the French philoso-pher Jacques Derrida, and perhaps its most representative texts are Derrida's collections *Of Grammatology* (Johns Hopkins, 1978) and *Margins of Philosophy*, Alan Bass, trans. (Harvester, 1982).

21. The main reason for this is that the worst consequences of the positions called "relativist" can only be generated by a prior (and unnecessary) commitment to what Barbara Herrnstein Smith calls "objectivist axiol-ogy": the strong view of objective truth sometimes associated with naive or commonsense realism. Her version of the relativism specter is a

mocking progression of dangers, sketched in *Contingencies of Value* (Harvard, 1988). It begins with charges of self-contradiction and fallacy, moves through "fatuous forebearance" and "Panglossism and status-qoism," and ends with "the breakdown of law and morality" and, therefore, "the Gulag, the Nazi death camps" (pp. 152–3). Her book's main point, shrewdly argued, is that noting the presence of contingency or variability in judgment—including interpretive judgment—does not lead to this gallery of horrors. It leads to better judgments.

22. Fish, "Play of Surfaces," p. 299.

23. Hirsch, "Counterfactuals in Interpretation," pp. 56–7.

24. Ronald Dworkin, "How Law is Like Literature," contained in *A Matter of Principle* (Harvard, 1985). This paper is a re-working of Dworkin's "Law as Interpretation," *Critical Inquiry* 9 (September 1982). See also his "On Interpretation and Objectivity," in *A Matter of Principle* and *Law's Empire* (Harvard, 1986).

25. Dworkin, "How Law is Like Literature," pp. 158–62.

26. An important ambiguity arises here, however, when we try to decide who the relevant authors are. Lawyers arguing cases, judges deciding them, legal theorists writing and teaching them, and legislators making new laws all seem to be possible candidates for authorhood in this sense. Dworkin focuses attention on judges, but even here we might want to ask, e.g., how judges at different levels of the court system relate their interpretations to one another and to the influential schools of interpretation. (I thank Todd Ducharme for clarifying this point.)

27. Dworkin, "How Law is Like Literature," pp. 149–54.

28. W. V. O. Quine, "Two Dogmas of Empiricism," in *From a Logical Point of View* (Harvard, 1953), and (with Joseph Ullian) *The Web of Belief* (Random House, 1978).

29. Georgia Warnke, "Legal Interpretation and Constraint," Chapter 4 of her *Justice and Interpretation* (MIT, 1993), p. 70.

30. For further discussion of Dworkin's integrity, see Denise Reaume, "Is Integrity a Virtue? Dworkin's Theory of Legal Obligation," *University of Toronto Law Journal*, 39: 380–409.

31. Warnke, "Legal Interpretation and Constraint," pp. 72–81.

32. The point of dispute in the case was the question of delay. The precedents, in which plaintiffs recovered damages for emotional injury, all involved shocks that happened at the scene and time of accidents.

33. Those who defend the broad continuity of text seem to me to underestimate this point: if law were just another genre (that is, of literature in the broad sense), it would not pose its special kind of interpretive difficulties. It is precisely because law comes wedded to social power, especially the "legitimate" use of force, that stopping at an identification of generic difference is not enough. Such a position leaves all the hard questions unasked.

34. Jessica Lane, "The Poetics of Legal Interpretation," in *Interpreting Law and Literature*, pp. 269–84, is an effective overview of Dworkin's recent work on legal interpretation. Lane is especially convincing in her demonstration that the superior rationality of the Hercules model (circa *Law's Empire*) is inconsistent with the chain-novel analogy developed in "How Law is Like Literature."

35. Fiss, "Objectivity and Interpretation," pp. 234–5.

36. Of course this may hold more in theory than in practice, where lower courts may depart from the "single answer" as a result of incompetence or interpretive differences. While, again in theory, such "errors" can be remedied through the appeal process, this often does not occur because of limitations on the resources of the parties, restricted access to competent counsel, and so on. (I thank Todd Ducharme for this point.)

37. Stanley Fish, "Fish v. Fiss," *Stanford Law Review* 36 (1984); reprinted in *Interpreting Law and Literature*, pp. 251–67.

38. Macmillan, 1953.

39. Bill Lee, the eccentric Boston Red Sox and Montreal Expos pitcher, reported in his memoirs that he once had a dream in which Tom Landry, then coach of the Dallas Cowboys football team, appeared and gave him just this imperative. My baseball example is clearly also derived from Fish's basketball example, where the given rule is "Always take the open shot."

40. Posner, *Law and Literature*, p. 242.

41. For a clear statement of the position that textual status is always conferred by contextual features of reading, see Walter Benn Michaels, "Against Formalism: Chickens and Rocks," in *Interpreting Law and Literature*, pp. 215–27.

42. Posner, *Law and Literature*, p. 261.

43. See Sanford Levinson, "Law as Literature," in *Interpreting Law and Literature*, p. 166. Levinson's disservice to the debate is to take interesting

notions—e.g., Rorty's distinction between strong and weak textualists; the literary theoretical claims about textual indeterminacy—and make them into a dogmatic position. So, for example, his argument that there is no uncontroversial set of public values does not entail (what he suggests) that there are no public values at all. Likewise, no determinate textual meaning is not equivalent to no meaning at all. Gerald Graff's reply to Levinson, "Keep off the Grass, Drop Dead, and Other Indeterminacies," in the same volume, makes the obvious point that *at the level of practice* the problem of meaning is no problem at all: our practical ability to do things with words is unimpaired by a failure to meet impossibly high standards of determinate meaning. I will have more to say on this point below.

44. Gadamer's magnum opus *Truth and Method*, Garrett Barden and John Cumming, trans. (Crossroad, 1975), is the basic text of this view. For a detailed treatment of its relevance for legal interpretation, including further citations, see David Couzens Hoy's excellent overview, "Interpreting the Law: Hermeneutical and Poststructuralist Perspectives," in *Interpreting Law and Literature*, pp. 319–38. See also Gerald L. Burns, "Law and Language: A Hermeneutics of the Legal Text," and Hoy's "Intentions and the Law: Defending Hermeneutics," both in *Legal Hermeneutics*.

45. Alan Wolfe, "Algorithmic Justice," in *Deconstruction and the Possibility of Justice*, pp. 361–86. But it is not enough, *pace* some critics (notably Terry Eagleton), to overturn law's status by drawing attention to an imagined desire for algorithm. Posner makes this point especially well, and uses it to bolster his objectivist position. What neither side of the choice makes clear is that, as I argue in section iii, we can still have validity without method.

46. Hoy, "Intentions and the Law," pp. 179–82. Gadamer does not believe that intention is recoverable as something *outside* the text, however. The emphasis on context—which is discerned by looking at other texts—means that we are never, in the celebrated phrase, outside the text. But that does not mean that the meaningfulness of communication, the intention to say something by means of words, is lost.

47. This point is surprisingly often mislaid, even by discerning commentators. See, e.g., Fish's chiding comments about Fred Dallmayr and E. D. Hirsch in "Play of Surfaces," p. 305.

48. Heidegger's discussion of the hermeneutic circle is at sections 31–33 of *Being and Time*, John Macquarrie and Edward Robinson, trans. (Harper and Row, 1962). The hermeneutic circle—where pre-understanding is

confirmed and/or modified by acts of understanding, and so necessary
for beginning the task of understanding—received earlier discussion in
nineteenth-century classics of hermeneutic theory, notably in the work
of Schleiermacher.

49. Habermas's specific objections begin with his review of *Truth and
Method* in *Zur Logic der Sozialwissenschaften* (Suhrkamp, 1970), where
he suggests that Gadamer's interpretive model is devoid of critical possibilities because it leaves no room for assessing deception and force. A
good English translation of the review is found in Brice Wacherthauser,
ed., *Hermeneutics and Modern Philosophy* (SUNY, 1986), together with
Gadamer's reply, "On the Scope and Function of Hermeneutic
Reflection." Habermas replied with several subsequent essays, the best of
which is "On Hermeneutics' Claim to Universality," a fusion of two early
papers published in the journal *Inquiry*. It can be found, together with
excerpts from *Truth and Method*, in Kurt Mueller-Vollmer, ed., *The
Hermeneutics Reader* (Continuum, 1990). Hoy's "Interpreting the Law"
provides a good overview of this debate.

50. Habermas's extensive work on this project began systematically with the
two-volume work *The Theory of Communicative Action* (Beacon,
1984–88) and continued, emphasizing its role in moral theory, with the
essays in *Moral Consciousness and Communicative Action* (MIT, 1990)
and *Justification and Application* (MIT, 1993).

51. Paul Ricoeur's interpretive theory, which goes beyond the Gadamer-
Habermas debate by, in effect, appropriating elements of each in a highly
original way, may represent a superior position to either. See, e.g., his
defence of "critical hermeneutics" in *Interpretation Theory* (Texas
Christian, 1976) and *The Conflict of Interpretations* (Northwestern, 1974).
Ricoeur attempts to reintegrate "method" with "truth" and thus build-
in a critical pivot for interpretation in the form of what he calls "the
dialectic of suspicion and recovery." For a short and accessible statement
of this program, see his "Hermeneutics and the Critique of Ideology," in
Hermeneutics and Modern Philosophy, pp. 300–339.

52. Hoy, "Interpreting the Law," p. 323; Georgia Warnke, "Habermas and the
Conflict of Interpretations," ch. 5 of her *Justice and Interpretation*.

53. See, for example, Brenda Baker's critical notice of *Law's Empire*,
"Empire-Building," *Dialogue* 32 (1993): 149–62.

54. I am following Baker's discussion in these points.

55. Notice that Dworkin's shying away from "conversational" models of

interpretation is motivated by a desire to avoid debates about discerning the intentions of temporally distant authors. His "constructive" model of interpretation concentrates on where I find myself, and whether I can construct an interpretive stance I feel comfortable ascribing to myself. But since intention need not be the problem Dworkin apparently thinks it is, and is not in practice excisable from a valid interpretation, there is no need to make this choice.

56. Rorty, "Pragmatism, Relativism, and Irrationalism," in *Consequences of Pragmatism* (Minnesota, 1982), p. 173.

57. Hoy makes this point in "Interpreting the Law." For an accessible treatment of Roberto Unger's views, especially his political realism about the law, see his *The Critical Legal Studies Movement* (Harvard, 1983). Views like Unger's, which argue that law is little more than a set of institutional power plays, find themselves sharing diagnostic (though not, of course, prescriptive) commitments with some right-wing political realists in the strong objectivist school.

58. To say this is, in some sense, to recapitulate Ricoeur's dialectic between suspicion and recovery: we note the pressures and limitations of institutions, not to shut down further discernment of meaning but precisely to make it possible. (I thank Matthew Parfitt for clarifying this point for me.)

59. Hoy, "Interpreting the Law," p. 325. Compare this view with Wacherthauser's notion that hermeneutics provides the following "rules of thumb" concerning valid interpretation: comprehensiveness; semantic depth; inclusivity; and teleological structure (i.e., anticipation of completeness). See his "Must We Be What We Say? Gadamer on Truth in the Human Sciences," in *Hermeneutics and Modern Philosophy*, pp. 219–41.

60. Steven Mailloux, "Rhetorical Hermeneutics," in *Interpreting Law and Literature*, p. 345. Another version of the "therapeutic" position is given by Steven Knapp and Walter Benn Michaels in their response to Hoy's hermeneutical position, "Intention, Identity, and the Constitution," in *Legal Hermeneutics*, pp. 187–99.

61. Hoy makes this point, that even therapists are theorists—though in some weaker sense than that for which they attack others. See his "Intentions and the Law," p. 173.

62. Smith, *Contingencies of Value*, especially ch. 4. Her claim is that certain Enlightenment tendencies, in particular those associated with Hume's

"natural standard of taste" and Kant's "pure judgment," have twisted subsequent philosophical reflection concerning judgment, leading to, among other things, a debilitating fact/value distinction. Another nuanced version of the middle position in the current fork is Stanley Rosen's *Hermeneutics as Politics* (Oxford, 1987), which criticizes Derridean deconstructionism by emphasizing the inevitable political and institutional features of interpretation.

63. Rorty's irony is the ability to be of two minds about a practice and its theoretical description. One version of this crucial distinction is thus that a pragmatist—favorite enemy of the objectivist—is not pragmatist about theory (in the practice-specific sense) but about philosophy: which is to say, his pragmatism is no threat to quantum physics, for example, but is a repudiation of certain philosophical attempts to hook quantum physics onto something called "the world" or "the nature of reality."

64. Posner, *Law and Literature*, pp. 263–4.

65. See, for example, W. J. T. Mitchell ed., *Against Theory: Literary Studies and the New Pragmatism*, (Chicago, 1985); also Steven Knapp and Walter Benn Michaels, "Against Theory 2: Hermeneutics and Deconstruction," *Critical Inquiry* 14 (1987): 49–68. Of course philosophical pragmatism is itself a theory, but one that undermines a certain kind of philosophical justification, and that is its central therapeutic claim.

14. The Theory Theory; or, The Fashion System Revisited

i. System

"Fashion must be beautiful first, and ugly afterwards," Jean Cocteau said. "Art must be ugly first, thus beautiful afterwards."

Is that right? Like a lot of what Cocteau said, it *sounds* right; but how much of that impression is because it is euphonious, deploying the obvious rhetorical device of parallelism? Euphony is beauty in sound and so, according to the logic of its own maxim, this artful remark is not art at all, just fashion. Cocteau himself can be faulted—indeed is faulted by some—for being too fashionable, which is to say overly conscious of, hence an unwitting slave to, mere fashion.

Is that fair? Surely not, because the sentiment, and more so the artist who uttered it, survive scrutiny. Consider *Diary of an Unknown, The Art of Cinema, Orphée, La belle et la bête.* Picasso. Édith Piaf. Cocteau's cleverness is never mere, and the wisdom of this observation, though it does not support the presumptive binary division of fashion and art, contains important grains of truth. Fashion by definition goes out of style, not least for the merely logical demand that to be in style implies the possibility, probably imminent, of being out of style. Art, by contrast, is understood to endure. *Ars longa vita brevis*, after all—or so we have often been told, in ways fashionable and unfashionable (prog-rock album, apothegm), by people in style and out of style (Hippocrates, The Nice). It might even be true—though the full original quotation speaks more to the difficulty of learning medicine in a lifetime than to anything about art. At the very least, art is meant to stretch existing boundaries, not conform to them. Hence its initial perceived ugliness, which is only judged so in a temporary fashion, because we cannot yet see, not having stretched with its stretchings, how beautiful it actually is.

Is that accurate? Some people, not just fashionable ones either, would distinguish violently between art and beauty, and suggest art need not, maybe need never, be beautiful. On the contrary, beauty is a trap for art. Others, just as violently, would distinguish between fashion and style, suggesting "true" or "authentic" style— the presentation of self as comfort in one's own skin, or intuitive grasp of what works/endures in personal beauty—are above, or beyond, mere fashion. This distinction between fashion and style, which tends swiftly to collapse on examination, is nevertheless a staple of all fashion magazines. That, and not their avowed "aspirational"—which is to say, envy-driven—status, is what makes them comprehensively self-contradictory and objectionable.

Neither beauty nor style is precisely the point this essay addresses, though the matter of *taste* as the arbiter of both is implicit. The precise issue is fashion, which must be understood, first, as not aesthetic at all but economic. Recall Roland Barthes's now canonical view of how the tropes of fashion function, in *Système de la mode*: "Calculating, industrial society is obliged to form consumers who do not calculate; if clothing's producers and consumers had the same consciousness, clothing would be bought (and produced) only at the very slow rate of its dilapidation."

Which is to say: the function of the fashion magazine, and of the system of which it is a frontline part, is to maintain the fiction, indeed to *erase its status as a fiction*, that the purveyors of fashion are dedicated to making women and men look beautiful. What the magazines are really doing is helping design houses sell clothing at absurdly inflated prices by constantly refreshing the demand for new clothes that must, per the system's demands, replace old ones.

The shorter the gap between old and new, the better the system functions, since demand is made almost constant. It follows that the notional ideal point of a fashion system is a piece of clothing that goes out of style, hence needs replacing, at the exact moment of sale, thus rendering demand both total and unfluctuating. Marxist economists like to point out that the genius of commodification is that it can assign exchange value to anything at all, including the flimsiest piece of sweatshop *shmatte* or, of course, nonmaterial things such as brands or position.

What this magic transformation gives with one hand it takes away with the other. Automobiles immediately depreciate 15 percent of their value just by being purchased, while many accountants depreciate miscellaneous small-ticket items (those less than five-hundred dollars, say) a full 100 percent at moment of sale. Like these, clothes paradoxically lose value precisely by being valued enough to be purchased. Fashion is, in this important sense, a form of thaumaturgic ritual, as spectral as divination or prayer. Commodification dovetails with neophilia to create the ideal form of capital market: one where the goods are beside the point.

It is not all sleight of hand. Value is a function of desire, and desire, short of death, must be forever renewed. Fashion depends, like much of life insofar as it is structured by desire, not on desire's *satisfaction* but on its *renewal*. The point is not, as it appears on the surface, to get what you want; it is to want what you will, as a result, then get. If desire were ever satisfied, demand would end. Given that the desires in question here—to appear beautiful, *au courant*, wealthy, tasteful, and sexually attractive all at once—are among the most powerful in human experience, the erotic charge running through the system is as close to absolute as civilization gets.

The purchased clothes cannot ever gain back the value they

have lost, can only forfeit value more or less quickly from the point of purchase. It thus falls to new clothes to act as the vehicles of renewed value. And yet, consumers cannot be counted on, just by their own untutored devices, to leach value from existing clothes, nor to renew value towards new clothes, as quickly as manufacturers would prefer. Thus the need for magazines as an essential part of the system. As Barthes points out, the text and images that form these glossy productions are never merely conveyors of information. They are structured so that their luxuriant appeal and breathless excitement exactly mirror both the coded messages manufacturers wish their clothes to bear *and* the attitude they hope to create in the consumer. If the system is functioning as it means to, in other words, the triangle will be equilaterally completed as a triumph of smooth social coding: clothes, prose and person will all be signatories of the same narrative covenant, acted out in ever-renewed exchanges.

Likewise, if the consumer were ever to defect from the implied code-contract, the system would break down as surely as if a sabot had been tossed into a power loom. Existing clothes would not lose value nearly as fast as before, since now value would be concentrated on use alone, with perhaps some idiosyncratic aesthetic sense lingering on a favored skirt or blouse. The slow pace of replacement would cause the spinning wheels of fashion-consciousness to spring loose of their mountings, and the witless admonitions, warnings, seductions and coaxings of the bright magazines would fall on ears of cloth, so to speak. The sullen pouts and beckoning smiles of the leggy mannequins dragooned into cultural servitude as proxies of permanent envy and dissatisfaction would subtly shift into rictuses of sour deception and cynicism. The glossy paper would fold and crumple beneath our fingers.

ii. Markets

Is that right? No, of course it isn't. But why not?

The problem is not merely the reductionism implicit in Barthes's analysis, though that is considerable. Barthes writes here as a structuralist semiotician, uncoding the messages of the magazines with the debunking methods shared by anthropologists and cultural critics alike. The idea, familiar now but novel at the time Barthes was writing, is to take the surface evidence of cultural production—the magazines, newspaper stories, advertisements, iconic images—and subject them to the close attention usually reserved for the magical rites and layered rituals of a foreign tribe. We alienate ourselves from cultural presuppositions in order to expose them as presuppositions, not nature. "The starting point of these reflections was usually a feeling of impatience at the sight of the 'naturalness' with which newspapers, art and common sense constantly dress up a reality which, even though it is the one we live in, is undoubtedly determined by history," Barthes wrote, introducing his celebrated collection of semio-cultural dismantlings, *Mythologies.* "I wanted to track down, in the decorative display of *what-goes-without-saying,* the ideological abuse which, in my view, is hidden there."

Note the language: the show of naturalness is not just magic, but *ideology.* The messages coded in culture are ones that maintain a system of thoughts, not just "natural" (or merely efficient) social relations. More precisely, the social relations themselves both act out and affirm the thoughts. They are not just any thoughts, though: the ideology is *abusive.* It structures a sense of what is beyond question, then obscures the fact of having done so, rendering the naturalization process itself so natural as to evade scrutiny. We all sign on to social givens precisely because we do not perceive that we have signed on, or that the givens are even given. The baseline aim of all ideology is to render itself so thoroughly a priori as to disappear from sight entirely. Resisting this tendency, bringing the taken-for-granted into sight for critical analysis if not outright rejection, is what critical thinking is all about.

There is much to value in this dedicated antinaturalism, even if we fear to subscribe to the Marxist logic implied by it. In fact, though, when it comes to the present example, Barthes resembles Thorstein Veblen more than he does Claude Lévi-Strauss or the

Karl Marx of *The German Ideology*. Like Veblen before him,
Barthes seems to think all allegedly aesthetic choices are really economic ones, and moreover that those making them do so from
within a duped state. Recall again the quotation from *Système de
la mode*: if consumers and manufacturers had the same "calculating
consciousness," the system would self-destruct. Thus an assumed
opposition between crafty manufacturers, calculating advantage,
and bovine consumers, placidly being duped. Questions of beauty
are all revealed as semi-conscious collisions of economic interest.

In fact, Veblen is subtler than Barthes on this point, though no
less reductive of beauty to social position. Veblen never suggests
there is a conspiratorial whiff in the system, or that consumers of
positional goods are in a state of false consciousness. He is not revelatory, moralistic or political in his rhetorical aims; he does not
uncover and condemn, he simply (and witheringly) analyzes. He
is fascinated by the way capital growth has made luxury goods,
especially leisure and its appurtenances, including fashion, which
were previously the preserve of the genuine (which is to say, land-
owning or court-favored) aristocracy, the object of upper-middle-
class longing. Money can now be translated into, if not taste exactly,
then at least the forms and signs of taste. Taste loses the essential
quality it had for eighteenth-century thinkers such as Shaftesbury
and even Hume, revealed now as a matter of class, not cultivation:
its trappings are for sale. From this point of view, the worst enemies
of the emergent American leisure class are not the purveyors of
goods, art dealers, and faux sophisticates who feed on their *par-
venu* insecurity. Their worst enemies are themselves. They cannot
see how foolish they are, but not because they are insufficiently
versed in critical social theory. Their deception is self-imposed. In
addition, it is very agreeable to them.

Barthes is working nearly a century later in a social field where
fashion, like much of leisure, has been even further democratized—
which is to say commodified, made available to even more in the
market of money. As a result, he is too much of an instinctive
Marxist to be such a clear-eyed anthropologist as Veblen. He

seems to believe critical theory will change behavior, whereas Veblen presents himself as entirely uninterested in changing anything. He may make fun, but it is black humor if anything; he does not satirize in order to improve. "In making use of the term 'invidious,'" he notes of his famous characterization of the comparisons afforded by conspicuous consumption, "it may perhaps be unnecessary to remark, there is no intention to extol or depreciate, or to commend or deplore any of the phenomena which the word is used to characterize."[1]

Barthes, by contrast, cannot help exhibiting a vestigial reformist urge. His revelations seem meant to change consciousness, if not behavior. And it is this presumptive reliance on the logic of appearance and reality, together with gestures towards a controversial theory of false consciousness, which finally trips up the cultural critic. Fashion magazines appear to be selling beauty but they are really shills for the clothes industry! You are a useful idiot to the system's needs! You think you are pursuing self-expression but you are only expressing the imperatives of producing consumption!

Sure. But here is the uncomfortable fact: barring the early entrants to the system (younger and younger to be sure), nobody in the fashion system is duped. Exposing the workings of the system does not challenge the system, because the consumers are as happy with their constant dissatisfactions of desire as are those who manufacture those dissatisfactions. Indeed, in an irony now more familiar even than the original critical theory, critical theorizing about the fashion system has the reverse of its intended effect. Instead of dispelling false consciousness, analysis of false consciousness now redoubles it by providing "savvy" consumers with the second-order delusion that they "get" the system despite their participation in it. Advertisers and magazines, no idiots in their own terms, quickly adopt this rhetorical position of "savviness" and serve it up as part of the luxuriant codings they carry.

There is one more effect, in fact the most interesting one. In addition to making critical savvy part of fashion's rhetoric, fashion also renders critical savvy itself fashionable—and hence, by fashion's own logic, subject to depreciation. This is a localized version of the general point that capitalism is much better at ideology than the first-generation critics gave it credit for. It is fully able, and more than willing, to enfold critical challenges into its own spheres of meaning, making those challenges into commodities and so assimilating them. The final irony of critical analysis of fashion is that fashion makes critical analysis itself a fashion. Once this is done, the original analysis can be celebrated as novel, then sloughed off as smoothly as last year's *pret-à-porter* line.

iii. Fashionable

Kant said: "It is better to be a fool in style than a fool out of style."

Is *that* right? It is recorded in Manfred Kuehn's monumental 2001 biography of Kant, a valiant attempt to humanize the Köningsberg sage, whose regularity of movement and careful, not to say painful, precision of thought has rendered him a cliché of philosophical disembodiment. Kant, Kuehn tells us, was quite a dedicated *bon vivant* and dandy in the first decades of his adult life. He was a much sought after dinner guest, enjoyed parties, and pursued a couple of fashionable love affairs with ladies of superior rank. If not quite the blade or rake of Regency fashion, he was at least a man more or less of mode.

At least until his fortieth year. That was when he met the expatriate Englishman Joseph Green, whose passionate punctuality found a ready psychological complement in Kant's growing mania for intellectual order. Thus Heinrich Heine was able, a few decades after the philosopher's 1804 demise, to describe him this way: "Getting up, drinking coffee, writing, giving lectures, eating, taking a walk—everything has its set time, and the neighbors knew precisely that the time was 3:30 p.m. when Kant stepped outside with his grey coat and the Spanish stick in his hand."

This serious, regular Kant, with his monumental critical philosophy now well under way, might seem to give the lie to the velvet-edged, lace-festooned coxcomb of frivolous days gone by. He might appear, indeed, the paradigm case of the worthwhile versus the merely fashionable—not least in his *Critique of Judgment*, which tried to put analysis of beauty on a more reliable cognitive footing than the taste-fashions of his contemporaries. And yet, Kant's earlier sentiment was not idle. Fashion, or style as he put it, does not itself affect the foolishness of a person or view. A stylish fool is at least stylish; an out-of-style fool has nothing to recommend him.[2] It is even possible Kant had in mind Colley Cibber's popular 1696 play *Love's Last Shift; or, The Fool in Fashion*, a moralistic work that introduced to the world the scruple-free dandy Sir Novelty Fashion. Though Shakespeare is credited with coining the adjective "fashionable," his own comedies rarely take on the subject directly as a moral issue. Not so Cibber. Sir Novelty gets most of the laughs in the play but the protagonist is the rake Loveless, who is reformed during the action into a dutiful husband. Playwright John Vanbrugh's *The Relapse*, written in response, has Loveless falling into his old ways when marriage palls.[3] (Together the two works produce a sort of either/or effect between the lures of seduction and fidelity that Kierkegaard would have appreciated, and perhaps did.)

More particularly, Kant's remark accepts that there is no necessary connection between style and anything else. That something is fashionable does not make it wrong any more than being unfashionable necessitates virtue, honesty or truth. Some received wisdom is wise, some is not; some new ideas are good ideas even as not all old ones are. The idea that something can be dismissed for being fashionable is part of an unexamined moral code that is actually subservient to the fashion system, not superior to it. Meanwhile, and more to the present point, every puritan is a dandy of his own convictions—as well as vice versa.

This can be hard to see. Fashion's practitioners and devotees like to consider it an applied art, along with architecture and design a valid member of that "third realm" of beauty thought to lie between the natural world and the art world. And yet, despite this kind of defense, fashion's status remains unstable.[4] Fashion undoubtedly adds to everyday life an aesthetic dimension that might otherwise be muted or even absent. A fashion system may hasten the obsolescence of novelty, but it also allows us to track ourselves and the cultural zeitgeist over time: we can cringe over past fashion mistakes, rehabilitate old haircuts, mix and match by decade or even year. Just as popular music and films provide a timeline of recent culture—or at least they did until the advent of the Internet downloads that render every cultural artifact achronic, the great mix tape in the sky—fashion illuminates change, and does so, sometimes, beautifully.

Nevertheless, its status remains unstable. Many if not most "serious" people consider fashion, or the category of the fashionable, inherently suspect. Excessive concern with aesthetic fashion, meaning clothing and makeup and so on, strikes many people as vulgar or trivial or even somehow lower class: superior people do not concern themselves with such superficialities. A man who has such a concern likewise shoulders the judgments, or suspicions, that he is effeminate as well as unserious: dandy or prissy or faggy.

By the same token, following fashion in ideas or culture is considered still more weak-minded or insecure or even *tragic*, as in the tragically hip when it was a phrase and not a band. We have a fat thesaurus of derogatory nouns for such people: trendy, fashion plate, fashionista, hipster, hipster doofus, faux hipster, fauxhemian and so on. Holden Caulfield's adolescent moralism of "phoniness" here joins forces with presumptions of intellectual seriousness, independent character, depth of purpose, and other "serious" virtues to condemn preoccupation with the fashionable.[5]

Two literary examples will suffice to make the point, though both are laced with a notable irony. In Barbara Pym's 1982 novel *An Unsuitable Attachment* we find this nicely turned bit of social observation:

> "My dear, this is a fashionable London parish, so called," said Randolph. He carved the saddle of mutton savagely, as if he

were rending his parishioners. "What hope is there for them this Lent? I suppose they can give up drinking *cocktails*."

Because she is deft with her chosen milieu of Anglican bourgeoisie, Pym gets this exactly right. Randolph's angry disapproval is neatly undercut by his evident need to condemn the fashionable. (The italicization of "cocktails" is perfect.)

Or consider this passage from another master of social tone and situation:

"Ah well, Thackeray, and George Eliot," said the young nobleman; "I haven't read much of them."

"Don't you suppose they know about society?" asked Bessie Alden.

"Oh, I daresay they know; they were so very clever. But these fashionable novels," said Lord Lambeth, "they are awful rot, you know."

This prosaic sentiment is expressed to young Bessie by Lord Lambeth, in Henry James's *An International Episode*, which details the flirtation between the dim young aristocrat and his lively Boston-born acquaintance. James manages to flirt with his own status as a fashionable society novelist even as he twits Lambeth for his aggressive anti-intellectualism. It is worth noting that Bessie's older sister, Mrs. Westgate, is given to explaining her banker husband's habitual absence from the social rounds of Newport and London by saying "in America there is no leisure class"—he has to remain at his Wall Street office. Likewise striking is that the narrator of the novel destined to give James his early fame, *Daisy Miller: A Study*, also published in 1878, remarks on the presence of "stylish" young girls in the resort town of Vevey—the "scare quote" inverted commas present in the original, as if to distance the narrator from such modish usage.

These passages, chosen not quite at random, show how "fashionable" and "stylish" function as adjectives of handy disapproval over the course of almost a century and on both sides of the Atlantic. Even if some distance is applied in the last example, it is clear that for a certain kind of moralist, such as Randolph, Lord Lambeth or the narrator of *Daisy Miller*, the aim is not to be *à la mode* but to establish mode by denouncing the modishness of others. Thus does fashion function not just as an economic system but also as a system of class distinction.

This is not news, and to repeat just these points would be neither fashionable nor functional. What else can be said about fashion? In pursuit of the idea mentioned at the end of the previous section, let us ask: what is it for an idea, a theory, or a discourse to be labeled "fashionable"?

Barthes himself offers an ironic case in point. The style of revelatory critical thinking at work in *Système de la mode*, and elsewhere, is no longer considered stylish. Per the observations made above, that judgment is only possible because it once *was* stylish. How is this possible? Surely the insights are as penetrating (or banal) as ever, the observations as perceptive (or slighting) as before? Surely a work of intellectual analysis is not like a pop song, subject to popularity followed by dismissal without ever changing a note? (Even in the case of a pop song, there is cause to wonder what has happened since nothing in the song can possibly have altered.)

These "surelies" are special pleading. There is nothing in principle to separate discourse from pop song, and no claims about essential features of the work will, in either case, prevent the rise and fall of fashion. In discourse the key has been the creation, or at least the allegation thereto, of a fashion system. Barthes, whatever his status in terms of being thought fashionable, is enduringly right that fashion—including the judgments, pro and con, asserting something is fashionable—requires and supports an economic field. If that field is not one of capital *simpliciter*, it must be one of some other form of capital: cultural, social, intellectual.

iv. Theory

Hence the creation of Theory with a capital "T," a marker borrowed here from various discussions of the topic from observers both sympathetic and caustic. As anyone even glancingly familiar with academic culture will know, Theory means the incursion into the vast North American university system, especially in language and literature departments, of certain texts and approaches, many with French provenance, during the period roughly from 1975 to 2005. The names will be familiar: Foucault, Derrida, Emmanuel Levinas, Deleuze, Baudrillard, Barthes, Lacan, Virilio. So will the schools: structuralism, poststructuralism, deconstruction, postcolonialism, new historicism. Some may even recognize those who rose to second-order prominence on the wave: Homi K. Bhabha, Judith Butler, Avital Ronell, Gayatri Chakravorty Spivak. And a few may know something of the intellectual line to which these thinkers belong: Heidegger, Edmund Husserl, Hegel, and especially the three masters of modern suspicion, Marx, Freud, Nietzsche.[6]

There is no need to rehearse the rise and fall of Theory in this sense, not least because it has been thoroughly documented in both fact and fiction. (David Lodge's career is unimaginable without Theory's supplied material.) More interesting are the diagnoses, really postmortems, concerning "what happened" to Theory. Take, as evidence, a recent article by Mark Bauerlein concerning *Theory's Empire: An Anthology of Dissent*, a large collection of articles published in 2005 by Columbia University Press. Explaining the relevance of this book, the only thing Bauerlein does not take to task is its suggestive, even kooky, title. (He is, for the record, one of the contributors.) The new book is necessary, Bauerlein argues, "[b]ecause in the last 30 years, theory has undergone a paradoxical decline, and the existing anthologies have failed to register the change." They simply offer up the usual suspects without noting that "Theory lost its novelty some two decades ago, and many years have passed since anybody except the theorists themselves took the latest versions seriously."

There you have it: there was novelty, then the novelty was

lost—as novelty always will be. The freshness was gone. Just as inevitably, we knew this because the once arcane had gone mainstream. Just as grunge music went from underground to Gap staple, Theory went from necromantic scholarly esoterica to the stuff of gee-whiz *New York Times Magazine* features and personality profiles. That is, one sort of fashion had leached into another, indeed had run them all together, creating the familiar media-age vortex from which all substance, especially of cultural dissent or challenge, is drained. Bauerlein:

> The cumulative result was that the social scene of Theory overwhelmed the intellectual thrust. Years earlier, the social dynamic could be seen in the cult that formed around deconstruction, and a comparison of "Différance" with the section in *The Post Card* in which Derrida ruminates over a late-night call from "Martini Heidegger" shows the toll celebrity can take on a brilliant mind. By the mid-Nineties, the social tendencies had spread all across the humanities, and its intellectual consequences surfaced in the desperation and boredom with which Theorists pondered the arrival of The Next Big Thing.

The Theorists had become, you might say, tragically hip. And don't forget the obligatory posthumous shot at poor Derrida, no longer around to defend himself against charges of "celebrity."

You might think such a diagnosis, if accurate, would obviate the need for another anthology. After all, if a subject is over, why bother to announce, at seven hundred pages of length, that it is? But Bauerlein and the book belong to a new moment: they are masters of the discourse *and* its fashion arc. Like executors of a disputed will, they pose as guardians of the true meaning, the genuine heft, beneath the fashionable chatter. Bauerlein wants to rehabilitate the real challenge of theoretical thinking.

There can be no quarrel with him on that score. As a philosopher rather than a literary critic, I have perhaps regarded the ideas and theories in question as more of a larger pattern than a sudden upsurge followed by an equally sudden decline. Indeed, the bothersome aspect is the easy acceptance of the judgment that such ideas were "fashionable" in the first place. I cannot exclude myself here. Now and then, I have used the adjective "fashionable" in a somewhat pejorative sense, though usually as an easy form of description to nonspecialists. A long time ago I called deconstruction "a fashionable theory" in a newspaper article; noted one academic's "fashionable special pleading"; complained about architecture's recent penchant for "fashionable philosophical ideas, mostly emanating from Paris"; and took issue with "fashionable talk about architectural renaissance" in the city of Toronto. I even, in the sort of brisk autopsy that Bauerlein would perhaps approve, spoke of "the once-fashionable theories of structuralism, deconstruction, poststructuralism, psychoanalysis, postcolonialism, and new historicism" and how they "have all run their course." Further, "nothing seems poised to generate the sort of excitement that formerly swirled around the merest utterance of Derrida or Foucault or Lacan."

In defense, in the last case at least I was trying to analyze the very thing I am analyzing now, namely the *cultural need* to see, and so consume and dispose of philosophical thought under the general economies of novelty, freshness and bigness. It happens that this last iteration of "fashionable" occurred in a column about a book called *Empire*—not *Theory's Empire*, but still—by Michael Hardt and Antonio Negri. People were saying it was The Next Big Thing and the article took leave to doubt it. "In common with every other fashion system, the world of intellectual trends is ruled by novelty and cool," I wrote. "Novelty and cool function in constant self-canceling spirals; things cease to be new and cool just as soon as they are labeled as such. You have now heard of *Empire*; ergo, *Empire* is over."[7]

I also said this: "[a]ll this talk about *Empire* being the Next Big Thing just obscures the deep truth, which is that there is no Next Big Thing coming. Or rather, the Next Big Thing is already here,

and its message is this: Big Things are over." Then added: "Any day
now, when I have a minute, I will get to work on *The Theory Theory*,
my massive, irritable, syntax-mangling monograph explaining
why." This was kidding, of course, trying to poke fun at the idea
that Big Things in Theory could be explained by some supercharged Big Thing Theory. Nevertheless, I received several e-mails
from readers who wanted to know who the publisher was. (And
hence the title of the present essay.)

There is no theory big enough to encompass Theory. Fashion
is not overmastered by further fashion. Despite all this, surely I fell
partly into the "fashionable" trap here. The article accepted, if only
ironically, the judgment that ideas could be dismissed for being
fashionable. Note, again, the irony of Barthes as an example: structuralist analysis of the fashion system itself rendered disposable by
an intellectual fashion system.

Not to make it all personal, but the bite of this judgment
touched home when I was a little offended recently to see the
essayist Phillip Lopate, reviewing a book of mine, remark on its
mastery of a "fashionable academic prose style" of cultural suspicion. Now, I was not aware I mastered any such thing. I thought I
was just, you know, thinking and writing—though it is some kind
of solace to know that the style had been mastered, as opposed to
just mimicked, pastiched or fallen into. That is probably often the
way. Some people consciously strive to be fashionable, and these
we dismiss as mere trendies; others fall into the category of fashion because of kinship or anxieties of influence concerning ideas
judged fashionable.

True, the style in question is a way of going on that seeks
beyond surface appearances in search of buried or obscured
meanings. It is tinged with misgiving—a hermeneutics of suspicion, to use Paul Ricoeur's once-fashionable phrase—but also
with optimism. There is no hint of conspiracy in it, though one
can see how a "plain talking" essayist like Lopate might choose to
see it that way—though his style too has its fashionable elements,
including a kind of high-minded anti-intellectualism. The lurking

background irony, meanwhile, is that this style, assuming my book exhibits it in the first place, is *not* fashionable. Bauerlein could inform Lopate that he is badly out of date: if one wished to master a fashionable academic style these days, the models would be Alain Badiou or Giorgio Agamben, not Barthes or Baudrillard. Not that you asked, but when it comes to influences the style of the book in question probably owes as much to Amis and P. G. Wodehouse as to Barthes or Baudrillard.

What offends is not the simple judgment of kinship. That's as may be in the universe of writing, where there really is nothing outside the text, however fashionable that phrase may sound. Architects are known to object violently to any judgments that imply they have a style, or still worse a "signature" style, but writers, whatever their other vices, are generally not so pretentious, pious or deluded.[8] Writing is, after all, a seeking after style, as the Latin *stylus*—pen, and hence the manner of wielding it—reminds us. No, what bothered me was rather the suggestion that something that sounds a certain way (whatever way it is) is wrong, or limited, *because* judged fashionable. Not wrong because wrong, but wrong because sounding as swayed by trends. Guilt by association, victim of fashion.

Nor is it merely a matter of leveling the judgment. The judgment confers superiority upon the judge; it establishes position. In this case, Lopate is letting readers know *he* would never succumb to such, or any, fashion. This becomes clearer still with another example, also personal.[9] In an article published in a philosophy journal, where almost no one could reasonably be expected to see it, my colleague Joseph Heath took aim at what he called "the structure of hip consumerism."[10] The article mostly targeted Naomi Klein and *Adbusters* magazine, but a work of mine on happiness and consumerism was also quoted. The overall argument was consonant with the position Heath defended, with Andrew Potter, in a popular book.[11] Being against consumerism, especially as governed by the Barthes-era fashion system, is itself a form of fashion. It is not simply that anti-WTO protest garb gets featured in fashion spreads. The very idea of hip political protest is fatally contaminated by its faulty conspiratorial analysis (The Man wants you to buy Nikes!) and its self-congratulation (I am *so* cool for not buying those shoes The Man wants me to think cool!).

The use of "hip" as a depreciation here runs parallel to the deployment of "fashionable" in the previous example. Both uses hint at the subtle links between economic and rhetorical depreciation that are my main interest here. The suggestion is that a person holding such views, or using such style, is only doing so because of some sad wish to be "with it," not realizing (a) this is the real motive behind the view or style or (b) the view or style is thus rendered dismissible. The two claims—rarely actually claimed— are distinct but usually run together. That is, as noted before, something is not judged wrong *and* stylish but wrong *because* stylish.

Stylish is wrong. Hip is deluded. The core of dissent is neither true nor false, merely some people's chosen way of being cool. Case closed.

v. Not So Fast

But not so fast. Note three important things about this style or fashion of intellectual insult as it functions in the play of discourse.

1. Thinkers of this stripe normally reject any idea of false consciousness as typical 1968-vintage Marxist hangover. They favor allegedly neutral "rational choice" models that presume economic actors always to act in ways that make sense to them. Thus the exposure of the fashion system does not lead to system failure, because consumers are pretty happy to be fashionable as long as you give them new "rebellious" ways of doing so.

That is just a false consciousness model in reverse. The agent is no longer deluded about the relation between his action and his economic interest (Marx was wrong); he is merely deluded about the relations between his reasons and his actions (Veblen was right). You didn't object to the wTo because you were passionate and committed, maybe even right; you did so simply because you wanted to be cool. And, as so often, the only people free of this new form of false consciousness are those who form the circle of initiates into the rhetorical position of the theory. Not even Veblen can forebear from judging his subjects now and then; as soon as he does, he goes from being a social anthropologist to being just one more fashionable, and superior, cultural critic.

2. As a result of (1), all this talk about the fashions of theory or dissent is subject to performative contradiction. It is itself no more than a fashion—and this *in its own terms*.

The most obvious feature of this reflexive ensnarement is that, no less than any fashion glossy or design-house press release, this sort of "analysis" at once depends on and perpetuates a necessary fiction of time-slice causality. A given theory or view rose to prominence for *this* reason: it established social position. Then it fell, for this reason: it no longer did so. It was new, then it was not. That, in itself, is new!

It is not new. The paucity of time-slice in play—thirty years—shows the idiocy of these claims. Ideas have risen and fallen in popularity from time immemorial; texts and schools have been taken up and dropped. Voltaire was an intellectual celebrity in his day, just as Schopenhauer was in his; the details of their dress and habits, even in the latter's case his choice of pet, were pored over endlessly by the impressionable and with-it publics of the time. Schools and thinkers have always gained and lost popularity for manifold reasons, including intellectual trendiness but also much more important things, like social networking, bold expression, luck and confluence with other forms of change.[12]

Thus, a theory of theory-fashion can itself never be anything other than a fashion.

3. As a corollary of (1) and (2), we can now say that any theory of the fashions in theory has all the hallmarks of what, for lack of a better term, we may call a superpositional good.

Part of the motivation here is that lots of people, including such critics, do not want to be told there is anything wrong with the current arrangement. If they took such claims seriously, something political might follow; if they can denigrate the claims, nothing political follows, everything stays the same. There is some tectonic shifting here concerning moments when dissent becomes orthodoxy, but in general criticism of ideas as fashionable is a right-wing preoccupation. It makes possible an off-load of counter-cultural dissent or unpalatable criticism into mere hipness.

That aside (if you wish), there is another motive. It is the simpler one of intellectual superiority. Deploying a critical account of "fashionable" ideas as positional goods—ideas or stances valued not in themselves but for the sake of the coolness, or hipness, they confer—offers the ultimate positional good. The critic so armed can both dismiss the first-order ideas and assure himself, at the second order, that he is smarter *because less concerned with cool* than the holder of the first-order ideas.

The only problem with superpositional goods of this sort is that they once more enact a performative contradiction, now in seeking cool as well as novelty. This new form of being smart by denouncing cool is quickly revealed as another way of saying: *Look how cool I am!* Like it or not, superpositional theoretical goods are still forms of intellectual and cultural capital, and they cannot escape their own analysis.

At this point, you might be thinking the present effort falls prey to the same objection, only now, as it were, at the third order: the super-superpositional good of having a fashionable theoretical account of why fashionable theoretical accounts of fashionable theories are misguided. Such an endgame might be an example of what has been called "Adorno's Ladder": the ascending imperatives of smartness, or critical-theoretic acumen, that must claim to see through all previous levels of smartness.[13] Or it might offer an instance of the general problem of mastery in intellectual discourse: just as a system is supposed to master a field, a theory (like Barthes's original one) masters the system. If that theory in turn is mastered by further readings of it as "fashionable," we are off to the races. All further interventions will simply multiply levels of attempted mastery, stepping aside and around previous forays in *an endless game of one-upmanship*, than which there is no better way of describing a fashion system!

Now, we could simply embrace the resulting contradiction, perhaps by giving it a more fashionable label such as "tension" or "lacuna," and leave it at that. Or we could decide mockery is the appropriate, unserious response; but this is too often the tactic of the critics of "fashionable" Theory.[14] Instead, consider something else: reading like a loser. I borrow the phrase from Malcolm Bull, who advanced it as a response to the problem of reading Nietzsche. "Reading to one's own overthrow, to convict oneself from the text is an unusual strategy," Bull says. "It differs equally from rejection of a text as mistaken or immoral and from the assimilation of a text as compatible with one's own being. Reading like a loser means assimilating a text in such a way that it is incompatible with one's self."[15]

What does that mean? Giving up on getting the better of things, not as a matter of intellectual jiu-jitsu but as a form of submission.[16] Feeling the jabs of critics without feeling, at the same time, a need to justify or explain. Giving back by giving over, a logic of gift rather than contract or contest. Rational choice economists have long been vexed by the "irrational" behavior exhibited by many economic actors in advanced postindustrial economies. Not only do they seem sometimes to act against personal interest—any Marxist could have predicted that—but they seem to act according to primitive rules of regard, care and longing, which are both definite and anticapitalist. Even when commodification threatens to overwhelm all aspects of economic life, agents reassert, however confusedly, concern for extra-capital value. Standard profit-and-loss economies, in other words, seem to coexist with gift economies, where exchanges are precisely not premised on exchange value. One cannot explain human behavior without reference to these nonexchange values, except at the cost of labeling humans comprehensively irrational.

Reading like a loser is a kind of gift. It wants nothing in return. It is not stylish, or fashionable, or hip, or cool. Nor, at the same

time, does it attempt to get the better of these categories by subverting, inverting, reverting or converting them. It proffers itself
without thought of effect or reward, a suspension of the logic of
mastery. There is no system, maybe even no theory, in play. This is
not a Theory Theory; nor is it a Theory Theory Theory; nor is it
even an Against Theory Theory. Just thinking without theory;
value without depreciation.

Has the present effort succeeded in doing this? Despite all
qualifications, probably not. Effort erases success, since *aiming*, as
J. D. Salinger's marble shooters remind us, is, like trying more generally, an admission of failure. In any event, it is not for me to say.
Let me only conclude with the reminder that the word "fashion,"
probed at some length here, has a complex etymology. It is a verb
as well as a noun; indeed it is also a compound adjective, walking
crab-fashion through the language in a manner that makes it
synonymous with wise. The verb form is even older and more
basic, since its Latin roots embrace facts as well as fashions. To
fashion is to make, to shape, to put in place. After a certain fashion, to say what is the case: a small gift to losers everywhere.

Notes

1. Thorstein Veblen, *The Theory of the Leisure Class: An Economic Study of
    Institutions* (Modern Library, 2001), p. 40. The most persuasive and
    influential recent analysis of fashion as it serves the ends of capitalism is
    Gilles Lipovetsky's *The Empire of Fashion: Dressing Modern Democracy*
    (Princeton, 1994), which updates Barthes and Veblen from a postmodern
    Marxist standpoint. Fashion, Lipovetsky argues, is a form of play that
    creates as well as reflects prevailing political conditions; its liberating
    possibilities are enhanced, rather than undermined, by its superficiality.
    (Note the use of the empire trope here, as with theory below.)

    Others have held simpler and even more powerful views. The
    futurist Vincenzo Fani, writing as "Volt" in 1920, proposed the "Futurist
    Manifesto of Women's Fashion," one of several sub-manifestos that
    followed Filippo Marinetti's famous general one in 1919. "Women's fash-
    ion has always been more or less Futurist," Fani began. "Fashion: the
    female equivalent of Futurism." It must be said, whatever the grain of
    truth there, that not many fashion-forward women have been inclined

to heed Fani's call for uneven shoes, spirals, triangles, hidden stingers, cameras, electric currents, and various other "gadgets fit to play the most wicked tricks and disconcerting pranks on maladroit suitors and sentimental fools." Nor have the machine-gun, tank, submarine, and airplane designs he favored come to the fore, let alone the demanded general shift away from silk—whose "reign must come to an end"— toward glass, cardboard, tinfoil and fish skin.

2. Kant may also have been thinking, in a different vein, of what John Locke had called "the law of fashion." This was Locke's phrase for the enforcement of custom, without recourse reason (or *nomos* versus *logos*, to use older language). In a Veblenesque twist, Locke notes how this law reduces virtue to mere social conformity: "what is everywhere called and esteemed virtue and vice is this approbation or dislike, praise or blame, which, by a secret and tacit consent, establishes itself in the several societies, tribes, and clubs of men in the world: whereby several actions come to find credit or disgrace amongst them, according to the judgments, maxims, or fashion of that place." (*An Essay Concerning Human Understanding* [Oxford, 1975], book II, ch. 28.) Like all clubs, this social one enforces its maxims, with great effectiveness, through a system of promised reward and feared punishment. The mature Kant, as with Plato before him, thought stable reason could rescue custom from its dangerous instability and arbitrariness.

3. Both men were men of fashion, though Cibber (poet laureate from 1730 to his death in 1757) was more concerned with reforming the standards of decency in English theater, widely known for its bawdiness. Vanbrugh, an architect as well as a playwright, working in the English Baroque style, designed both Blenheim Palace and Castle Howard in Yorkshire. The latter pile, if readers will recall, stands in for that safe house of twentieth-century dandies, Brideshead, in the 1981 television adaptation of Evelyn Waugh's novel *Brideshead Revisited*, starring Jeremy Irons and Anthony Andrews. Nickolas Grace's portrayal of Anthony Blanche, the louche dandy loosely based on Brian Howard, perfects the pronunciation of "bavoque"—the sure signal, as analyzed by Kenneth Tynan in his diaries, of high-toned histrionic English pansydom.

4. Arthur Danto details the sometimes porous lines between the three realms of beauty in *The Abuse of Beauty: Aesthetics and the Concept of Art* (Open Court, 2003).

5. There is a separate study to be made of the trope of *seriousness* as it arises in philosophical discourse. We can think here, for instance, of Derrida's

playful dismantling of ordinary-language philosophy in *Limited Inc*
(Northwestern, 1988), a book that comprehensively refuses to accept the
prescriptive distinction, found in J. L. Austin and John Searle, between
"serious" and "unserious" iterations. Austin likes to think of himself as
playful, even if Searle emphatically does not; Derrida's play with both
shows them, and us, what doing things with words really is. Style, in
other words, is not the enemy or even the mere vehicle of philosophy—
whatever that could mean. Style *is* the basic philosophical issue.

6. Note that there would be no such easy narrative of "theory fashion"
    available in the more analytic stream of academic philosophy. If A. J.
    Ayer or R. G. Collingwood are not read today, it is not because they are
    out of fashion; rather, they are uninteresting, or wrong, or merely taken
    for granted.

7. Mark Kingwell, "You have now heard of *Empire*; *Empire* is over,"
    National Post (1 July 2001); reprinted in *Nothing for Granted* (Penguin,
    2005), pp. 97–100.

8. Witold Rybczynski's *The Look of Architecture* (Oxford, 2001) contains a
    deft analysis of this predilection against style in architecture, using the
    block south of Bryant Park and the Manhattan Public Library as a
    springboard to a general discussion of style and gesture in architecture.
    Whatever architects say, or choose to believe, architecture exhibits style.

9. I will spare the reader any tedious discussion of the two bloggers' judg-
    ments that disparaged my book about fly fishing for treating it as "a
    fashionable sport, that is, a sport of fashion" even as the narrator of the
    book went "from hipster doofus to crusty uncle in a single trout season."
    Nobody is more prone to the fashion performative contradiction than
    anglers: the reigning fashion is always to insult as fashionable those who
    take up the sport after you. It follows that, for true authenticity, you
    must always already be an angler; thus it is never possible to fish for the
    first time.

10. *Philosophy and Social Criticism* 27 (2001): 1-17.

11. Andrew Potter and Joseph Heath, *The Rebel Sell: Why the Culture Can't
    Be Jammed* (Random House, 2005).

12. The best analysis of this process that I know is Randall Collins's monu-
    mental work *The Sociology of Philosophies: A Global Theory of
    Intellectual Change* (Harvard, 1998), which tracks the rise and fall of
    philosophical schools, East and West, over two and a half millennia.

13. "Nothing is more unfitting for an intellectual resolved on practising

what was earlier called philosophy," Adorno says in *Minima Moralia* (Verso, 1996), "than to wish, in discussion, and one might almost say in argumentation, to be right.... When philosophers, who are well known to have difficulty in keeping silent, engage in conversation, they should try always to lose the argument, but in such a way as to convict their opponent of untruth. The point should not be to have absolutely correct, irrefutable, water-tight cognitions—for they inevitably boil down to tautologies—but insights which cause the question of their justness to judge itself."

14. Nobody is immune from this temptation. Some years ago, at a symposium in Stuttgart on the topic of interpretation, a group of distinguished poets and scholars, plus a few academic *Üntermenschen* of considerably less distinction, could be observed on a hotel terrace competing in their efforts to imitate Homi Bhabha deconstructing the lyrics of Earth, Wind, and Fire songs. During one general convulsion of laughter, Bhabha walked onto the terrace and the laughter braked into an embarrassed silence. He turned and left without a word: his most effective intervention of the entire symposium.

15. Malcolm Bull, "Where Is the Anti-Nietzsche?" *New Left Review* 3 (May/June 2000), pp. 121–45. The weakness in Bull's ironic position is that such a reading, offered here as a way of reacting to Nietzsche, still suggests itself as the *superior* way of going on. I suggest that this is probably the limit-case of all intellectual suggestion. And Bull is nothing if not consistent. He concludes his article with a suggestion that we losers extend society to non-human species, and divert the resources of now-redundant cultural institutions to these new citizens: "Perhaps the Louvre, and its collections, could be put at the disposal of apes freed from zoos and research laboratories: the long galleries could be used for sleeping and recreation, the Jardin des Tuileries for foraging."

16. The tactic of "culture-jamming" that Heath and Potter so disdain in *The Rebel Sell* is sometimes described, by the *Adbusters* crowd, as a form of political jiu jitsu.

Acknowledgments

When, some years ago, I began to think, teach and write about art and architecture, friends wondered how these interests squared with the political theory which had been, until then, my evident specialty. One sort of answer is to claim that art and especially architecture are themselves political features of life. In making its own versions of that claim, the present volume is an extension of, or companion to, the positions worked out in earlier works, especially *Practical Judgments* (University of Toronto, 2002), *Nearest Thing to Heaven* (Yale, 2006) and *Concrete Reveries* (Viking, 2008).

But there is a simpler reason for this branching of focus into the aesthetic. My teachers in graduate school, particularly Karsten Harries, Georgia Warnke, and the late Maurice Natanson continue to exert an influence they may not favour in conclusion but I hope they will accept as inspiration. Karsten's lectures on aesthetics at Yale in the late 1980s stay with me, not least in the basic orientation of my own teaching in philosophy of art, as do Georgia's seminars on the paradoxes of interpretation and Maury's inspiring, boisterous literature and philosophy classes. Though none of these scholars

was or is especially meta-philosophical in orientation, their thinking has allowed mine to move in second-order directions that now
seem natural. I would add, too, the earlier influence of Ronald
Hepburn of Edinburgh University who taught me and others
much about the experience of natural beauty. I thank all of them
here, alas in one case too late for him to see it.

With the exception of the introduction, the pieces collected in
this book have all been previously published, either in journals or
as essays in artist's catalogues and books. They were written over a
period of eighteen years, since the oldest of them was first published in 1994, though that span is misleading, because the bulk of
the material was composed and published between 2004 and 2008.
This is true of all essays in the first part, those concerned explicitly
with art and architecture. In addition, a number of these essays
either started or were subsequently delivered as public talks. The
details may be found below.

I thank Linda Pruessen of Key Porter for her enthusiasm and
interest in a book that she could not reasonably expect to earn her
firm, or anyone, a lot of money; also Martha Sharpe for a thorough and helpful copyedit of the manuscript, and Esther Shubert
and David Owen Morgan for proofing and help with the images.
The editors of the various journals and books, especially Karen
Mulhallen at *Descant*, Roger Hodge and Jennifer Szalai at *Harper's*,
and Boris Castell at *Queen's Quarterly*, continue to offer wonderful places to work out idiosyncratic ideas about thought itself.
Artists who have become friends both over their work and apart
from it include James Lahey, Edward Burtynsky, Iris Häussler,
Geoffrey James, and the late David Bierk. I thank them all for
inspiration and for the occasions their work presented for
thought. Other friends, artists, and colleagues to whom I am
indebted (with apologies to any I have forgotten) are: Blue
Republic, Richard Rhodes, Sylvère Lotringer, Eldon Garnet,
Leanne Shapton, Carolyn Bell Farrell, Steven Matijcio, Sylvette
Babin, Niamh O'Laoghaire, Charlie Foran, Mary Ladky, Victoria
Jackman, Lonti Ebers, John Hartman, Kate Hollett, Lisa Klapstock,

Marianne Lovink, Julian Siggers, Shelley Adler, Janice Zawerbny and Pym Buitenhuis.

As always, Molly, Chloe and Clara sustain me with their multiform beauty, the visible kind and otherwise. They bring me joy.

Details of Publication

Part One: Art and Its Objects

"Art Will Eat Itself," *Harper's Magazine* (August 2003), pp. 80-85.

"Monumental-Conceptual Architecture," *Harvard Design Magazine* 19 (Fall 2003/Winter 2004). A polemical version of the argument was published as "Redesigning Toronto: the $195-million scribble," *Toronto Life* (June 2004), pp. 70–75. Combined and abridged as a talk, Faculty of Architecture, Landscape and Design, University of Toronto, 2004.

"Modernism à la Mode," *Harper's Magazine* (November 2007), pp. 83–88.

"Earth and World in James Lahey's Index Abstractions," in *James Lahey: Index* (MacLaren Art Gallery, 2005), pp. 34–46. Abridged as part of a conversation with the artist, University of Toronto Art Centre, 2007.

"David Bierk and Appropriate Beauty / David Bierk et la beauté approprié," in *David Bierk 2006* (Galerie de Bellefeuille, 2006), pp. 7–16.

"The Truth in Photographs: Edward Burtynsky's Revelations of Excess," in *Burtynsky—China* (Steidl, 2005), pp. 16–19.

"Unlearned: Losing Your Way, Finding Yourself," in Steven Matijcio, ed., *Unlearn* (Plug In ICA, 2006), pp. 6–11. The basis for "Who Owns Art?", Christina Sabat Memorial Lecture, Beaverbrook Art Gallery, Fredericton, New Brunswick, 2005.

"Imaging the Artist: Going to Eleven," *Canadian Art* (Summer 2005), pp. 60–63. Delivered as a contribution to *Canadian Art* Imaging the Artist Conference, Toronto, 2005, and adapted for "The Conspiracy of Art" (with Sylvère Lotringer), *Impulse* Archaeology Symposium, Toronto, 2005.

"The Legacies of Joseph Wagenbach [Sur les traces de Joseph Wagenbach]," *esse arts + opinions* 60 CANULAR (Summer 2007), pp. 14–17. Abridged as "The Artist Has Left the Building," panel discussion at the Goethe-Institut, Toronto, 2006.

"Five Stops: Homesick and Wanting in the Blue Republic," in *Nostalgia for the Future* (The Koffler Gallery, 2008). Adapted as keynote address, Provost's Symposium on the Future of the Arts, Faculty of Fine Arts, University of Calgary, 2006; also Catherine Parr Traill College, Trent University, 2006; Humanities Research Group Distinguished Speakers Series, University of Windsor, 2007.

Part Two: Philosophy After Art

"Love and Philosophy," *Queen's Quarterly* 111:3 (Fall 2004): 343–57. Delivered as a lecture, Trinity College, University of Toronto, 2003; Royal Ontario Museum Institute for Contemporary Culture, 2004; Philosophy Course Union Symposium on Love, University of Toronto, 2008.

"Anguish as a Second Language," *Descant* 32:4 (Winter 2001): 155–70. Keynote address, Alberta Teachers of English as a Second Language Conference, Edmonton, 2000; Saskatchewan Book Awards, Regina, 2000.

"Crayon in the Brain: Machining Happiness in the Time of Homer," *Descant* 37:2 (Summer 2006): 68–87. Also published as "'Free Drinks Tomorrow': Machining Dreams of Happiness in the Time of Homer," *Filosofie in Bedrijf* 3/4 (Summer 2006): 8–17. Keynote address, *Congres over Geluk* (Conference on Happiness), Utrecht University, Holland, 2005; as a lecture, Senior Fellows' Lecture Series, Massey College, University of Toronto, 2005; Perth International Arts Festival, Australia, 2006; Vanier College, Montreal, 2006; *Noesis* Undergraduate Philosophy Group, University of Toronto, 2006.

"Let's Ask Again: Is Law Like Literature?" *Yale Journal of Law and the Humanities* 6:2 (Spring 1994): 317–52.

"The Theory Theory; or, The Fashion System Revisited," *Descant* 38:3 (Fall 2007): 225–48. Abridged as keynote address, *Noesis* Mini-Conference, Philosophy Course Union, University of Toronto, 2007.

Image Credits

Gerhard Richter works reproduced courtesy of Marion Goodman Gallery.
Fluxus *Fluxkit* courtesy of Gilbert & Lila Silverman, Detroit. Photographs
of Libeskind & Gehry works from Flickr Creative Commons: (clockwise
from top right) http://www.flickr.com/photos/suwatch/503962974/,
http://www.flickr.com/photos/rosaydani/1878072109/,
http://www.flickr.com/photos/patio/565600993/,
http://www.flickr.com/photos/henley24/530884968/,
http://www.flickr.com/photos/patio/565236542/,
http://www.flickr.com/photos/laurenmanning/2254664583/. James Lahey
works from private collection, courtesy of the artist. David Bierk images
courtesy of Estate of David Bierk. Edward Burtynsky's images copyright
Edward Burtynsky, courtesy Nicholas Metivier Gallery, Toronto. Image of
Ken Lum's work appears courtesy of the artist and Galerie Nelson, Paris,
photograph by Kleinefenn. Image of Kelly Mark's photograph courtesy of
the artist and Wynick/Tuck Gallery, Toronto. Michel de Broin's work photographed by the artist appears courtesy of the artist, ArtTexte, and the City
of Montreal. Photographs by Germaine Koh appear courtesy of the artist.
Photographs by Iris Häussler courtesy of the artist. Blue Republic's work
photographed by The Art Gallery of Sudbury, courtesy of the artist.